Understanding Gender Violence

Understanding Gender Violence

A Comprehensive Approach

Jenn Freitag

ROWMAN & LITTLEFIELD

Lanham • Boulder • New York • London

Published by Rowman & Littlefield
An imprint of The Rowman & Littlefield Publishing Group, Inc.
4501 Forbes Boulevard, Suite 200, Lanham, Maryland 20706
www.rowman.com

86-90 Paul Street, London EC2A 4NE

British Library Cataloguing in Publication Information Available

Library of Congress Cataloging-in-Publication Data

Names: Freitag, Jenn, 1982– author.
Title: Understanding gender violence : a comprehensive approach / Jenn Freitag.
Description: Lanham : Rowman & Littlefield, [2025] | Includes bibliographical references and index.
Identifiers: LCCN 2024045242 (print) | LCCN 2024045243 (ebook) |
    ISBN 9781538197011 (cloth) | ISBN 9781538197028 (paperback) |
    ISBN 9781538197035 (epub)
Subjects: LCSH: Gender-based violence.
Classification: LCC HV6250.4.W65 F746 2025 (print) | LCC HV6250.4.W65 (ebook) |
    DDC 303.6081—dc23/eng/20241127
LC record available at https://lccn.loc.gov/2024045242
LC ebook record available at https://lccn.loc.gov/2024045243

♾️™ The paper used in this publication meets the minimum requirements of American National Standard for Information Sciences—Permanence of Paper for Printed Library Materials, ANSI/NISO Z39.48-1992.

Contents

Preface

I have taken on various roles in the movement to end gender violence since 2002, when I first began reading about these issues as a college student. It was then I became a student peer educator and began learning as much as possible so I could contribute as a practitioner, performer, researcher, professor, and public speaker. I have worked through my own experiences of gender violence and witnessed its effects on family members, friends, students, colleagues, clients, and countless others. I have facilitated public conversations about high-profile cases, media treatment of people who have experienced gender violence, and engagement of these issues in pop culture. I have devoted a huge chunk of my personal life to thinking about gender violence and most of my professional life to educating others about it.

I know I am not alone in my frustration and disappointment that, as a movement, we have not yet been successful in initiating any widespread decrease of gender violence in the United States or around the world. We've made a lot of progress, but we have far to go. In this book, I draw on what we have learned in the movement to end gender violence over the last fifty years and offer a new way of thinking about it. Considering the problem of gender violence using a comprehensive approach has the potential to completely shift our prevention and response efforts and reinvigorate our work. It could unite us and increase our collective effectiveness like never before.

Whether you have been involved in this work for years or are just beginning to learn about gender violence, this book introduces the key components of a comprehensive approach in a clear and invitational way. I explain research, break down academic concepts, and apply my expertise working in the field. Crisis workers and activists will appreciate that I avoid flashy jargon and prioritize the use of accessible language; researchers will appreciate that I cite my sources throughout this book. Anyone without prior knowledge will gain a thorough awareness of the types, prevalence, impact, causes, and complexities of gender violence. Those already familiar with gender violence dynamics will likely recognize much of the terminology and information I offer, but with different framing. This book can be read and understood on its own or processed with a group or class. It is useful for examining any type of gender-based violence, including discrimination, sexual violence, partner violence, stalking, ideologically motivated violence, and hate crimes against people who identify across the LGBTIQA+ spectrum. And whatever your prior knowledge of gender violence issues, you can use my notes to do further reading on your own.

I am a White, cisgender, pansexual woman who grew up working class to become a first-generation college student. This perspective undoubtedly impacts how I have written this book. I continue to grapple with the ways I move through the world with many privileges and challenges, and I am thankful to reviewers of this book who helped to keep me accountable to my own commitment to self-reflexivity. Because my work with gender violence has taken place on local and statewide levels within the United States, I focus this book primarily on US-based research and trends within a larger global context. My hope is that as we engage the idea of a comprehensive approach to gender violence together, we will expand and refine this framework and its applications beyond one area of the world. Rather than an end-all, be-all approach, I intend for this book to be an invitation for honest and critical discussion about gender violence. I anticipate that this framework will shift with your contributions. I am grateful to those who have challenged and expanded my own understandings of gender violence throughout my adult life, and I offer this book in the same spirit of humility.

I am encouraged by your interest in understanding gender violence in a deeper way. Like you, I am committed to identifying ways to do better in this work. Perhaps this book moves us further in that direction. Share what you find helpful with your colleagues, students, volunteers, leaders, stakeholders, funders, elected officials, and collaborators. Invite one another to address the limitations of this approach, and bring more voices into this very necessary conversation. I am excited to be a part of this dialogue with you. Together, let's take a comprehensive look at gender violence and ask: what now?

Acknowledgments

If it wasn't for the early activists and trailblazers in the Gay Liberation and Anti–Violence against Women Movements, I would not be writing about these issues today or outing myself as pansexual for the first time in print. There are many countless others who pushed these issues forward before and after that time to whom I am also indebted. Thank you.

As I have reflected on writing this book, I kept returning to my own beginnings. I offer heartfelt thanks to the professors who got me thinking about gender issues when I was a college student—a strong group of women mentors at the University of Northern Iowa that included Dr. Victoria DeFranciso, Dr. Susan Hill, Dr. Catherine MacGillivray, Dr. Karen Mitchell, and Dr. April Chatham-Carpenter. I am grateful to the campus offices and local organizations in northeast Iowa that gave me early opportunities to get involved in crisis advocacy and prevention. Thanks to all of the co-activists who helped me hone my skills in educating others about these issues—especially Karen Mitchell, Amandajean Freking Nolte, Dr. Danielle Dick McGeough, Megan Jones-Williams, and Adam McCallister.

Thank you to Dr. Leland Spencer, Dr. Kathy Miller, Shanthi Blanchard, Dr. Shawna Mulvani Reddin, Kathryn Miller Goldman, and Dr. Chad Painter for your advice and help navigating book publishing for the first time. To Karen Mitchell, Brad Trainer, and students in my Ending Gender Violence class over the past few years, thank you for your early feedback on this book and the ways you helped me make it better. To Dr. Susan M. Weaver at the University of Dayton, Dr. Jenny Guthrie at Through the Fray Coaching, Dr. Sarah Jane Brubaker at Virginia Commonwealth University, Dr. Marcella L. Mulhollem at Drake University, Dr. Leland G. Spencer at the University of South Carolina, and anonymous reviewers through Rowman & Littlefield: I am incredibly grateful for your time spent reading parts of my manuscript and for your thoughtful considerations and challenges. Leland, your feedback on the entire book was invaluable. Thanks to Joe Sarver for your fantastic illustration work and to Allison Moon-Shope for connecting us. Thank you to my editor, Alyssa Palazzo, for believing in this project and answering my endless questions, and to Hannah Eveland, Jehanne Schweitzer, and the Rowman & Littlefield staff for assisting me through this process. Thanks also to Jesseca Ynez Simmons, Dr. Susan Weaver, and Dr. Jen Ptacek for your friendship—it has been meaningful to reflect with you on my progress.

Perhaps no three individuals have heard me discuss the ideas in this book more than Dr. Siri R. K. Lebaron, Dr. Jenny Guthrie, and Brad Trainer. I appreciate your embrace of my simultaneous ambition, frustration, and excitement over the past ten years as I've written this book. Your support means the world. Brad, your love for me and unwavering commitment to helping me finish this project are unmatched. Thank you.

CHAPTER 1

The Necessity of a Comprehensive Approach

I have been doing gender violence prevention and response work since the early 2000s. As a college student in Iowa—and years later as a crisis services coordinator at a midwestern university—I can recall specific instances of my anger and frustration at the difficulty of doing this work. I would take brief moments to marvel with my classmates and rant with my colleagues, then return to the daily grind of chipping away at the problem of gender violence one hotline call, legal change, or awareness-raising event at a time. Like others across the country and around the world, I cared deeply about these issues, but I struggled to stay optimistic about our collective capacity to end gender violence. Was it even possible?

This led me to wonder what is at the center of this monstrously large problem that seems impossible to unravel. It turns out that the same root causes and contributors are at the heart of any gender violence issue engaged by crisis counselors, nonprofit staff, campus educators, activists, and first responders. By reframing all types of gender violence as offshoots of one huge and complex problem, we can analyze it with more clarity. We can study all of its interlocking mechanisms and explore more effective and collaborative ways to take it on at its core. Gender violence *is* a massive problem, but understanding *why* it is so incredibly difficult to solve is the first and most important action we can take toward a future without it. This realization has given me renewed hope for ending gender violence. Over twenty years after I began this work, I am more invigorated than ever before to face this problem head-on.

The Problem of Gender Violence

Despite fifty years of activism, legal changes, and crisis service provision, there is no evidence to suggest any widespread decrease in rates of gender violence.[1] The internet age has meant more visibility and discussion of these issues than ever before, but the difficult reality remains: even after #MeToo went viral, people still experience gender violence at alarming rates, are often not believed when they tell others, and encounter countless obstacles in navigating medical, criminal system, media, and other institutional responses to their disclosures. The impact, dynamics, and causes of gender violence remain largely misunderstood by the general public. Groups who experience the highest rates of gender violence—like women of color, people who identify as transgender or gender nonconforming, Indigenous populations, and women with disabilities—are often unacknowledged. Individuals who commit acts of gender violence are rarely held accountable, especially if they are White, wealthy, and popular (cis)heterosexual men. Institutions struggle with how to respond to gender violence, economies suffer, and criminal processes often aren't effective. In addition to these challenges, we currently face losses of legal protections, widespread cuts to nonprofit services, and high-profile gender violence cases to which most members of the public do not know how to respond.

Social science researchers have published singular studies that suggest shifts in attitude and behavior change, demonstrate promising practices, and show that efforts on specific issues in some communities seem to be working. Even so, gender violence remains one of the most pervasive and complicated global social justice issues we face today, affecting the lives of countless individuals, their loved ones, and the communities to which they belong. It is necessary for us to ask why we aren't making more progress and what we can do about it.

What makes the problem of gender violence so massive, so difficult to engage, so hard to prevent? Why haven't incidences of gender violence decreased with the establishment of stronger laws and policies? Why do people who have experienced gender violence

---

[1] Sally Engle Merry, *Gender Violence: A Cultural Perspective* (Chichester, UK: Wiley-Blackwell, 2009), 2.

continue to be stigmatized? A broad and big-picture analysis of this problem begins with acknowledging four truths about gender violence.

1. **Gender violence is a problem of pandemic proportions.** Gender violence is a worldwide issue directly harming massive amounts of our global population. People who directly experience gender violence may endure a variety of physical and psychological effects—including severe trauma—that impact their health, jobs, financial well-being, and relationships with others. Those left unscathed by direct violence are often indirectly affected by witnessing and supporting loved ones and family members through and after these experiences; others vicariously experience trauma through their roles as first responders, crisis advocates, medical staff, law enforcement, or mental health professionals. Communities struggle with how to respond to and prevent gender violence effectively, and on state and federal levels, these issues have major economic impacts on employment, education, and health care. Considered within a global context, gender violence has monstrous repercussions with tangible, intangible, and unknowable effects. As such, we must simultaneously ensure supportive measures to help those affected by gender violence, process the collective trauma of dealing with these issues day in and day out, and also work to stop these things from happening in the first place. This is not an easy task, and this is why gender violence response work is often plagued with hopelessness and burnout.

2. **Gender violence is complex.** It is a complicated social phenomenon without one clear and simple cause. The best explanation for why it occurs begins with how cultural expectations of gender influence individual behavior and shape widespread gendered power dynamics and inequality. This is further complicated by various factors like early life experiences, underdeveloped social and emotional skills, difficult life experiences, ideas about sex, and misuses of power that may contribute to why an individual or group commits gender violence. Many cultures have historically placed responsibility for this problem on individual behavior, but social institutions—like media,

education, religion, the criminal system, the military, and others—play large roles in contributing to the acceptance and perpetration of gender violence. For these reasons, narrow, reductionist, and one-size-fits-all explanations about gender violence cannot meet the challenges of preventing and responding to it.[2] We need a comprehensive approach that responds to its multilayered complexities on individual, institutional, and collective levels.

3. **Gender violence is part of everyday culture.** More than a series of scary statistics or things that happen *somewhere else*, gender violence is ingrained in the everyday experiences of people across the United States and around the world. Subtle forms of gender violence—and language that makes it more acceptable—permeate our daily lives. When explicit forms of gender violence occur, the people who experience it are often met with disbelief and poor treatment. Victim-blame stems from belief in false truths about gender violence as well as unproductive attitudes and beliefs about gender itself. Widespread victim-blame has often meant that individuals stay silent about their experiences, fear disclosure to others, refuse to report to law enforcement and disciplinary officials, and decide against seeking medical or psychological help. Rather than a series of isolated events, a *culture of gender violence* normalizes subtle and explicit forms of gender violence, blames and silences victims, and maintains a social environment in which gender violence is accepted and sometimes even encouraged. We need to examine the foundational root of gender violence—the system of gender itself—and everyday ways traditional gender roles, gendered power dynamics, and limited understandings of sexuality and sexual expression lead to the everyday cultural acceptance of gender violence.

4. **Gender violence is interwoven with other forms of oppression.** A culture of gender violence is supported and maintained by other systems of power and control. Sexism (discrimination based on gender), heterosexism (discrimination based on sexual

---

[2] Laura L. O'Toole, Jessica R. Schiffman, and Margie L. Kiter Edwards, preface to *Gender Violence: Interdisciplinary Perspectives*, ed. Laura L. O'Toole, Jessica R. Schiffman, and Margie L. Kiter Edwards, 2nd ed. (New York: New York University Press, 2007), xi–xiv.

orientation), and cissexism (discrimination based on gender identity) all relate to issues of gender performance, gender roles, sexual identity, and sexual decision-making; these forms of oppression have a direct relationship with attitudes about gender violence, the people who experience it, and those who harm others. Other systems of oppression like those based on race, class, religion, age, ethnicity, ability, body size, nationality, and citizenship also overlap with a culture of gender violence in a complex web of tightly woven, intersecting threads.[3] War, colonization, and slavery in the United States and around the world have always included sexual violence.[4] Low socioeconomic status and financial hardship make certain populations more vulnerable to sexual exploitation, trafficking, and forced sterilization. Homophobia and transphobia contribute to the severity of street harassment and hate crimes. Appearance- and ability-based prejudices complicate and worsen how stalking is experienced. Engaging gender violence independently from other systems of oppression means oversimplifying its complex dynamics, ignoring the diverse aspects of how it may be committed or experienced, and failing to respond to it in the most productive ways possible. In order to deal with the problem of gender violence effectively, we must acknowledge, examine, and combat all systems of oppression. This means taking on the simultaneity of gender violence and prejudice in various forms and considering the ways that crisis services, criminal processes, institutional policies, and prevention efforts can be more equitable and inclusive.

---

[3] Kimberlé Crenshaw, "Mapping the Margins: Intersectionality, Identity Politics, and Violence against Women of Color," *Stanford Law Review* 43, no. 6 (1991): 1241–99, doi:10.2307/1229039; Patricia Hill Collins, *Black Feminist Thought: Knowledge, Consciousness, and the Politics of Empowerment*, 2nd ed. (New York: Routledge, 1999); Gayle Rubin, "Thinking Sex: Notes for a Radical Theory of the Politics of Sexuality," in *The Lesbian and Gay Studies Reader*, ed. Henry Abelov, Michèle Aina Barale, and David M. Halperin (New York: Routledge, 1993), 3–44; Jennifer Patterson, introduction to *Queering Sexual Violence: Radical Voices from Within the Anti-Violence Movement*, ed. Jennifer Patterson (New York: Riverdale Avenue Books, 2016), 5–13; Carmen Vazquez, "Spirit and Passion," in *Queer Cultures*, ed. D. Carlin and J. DiGrazia (Upper Saddle River, NJ: Pearson/Prentice Hall, 2004), 689–98.

[4] O'Toole, Schiffman, and Kiter Edwards, preface to *Gender Violence*.

Additional Information

The Problem of Gender Violence

- Pandemic-sized issue
- Super complex
- Part of everyday culture
- Overlaps with intersecting oppressions

These realities paint a stark picture of what we are up against. Unfortunately, gender violence has been a part of many cultures around the world for centuries. We can learn a lot, however, from the past fifty years of dedicated work on these issues. In the following sections I offer a brief history of how contemporary gender violence prevention and response efforts in the United States developed and a summary of our progress and current limitations. Then, I introduce the framework that will propel us forward: a comprehensive approach to understanding gender violence.

How the Modern Movement to End Gender Violence Began

Contemporary efforts to respond to and prevent gender violence in the United States began in the 1960s and 1970s alongside civil rights, women's rights, antiwar, and other social activism.[5] A variety of local, grassroots groups engaged issues of gender violence—primarily rape, spousal abuse, and discrimination against gay men and lesbians—with different interests, goals, and strategies. Even organizations united in the same cause, like creating support services for people who experienced sexual violence, often had very different motivations and priorities.[6] What they often shared, however, was a focus on systemic issues and the roles that

---

[5] Jami Ake and Gretchen Arnold, "A Brief History of Anti-Violence against Women Movements in the United States," in *Sourcebook on Violence against Women*, ed. Claire M. Renzetti, Jeffrey L. Edleson, and Raquel K. Bergen, 3rd ed. (Thousand Oaks, CA: Sage, 2018), 3–25.

[6] Ibid., 8; Merry, *Gender Violence*, 43.

institutions—formal social structures—played in perpetuating violence and discrimination.[7]

Anti–Violence against Women

Two trajectories of activism and organizing—the Anti-Rape Movement and the Battered Women's Movement—began in response to growing awareness of sexual violence and spousal abuse. Women gathered to discuss their common experiences through consciousness-raising groups, activists organized public awareness-raising events like speak-outs and marches, and volunteers created formal and informal rape crisis centers, hotlines, legal assistance networks, and shelters for women fleeing abusive relationships. People advocated for legal changes related to sexual assault, domestic violence, self-defense, and government funding for prevention and response efforts.[8]

Many successes are credited to anti–violence against women work during this time, including the institutionalization of crisis services (making them more permanent through state and federal funding), creation of better laws, and provision of educational and self-defense programs to local communities. By the mid-1970s, anti–violence against women activists had created state and national organizations, established national conferences, and attained governmental support.[9] Unfortunately, most of these efforts were focused on White and middle-class cisheterosexual women. Lesbian and bisexual women faced barriers in visibility and inclusion across local and national levels to the extent that they often protested the organizations to which they belonged or started their own groups so their interests would be represented.[10] There was also a heavy reliance on mainstream service provision that excluded marginalized populations and criminal system solutions that failed to take the concerns of Indigenous people and people of color into account.[11]

---

[7] Merry, *Gender Violence*, 43; Jonathan Alexander, Deborah T. Meem, and Michelle A. Gibson, *Finding Out: An Introduction to LGBTQ Studies*, 3rd ed. (Thousand Oaks, CA: Sage, 2018), 68.

[8] Ake and Arnold, "Brief History"; Emily Thuma, "Lessons in Self-Defense: Gender Violence, Racial Criminalization, and Anticarceral Feminism," *Women's Studies Quarterly* 43, no. 3/4 (2015): 52–71, https://www.jstor.org/stable/43958549.

[9] Ake and Arnold, "Brief History"; Thuma, "Lessons in Self-Defense."

[10] Merry, *Gender Violence*, 13.

[11] Ake and Arnold, "Brief History," 4.

Case Example

Self-Defense against Sexual Violence

At different points across the 1970s, a variety of Indigenous, Black, Chicano, Puerto Rican, gay Latino, farmworker, and feminist activist groups across the United States organized in support of four women who were charged with crimes after defending themselves from sexual violence. Yvonne Wanrow, a Sinixt woman, killed a White man and known sexual predator who broke into her babysitter's home. Joan Little, an incarcerated Black woman, killed a White prison guard during his attempted rape. Inez García, a Cuban Puerto Rican woman, killed a man physically assaulting her roommate after beating and raping García. Dessie Woods, a Black woman, killed a White man who attempted to rape her and another woman. Grassroots organizers and fundraisers marched for Wood's freedom, helped Wanrow get a retrial, and campaigned for the successful acquittals of Little and García. Their work set helpful legal precedents for future self-defense cases and initiated a decades-long critique of carceral justice within the movement to end gender violence [a]

[a] Emily Thuma, "Lessons in Self-Defense: Gender Violence, Racial Criminalization, and Anticarceral Feminism," *Women's Studies Quarterly* 43, no. 3/4 (2015): 52–71, https://www.jstor.org/stable/43958549

Gay Liberation

Largely distinct from anti–violence against women efforts, the Gay Liberation Movement grew from what was known as the Homophile Movement in the 1940s and 1950s in response to job and housing discrimination, the criminalization of same-gender sexual activity, and the mainstream media's representation of gays, lesbians, and gender nonconforming people as dirty, sick, and dangerous.[12] A large impetus of increased activity in the 1960s was repression by police, who would frequently raid gatherings of gays, lesbians, and gender nonconforming individuals at bars,

---

[12] Alexander, Meem, and Gibson, *Finding Out*, 65.

hotels, bathhouses, and costume balls; this harassment often involved arrests and sometimes led to job loss when newspapers published the names of arrested individuals.[13] In contrast to the conformist strategies of earlier organizers, many people began to fight back through protests and riots. The 1969 Stonewall Uprising in New York City became a galvanizing symbol for gay liberation when bar patrons and community members violently resisted police, then rioted for days in response to the initial event and homophobic and derogatory news coverage about it.[14] Activists—many of them young people—created organizations across the United States that worked to end police harassment, decriminalize gay sexual activity, increase job protection, critique gender roles, and challenge traditional family structures and understandings of sexual desire.[15] They planned public protests like the 1970 Christopher Street Liberation Day March commemorating Stonewall and the 1979 National March on Washington for Lesbian and Gay Rights. The March on Washington happened after the assassination of Harvey Milk— one of the first openly gay politicians to get elected to office in the United States—and the subsequent White Night Riots after a jury gave his assassin a lenient verdict. The rally advocated for legal changes and featured speakers who were gay and lesbian writers, feminist and civil rights activists, and out members of Congress and former military.[16]

The Gay Liberation Movement was successful in promoting the visibility of gay and lesbian issues and creating a strong agenda for legislative change. Many of the efforts at the time, however, centered the experiences of White, middle-class gay men and excluded the experiences of lesbians and transgender people who were low income, incarcerated, or worked in the sex industry.[17] Decisions

---

[13] Elizabeth A. Armstrong and Suzanna M. Crage, "Movements and Memory: The Making of the Stonewall Myth," *American Sociological Review* 71, no. 5 (2006): 728, doi:10.1177/000312240607100502.

[14] Ibid.

[15] Alexander, Meem, and Gibson, *Finding Out*, 67; Colin P. Ashley, "Gay Liberation: How a Once Radical Movement Got Married and Settled Down," *New Labor Forum* 24, no. 3 (2015): 30, doi:10.1177/1095796015597453.

[16] Alexander, Meem, and Gibson, *Finding Out*, 71–72.

[17] Armstrong and Crage, "Movements and Memory," 744; Patterson, introduction to *Queering Sexual Violence*, 8; Stephanie Gilmore and Elizabeth Kaminski, "A Part and Apart: Lesbian and Straight Feminist Activists Negotiate Identity in a Second-Wave Organization," *Journal of the History of Sexuality* 16, no. 1 (2007): 95–113, doi:10.1353/sex.2007.0038.

within the Gay Liberation Movement to include Black leaders in high-profile events were often met with controversy, and many activist groups outside the movement distanced themselves from associating with gay rights altogether.[18]

The 1970s and Beyond

Anti–violence against women and gay liberation efforts formed a strong but incredibly flawed foundation for the modern movement to end gender violence in the United States. Their contributions to crisis services, legal advocacy, and public visibility of gender violence issues were unprecedented and influenced the academic study of gender violence through women's studies programs and lesbian and gay studies courses at universities.[19] Though many people of color, Indigenous groups, poor and working-class people, and individuals working in taboo professions like the sex industry were involved in laying this groundwork, their efforts often went unrecognized and their interests underrepresented—an unfortunate reality of intersectional oppression that carried over into scholarly research. The contributions of traditionally marginalized groups remain unacknowledged even in recently published historical accounts, and the concerns of these groups are still underprioritized in studies on gender violence.

The 1980s into the new millennium were a mixed bag for gender violence prevention and response. Important legal advancements were made, more governmental funding was allocated than ever before, and a large body of research on gender, sexuality, and violence was generated alongside decades of services and education provided by nonprofit organizations. Anti–violence against women activism continued, but not with the fervor of the 1970s. Bisexual activists were successful in making their identities more visible,[20]

---

[18] Alexander, Meem, and Gibson, *Finding Out*, 72.

[19] Marilyn J. Boxer, "Women's Studies as Women's History," *Women's Studies Quarterly* 30, no. 3/4 (2002): 42–51, https://www.jstor.org/stable/40003241; Jennifer Miller, "Thirty Years of Queer Theory," in *Introduction to LGBTQ+ Studies: A Cross-Disciplinary Approach*, ed. Deborah P. Amory, Sean G. Massey, Jennifer Miller, and Allison P. Brown (Geneseo, NY: Milne, 2022), https://milnepublishing.geneseo.edu/introlgbtqstudies/chapter/thirty-years-of-queer-theory/.

[20] Loraine Hutchins, "Making Bisexuals Visible," in *Identities and Place: Changing Labels and Intersectional Communities of LGBTQ and Two-Spirit People in the United States*, ed. Katherine Crawford-Lackey and Megan E. Springate (New York: Berghahn Books, 2020), https://doi.org/10.3167/9781789204797.

but the AIDS crisis of the 1980s shifted most gay rights work toward those of survival, health care, and responding to public antigay sentiment.[21] The Second National March on Washington for Gay and Lesbian Rights in 1987, attended by more than four times as many people as the first march, reinvigorated grassroots local activism through organizations like ACT UP.[22]

As feminist activism was reignited in the 1990s and 2000s with a stronger focus on intersectionality, media critique, and more open discussion of sex and gender violence, additional topics became a part of public discussion, like sexual harassment, sexist language, and discrimination in education. Youth activism, debates about gay individuals in the military, and attention to hate crimes increased.[23] In the 2000s into the 2010s the internet and social media simultaneously created new opportunities for crisis centers, activists, and people affected by gender violence to reach audiences and presented new challenges related to the use of technology-assisted harassment, stalking, nonconsensual distribution of pornography, and other forms of gender violence. There were also advancements in the legality of same-gender marriage in the United States and increased visibility of transgender identities.[24]

Over the past decade, many activists, organizations, and scholars have advocated for even more inclusivity in what we consider gender violence and who experiences it. Many crisis centers have changed their names and strategies in rejection of an exclusive focus on women, and the scope of queer liberation issues has become a spectrum that includes intersex, asexual, and a broad range of gender nonconforming identities. More LGBTIQA+ (lesbian, gay, bisexual, transgender, intersex, queer, asexual/aromatic, and other) programs and services include an explicit focus on sexual and partner violence, and more sexual and partner violence–focused efforts are LGBTIQA+ inclusive. We've got a lot to show for where the movement to end gender violence is now, but we still have a lot of work to do.

---

[21] Alexander, Meem, and Gibson, *Finding Out*, 93–96.
[22] John D'Emilio, "After Stonewall," in *Queer Cultures*, ed. Deborah Carlin and Jennifer DiGrazia (Upper Saddle River, NJ: Pearson Education, 2004), 3–38.
[23] Alexander, Meem, and Gibson, *Finding Out*, 93–104.
[24] Ibid., 101–5.

Where We Are after Fifty Years

Building on the previous fifty years, our current efforts in the movement to end gender violence primarily involve five areas: crisis services, legal advocacy, criminal prosecution, institutional policy and procedure, and education and awareness raising. In this section, I explore key successes and limitations of our work that necessitate a new framework for prevention and response.

Crisis Services

Trauma-informed crisis services in brick-and-mortar centers, through hotlines, and across the internet provide integral support for people affected by gender violence and serve as symbolic representations of the public's acknowledgment of the problem.[25] They demonstrate the impact of gender violence on victims, remind others that gender violence occurs, and often operate as sites of resistance against the silencing of victims' voices and needs. In addition to offering emergency shelter, many partner-violence-focused programs provide crisis advocates who assist individuals with filing legal paperwork and navigating court processes after reporting. Sexual-violence-focused programs often dispatch victim advocates to hospitals to support individuals through emergency medical treatment and forensic evidence collection; they may also coordinate community- or countywide SARTs (sexual assault response teams) to increase communication among police, hospital staff, and other social service agencies assisting victims. Many sexual and partner violence programs also provide support for people who experience stalking, sex trafficking, and sexual exploitation. National and regional hotlines provide anonymous help for those in crisis, support people navigating LGBTIQA+ identities, or offer ways to report suspected human trafficking. Child marriage, genital cutting, bullying, hate crimes, and online harassment are also engaged by a variety of separate programs and centers. Many educational institutions and places of employment have integrated support services into their human resources or equity offices.

---

[25] Ake and Arnold, "Brief History," 8.

Many of these programs have become permanent and streamlined through federal and state funding allocated through legislation like the Violence Against Women Act (VAWA), which was first passed in 1994 to set national priorities for responding to sexual and partner violence and ensure financial support for prevention and response, accountability for offenders, and safety for victims.[26] With institutionalization, however, programs became more limited by funding-specific requirements that narrow the scope of who they serve, necessitate resource-intensive grant writing and reporting, and encourage traditional approaches over creative, cutting-edge strategies that break with status quo thinking about the issues. In addition, type-specific programs that focus on sexual violence, partner violence, trafficking, LGBTIQA+ populations, or culturally specific issues are often put in competition with one another through funding structures established in the 1970s, resulting in less collaboration and more isolated efforts.

Crisis services are not always physically accessible for the populations they serve, especially in rural and low-income areas. Many programs have staff not trained in areas of gender violence less common but still present in the United States, like forced sterilization, forced marriage, and honor killings. Many partner violence shelters exclude men, transgender individuals, and people who are gender nonconforming. And many still primarily focus on the needs of White, cisgender, heterosexual women and do not adequately address the challenges of LGBTIQA+ individuals, people of color, Indigenous populations, people with disabilities, immigrants, and those living in poverty who have experienced gender violence. Employers and institutions may claim to support people who experience discrimination or violence through human resources or equity offices, but most exist primarily to protect the legal interests and image of the organization.

---

[26] Angela R. Gover and Angela M. Moore, "The 1994 Violence Against Women Act: A Historic Response to Gender Violence," *Violence against Women* 27, no. 1 (2021): 8–29, doi:10.1177/1077801220949705.

Additional Information

The Language of Victim and Survivor

Many nonprofit organizations and activists use the label *survivor* to describe someone who is moving forward after experiencing gender violence. Legal and criminal system professionals use *victim* almost exclusively. Which term is best? Both labels can be limiting: each has been used to shape public narratives about gender violence, pressure individuals to process their experiences a certain way, and even exclude people from the support and accountability they deserve.[a] In general, I recommend using person-first language instead of either term as an inclusive way to refer to *people who have experienced gender violence.*[b] If someone uses *victim* or *survivor* to describe themselves, you can follow suit in how you refer to them. In this book, I use both victim terminology and person-first language to call attention to the impact of gender violence (that these experiences are violent and often involve violation of emotional and physical boundaries) and invite broader accessibility for people who may have experienced gender violence but do not identify with the survivor label.

[a] Jennifer L. Freitag, "Four Transgressive Declarations for Ending Gender Violence," in *Transgressing Feminist Theory and Discourse*, ed. Jennifer Dunn and Jimmie Manning (London: Routledge, 2018), 134–50.

[b] Ibid.

Legal Advocacy

Changes to numerous gender-violence-related laws in the United States have been made as a result of legal advocacy that began in the 1970s. Activists and partner abuse shelters, for example, helped make spousal rape illegal in all fifty states by 1993.[27] Today, many state coalitions and gender-violence-focused organizations hire attorneys to lead efforts in creating laws to improve crisis services, increase victims' rights in court, and hold people who commit gender violence more accountable; they also publish and distribute

---

[27] Raquel K. Bergen and Elizabeth Barnhill, "Marital Rape: New Research and Directions," VAWnet, February 2006, https://vawnet.org/material/marital-rape-new-research-and-directions.

materials about laws and cases to individual centers and programs. Legal successes over the past two decades include the *Lawrence v. Texas* ruling in 2003 that made laws against consensual same-gender sex unconstitutional, the Matthew Shepard and James Byrd Jr. Hate Crimes Protection Act passed in 2009 to improve investigation and prosecution of hate crimes, the repeal of Don't Ask, Don't Tell in 2010 that allowed lesbian, gay, and bisexual individuals to serve openly in the military, *United States v. Windsor* in 2013 and *Obergefell v. Hodges* in 2015 that made advances in marriage equality for same-gender couples, and the *Bostock v. Clayton County* ruling in 2020 that prohibits employment discrimination based on sexual orientation and gender identity.[28] VAWA has also been updated over the years to increase support for culturally specific services, people with disabilities, LGBTIQA+ populations, and Indigenous communities as well as address technology-assisted abuse, housing and economic stability, and violence in rural areas.[29]

Changes in laws, however, do not always mean updates in implementation. Though law can help facilitate shifts in public opinion, attitudes about gender violence do not change quickly. Affirmative consent laws, for example, may give prosecutors the ability to hold perpetrators of rape more accountable due to clearer definitions of sexual consent, but negative stereotypes about sexual violence and victims held by investigators, arbitrators, judges, and juries still dramatically affect the way that laws are interpreted. Legal loopholes and differing interpretations of crimes can also limit their effectiveness. Some legislation may require certain actions on the part of schools, college campuses, and other public institutions—such as mandatory prevention programs—but lack the funding necessary for realistic or effective implementation. Other laws might institute policies but offer no recourse if mandated measures are ignored, like crime victims' right to be notified when their attackers are released on bail. Some laws also have unintended consequences: hate crime

---

[28] Alexander, Meem, and Gibson, *Finding Out*, 98–107; U.S. Department of Justice Civil Rights Division, "The Matthew Shepard and James Byrd, Jr., Hate Crimes Prevention Act of 2009," May 30, 2023, https://www.justice.gov/crt/matthew-shepard-and-james-byrd-jr-hate-crimes-prevention-act-2009-0; *Bostock v. Clayton County*, No. 17-1618 (U.S. June 15, 2020).

[29] Office on Violence against Women, "Violence Against Women Act: Milestones Achieved and the Road Ahead," U.S. Department of Justice, September 13, 2023, https://www.justice.gov/ovw/blog/violence-against-women-act-milestones-achieved-and-road-ahead.

legislation, for example, may make violence against LGBTIQA+ individuals more prosecutable but do so within a criminal system context typically biased against members of marginalized populations. Well-intentioned mandatory arrest policies for domestic violence calls to police may deter reporting. Other laws are still terribly inefficient. In Indigenous communities, the historical lack of jurisdiction and limited resources has often meant zero accountability for non-Native people who commit sexual assault against Natives.[30] Add to these current challenges numerous legal battles in the 2020s around Title IX, restroom access, gender-affirming health care, reproductive rights, and LGBTIQA+-inclusive education.

Criminal Prosecution

Changes to gender violence laws in the United States have coincided with an emphasis on victim empowerment and committer accountability through the criminal system. Better laws have meant that police can respond more swiftly and effectively to calls and reports. Improvements in forensic evidence collection and testing assist prosecutors in convicting sexually violent crimes. Victims have more rights as they move through court proceedings, and judges can file restraining orders against abusers to help ensure victim safety. In theory, these changes should mean more accountability for people who commit gender violence as well as more safety and justice for people who experience it, but this is far from the reality. Continued mistreatment of people who experience gender violence—especially those who belong to marginalized groups—deters reporting. Misperceptions about gender violence influence rates of arrest and thoroughness of investigations. Victims of some crimes are still stigmatized to the extent that they themselves are arrested, as is often the case with sex trafficking and sexual exploitation. Abusers violate restraining orders without consequences. Lack of resources leaves forensic evidence unpreserved and untested. Judges and juries may be lenient when criminals are White, cisheterosexual, upper-class, well-known members of their communities, making people of color the ones most likely to be incarcerated and

---

[30] Sarah Deer, *The Beginning and End of Rape: Confronting Violence in Native Communities* (Minneapolis: University of Minnesota Press, 2015).

economically exploited through the US criminal system.[31] Prejudice based on sexual orientation, gender identity, social class, and citizenship may increase an individual's likelihood of serving prison time. Few programs exist for successful rehabilitation of people who commit gender violence, and being in prison may increase an individual's vulnerability to sexual violence, anti-LGBTIQA+ discrimination, and forced sterilization.

Institutional Policy and Procedure

Even successful prosecution may leave people feeling disempowered, further traumatized, and unsatisfied in their quest for justice because of the nature of the process. Institutional policies and procedures in educational, work, and organizational environments may offer some recourse: their facilitation of accountability for gender violence may take place concurrently with criminal proceedings but do so on a completely separate basis. Employers might terminate positions, organizations may remove people from leadership, athletic teams might drop players, and professional networks may release statements condemning behavior. Should employers or organizations fail to respond to gender violence appropriately, individuals, families, and groups can file civil lawsuits or make complaints with the Equal Employment Opportunity Commission.

In educational contexts, universities and grade schools can discipline students and staff for committing gender violence. Title IX offices are becoming more common in PreK–12 school districts to enforce violations of gender-based discrimination, and students and their families are using lawsuits to respond to dress-code discrimination, inequitable restroom access, and homophobic policies by schools themselves. In higher education, changes to gender violence definitions and policies in the early 2000s and beyond mean that college campuses can respond more effectively to student accusations. Complaints can be investigated and arbitrated through campus processes involving Title IX staff, hearing boards, and judicial officers—and since these cases require a lower burden of proof than in criminal proceedings, students who experience

---

[31] Avery F. Gordon, "Globalism and the Prison Industrial Complex: An Interview with Angela Davis," *Race & Class* 40, no. 2/3 (1998): 145–57, doi:10.1177/030639689904000210.

gender violence can seek more accessible routes to safety or justice whether or not they pursue court processes outside the institution. College campuses can punish students who commit gender violence by withdrawing scholarships, requiring changes to class schedules, mandating issue-specific education, or removing them from campus through suspension or expulsion. If students do not feel that their accusations of gender violence are adequately addressed, they can file lawsuits against universities and prompt institution-wide investigations by the US Department of Education.

The US military punishes people who commit gender violence through the Uniform Code of Military Justice. Separate from the civilian criminal system, servicepeople can be held accountable by military commanders through a variety of methods including administrative action (like a reprimand or requirement to attend counseling), nonjudicial punishment (immediate corrective action), or court-martial (a formal trial).[32] The military has its own anonymous helpline to assist victims of sexual assault, specific offices related to sexual and domestic abuse, a confidential option for reporting, and military-specific advocates who provide support. Still, navigating this system can be difficult since commanders have sole discretion in determining how accusations of gender violence are handled.

Whatever the context, ineffective institutional response still occurs in a variety of forms. Rules and policies may lack clear definitions or fail to include all forms of gender violence. Employers, supervisors, leaders, teachers, boards of directors, administrators, commanding officers, and human resources staff may not take reports seriously, conduct thorough investigations, or enforce meaningful consequences for people who violate policies. Some institutions may respond to accusations by requiring the individual who experienced gender violence to change jobs, classes, or schedules instead of the person who committed the behavior; others may allow instigators to quietly resign and easily move on to positions at other places. Again, all of these issues contribute to less reporting of gender violence.

Education and Awareness Raising

In the United States, most gender violence prevention education and training is provided by crisis service agencies, state coalitions, college

---

[32] U.S. Department of Defense, "Military Justice Overview," https://vwac.defense.gov/military.aspx.

campuses, and gender-focused organizations. Sexual and partner violence prevention is mandated at many educational institutions through state and federal law, and college campuses and military bases often pay their own staff to implement programming. Crisis service agencies collaborate with schools, law enforcement, county prosecutors, and community partners. State coalitions create print and electronic curricula for prevention. Social media platforms allow for quick distribution of current events, proposed legal changes, and news related to gender violence. Online support networks, hashtag campaigns, and viral videos empower countless victims to disclose their experiences in virtual spaces, challenge misconceptions about gender violence, and inspire creative responses to these issues. Awareness months, visibility days, Pride parades, and national and international campaigns encourage around-the-year involvement.

Still, attitudes about gender violence continue to be influenced by political rhetoric, news coverage, and court decisions. Many companies have been under fire for supporting Pride campaigns; others express support of LGBTIQA+ communities only to sell more products. Many high-profile celebrities accused of gender violence still garner the support of the general public. And many people believe that the increase in visibility of gender violence issues corresponds to overreaction by victims, overly strict policies, and unfair treatment of the accused—the very opposite of the usual reality of these issues.

Isolated funding streams and cuts to resources limit educational efforts. Institutionalization has meant more competition, less collaboration and creativity, and narrow focus on type-specific prevention for sexual or partner violence. Many training and awareness-raising efforts leave out violence against LGBTIQA+ individuals and fail to address how gender violence affects marginalized populations and people who don't fit the victim stereotype (like people of color, men, individuals who are especially muscular or athletic, and sex workers). Additionally, many programs choose to deprioritize prevention when financial resources dwindle. College campuses are under pressure to implement cost-saving programming that compromises educational quality. Grade schools often lack trained staff and strategies for sustainable implementation. And even when companies and organizations do have the financial support for training and education, leaders often opt for the quickest and least expensive ways to meet requirements.

Case Example

Tarana Burke and the Me Too Movement

Many people believe that the Me Too Movement began in 2017 after actor Alyssa Milano asked her Twitter followers to reply "me too" if they had experienced sexual harassment or assault. Milano's high-profile status helped draw attention to the recently reported allegations against Harvey Weinstein and other powerful men, but she was not the first to start this conversation or use the powerfully galvanizing "me too" phrase to do so. In actuality, an activist named Tarana Burke started the Me Too Movement in 2006 to support young Black women and girls from low-wealth communities who had experienced sexual violence.[a] For Burke, the idea of "me too" is focused on empowerment through empathy.[b] She says, "I thought about how powerful it feels to not be alone. How empowering it is to know you don't have to walk a journey by yourself, to know that you're not the only one. And how inherently powerful it is to do things collectively."[c]

Even after learning that Burke was the creator of the Me Too Movement, news sources repeatedly credited Milano with being its champion. Even now, when people think about #MeToo, it is likely they think about a group of White celebrities.[d] In 2018, Allyson Hobbs made the point that "despite the enduring legacy of testimony by Black women, White women have often played the protagonists in the history of sexual violence, and Black women have been relegated to the supporting cast. Harriet Jacobs, Recy Taylor, Fannie Lou Hamer, and countless others took great risk and made great sacrifices, making it possible for more women to tell their stories, but many of us do not know their names."[e] It is important, therefore, to acknowledge Tarana Burke's legacy, and the legacy of Black women, in our collective work to end gender violence.

[a]   Me Too Movement, "History & Inception," 2024, https://metoomvmt.org/get-to-know-us/history-inception/.

[b]   Tarana Burke, *Unbound: My Story of Liberation and the Birth of the Me Too Movement* (New York: Flatiron, 2021).

[c]   Nicole Carroll, "Tarana Burke on the Power of Empathy, the Building Block of the Me Too Movement," *USA Today*, August 19, 2020, https://www.usatoday.com/in-depth/life/women-of-the-century/2020/08/19/tarana-burke-me-too-movement-19th-amendment-women-of-century/5535976002/.

d Thalia Charles, "The White Washing of #MeToo," *Medium*, November 9, 2018, https://medium.com/periodmovement/the-white-washing-of-metoo-bf778620f29.

e Allyson Hobbs, "One Year of #MeToo: The Legacy of Black Women's Testimonies," *New Yorker*, October 10, 2018, https://www.newyorker.com/culture/personal-history/one-year-of-metoo-the-legacy-of-black-womens-testimonies.

A Comprehensive Approach to Gender Violence

When it comes to the problem of gender violence, one thing is clear: we have a lot of work to do. We need to meet the challenges of effectively responding to and preventing gender violence with a massive amount of creative and intellectual energy. We must think bigger and broader and be more innovative and imaginative if we truly hope to decrease rates of gender violence and mitigate its effects on millions of people around the world. We must engage in thoughtful dialogue about what we are doing, what is not working, and how we can do it better. We must collaboratively address the challenges involved with taking on such an enormous issue, especially when financial support is limited. We must generate new ideas and approaches that reinvigorate the work and help it become more sustainable. These realities necessitate a new framework for how we think about gender violence that informs the strategies we use to end it.

A comprehensive approach to understanding gender violence involves (1) viewing all forms of gender violence as issues that stem from the same root causes and contributors; (2) examining the defining characteristics, types, prevalence, and impact of gender violence as a whole rather than separately; and (3) analyzing how the relationship between all of these aspects contributes to the immensity, complexity, and regularity of gender violence and its overlap with other systems of oppression. Envision the ongoing problem of gender violence as a rotating, smooth-running wheel and each specific form of it a spoke that radiates from a central hub (see figure 1.1). In a wheel, the spokes work collectively to keep it rolling, but the hub bears most of the load. In this visualization,

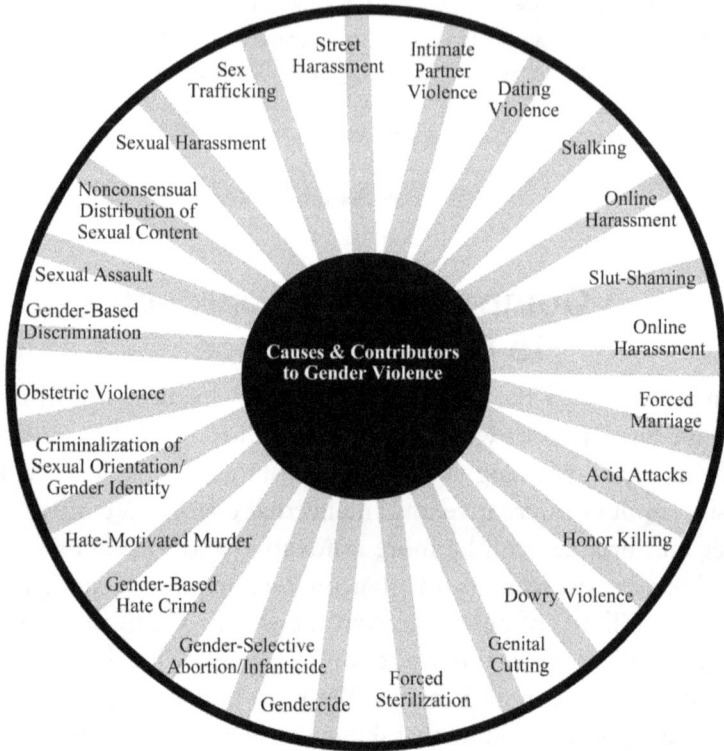

Figure 1.1. The Wheel of Gender Violence
Note: Not an exhaustive list of all types of gender violence

each type of gender violence is a spoke rooted in the same causes and contributors at the hub. Instead of isolated social phenomena, all forms of gender violence involve similar dynamics of power and control, apply similar understandings of gender roles and expectations, and are more likely to occur if certain contributing factors are present. Regardless of type, individuals experience similar emotional and psychological responses to gender violence and are often treated similarly by others after sharing about their experiences. This impact is also felt in their relationships, their communities, and the institutions to which they belong. The same underlying misperceptions about gender violence influence prevailing cultural attitudes about how often it occurs, what causes it, who commits it, who experiences it, and how it is disclosed to others. Each form of gender violence—and its degree of cultural acceptance—is reinforced by its relationship to other forms. They all help the wheel keep rolling. Unfortunately, there are so many spokes that focusing on them individually doesn't actually slow the wheel down all that much. Activists and educators have put a tremendous amount of energy into bending or breaking spokes over the last several decades, but the wheel keeps rolling because it is powered by a strong hub of root causes without which the wheel could not function.

A comprehensive approach to understanding gender violence has two main implications for response and prevention. First, it makes the problem of gender violence much harder to ignore. Independently, each form of gender violence is deserving of public attention, engagement, and change-making efforts on national and global scales. When considered together, however, they represent pieces of a more massive pandemic-sized problem worthy of an equally proportionate amount of energy and resources. A comprehensive approach makes it easier to communicate which groups of people experience the highest rates of gender violence across all forms because of intersecting prejudice and oppression—and how this reality should inform our efforts moving forward. Put another way, *we can argue a better case for the work we are doing*. Second, engaging gender violence as a ginormous system demonstrates why the problem is difficult to solve despite a multitude of type-specific prevention and response efforts. Shifting our focus to the main causes and contributors of gender violence can help us become more efficient with our resources, less isolated in our work, better equipped to challenge misperceptions and engage complexities, and more focused on cultural change at the problem's place of origin. We can more strategically combine efforts to attack the problem at its source and *shut the system down*.

I have written each chapter in this book as a building block of this comprehensive approach. The first five chapters are foundational for understanding the *what* of gender violence. I start with definitions and a holistic discussion of types to clarify what it is we are addressing; then I move into what we know about gender violence across all types: which groups are affected by it most, how people experience it on an individual level, and what this means on a broader, collective scale. The last five chapters are the *why* of gender violence. I explain how the system of gender is the primary root cause, how cultural acceptance of gender violence capitalizes on this system, and how a variety of other contributors add to this cycle. I address how misperceptions about gender violence that stem from these causes and contributors distort, oversimplify, and misrepresent the problem and the people involved. I end with ways to apply this comprehensive understanding, whatever your role in the movement to end gender violence.

Throughout this book, I draw from both my on-the-ground work as a prevention and response practitioner and my training as a communication researcher with an interdisciplinary social science focus that brings together perspectives from sociology, psychology, anthropology, criminology, and gender and sexuality studies. You will read about what we've learned—and have yet to investigate—through research and examples of how the realities of gender violence play out in people's lives and popular culture. My hope is that you become better equipped to talk about and engage these issues in a deeper and more holistic way.

Take Care as You Read This Book

I suspect that taking on this big-picture approach to gender violence might be overwhelming at times. Whether you are an educator, crisis advocate, first responder, activist, researcher, stakeholder, student, or person directly impacted by issues of gender violence yourself, it requires a lot of energy to take on the world's trauma. I recommend you proceed through this book with caution and care for your own well-being. Take breaks when you need them, and find ways to process what you are reading with others. Explore ways to connect with those who care about these issues, and consider what actions you can take for self-care and preservation.

When I teach semester-long courses on gender violence, I often end each class session with a video, image, or anecdote that takes us out of the trauma and into the rest of the day; perhaps you might begin a regular practice of doing something that contributes to your happiness as you conclude each chapter. One of my favorite videos is a narrated illustration by Chanel Miller called "Courage."[33] As in

---

[33] Chanel Miller, "Courage by Chanel Miller," YouTube video, from a presentation for Futures without Violence Night of Courage in February 2020, posted by New Revolution Media, May 11, 2020, https://www.youtube.com/watch?v=bmNArab8I6Y.

much of her art, Chanel's honesty and vulnerability in this piece is intermingled with a lightheartedness and hope that keeps me going. This is to say: keep returning to whatever motivates you forward. You will need it as we confront the problem of gender violence in and beyond the pages of this book.

CHAPTER 2

Defining Gender Violence

I believe that a comprehensive approach to gender violence begins with the language used to describe it. Gender-based violence, or gender violence, is a continuum of harmful and violent actions in which gender plays a significant role. More than a simple umbrella term for a group of related phenomena, *gender violence* is the most direct, concise, and inclusive way to emphasize the impact of these issues and why they occur in the patterned ways that they do. This is why I use this wording rather than *violence against women.*

Gender suggests the underlying significance of gendered social roles, expectations, and power dynamics. Most acts of gender violence are committed by heterosexual men toward women, transgender and gender nonconforming individuals, and men; for some types of gender violence, like sexual assault, partner violence, and stalking, men are responsible for nearly 90 percent of victimizations.[1] Women disproportionately experience gender violence far more than men, and incidences are even higher for gay, bisexual, and transgender women. Though gender violence may be committed by anyone of any gender identity or sexual orientation toward someone else of any identity, the unequal distribution of who is primarily committing the acts—and who is being victimized by them—points to gendered power dynamics characteristic of a system that privileges men's bodies, heterosexuality, cisgender identity, and traditional expressions of masculinity.

In a *system of gender*, rigid gender roles and expectations influence individual expressions of identity, interpersonal

---

[1] Patricia Tjaden and Nancy Thoennes, "Stalking in America: Findings from the National Violence against Women Survey," U.S. Department of Justice, 1998, https://www.ncjrs.gov/pdffiles/169592.pdf.

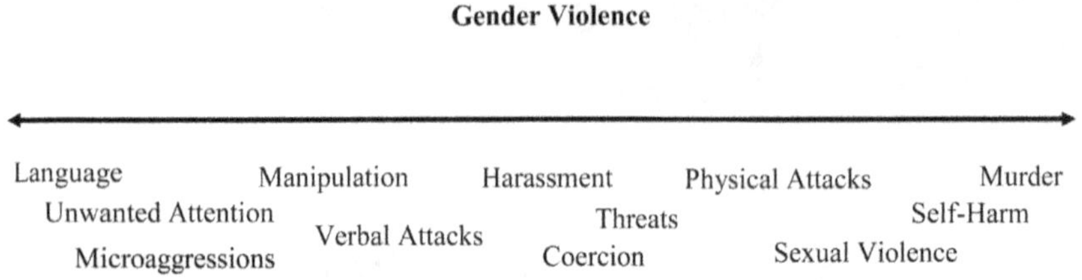

Gender Violence

Language   Manipulation   Harassment   Physical Attacks   Murder
    Unwanted Attention   Threats   Self-Harm
               Verbal Attacks
     Microaggressions   Coercion   Sexual Violence

Figure 2.1. Continuum of Gender Violence
Note: Depending on the frequency, context, and other specific factors involved in acts of gender violence, this continuum may look and feel different from person to person. For more on individual differences in the experience of gender violence, see chapter 4.

communication, group and family dynamics, institutional norms, and socialized patterns of participation in society.[2] Most people who commit gender violence do so as a way to assert, maintain, or regain power and control in this gendered system; in other words, gender violence is a way that some individuals *do gender* through violent power dynamics.[3] This explains why acts of gender violence are often enacted by those with more systemic power and privilege against those with less when it comes to gender, gender identity, gender expression, sexual orientation, and sexual behavior.

Violence suggests the serious physical, emotional, psychological, economic, or other effects suffered by those on the receiving end of gendered exertions of power or force. Best thought of across a continuum (see figure 2.1),[4] violence in gendered contexts can range from subtle microaggressions to injurious or fatal physical force. *Gendered microaggressions* are nonverbal behaviors, written and spoken language, and other actions that indirectly or sometimes unintentionally discriminate against members of marginalized groups, like women, LGBTIQA+ individuals, or men not perceived as upholding expectations for traditional masculinity. Though subtle, microaggressions reinforce power dynamics, contribute to other

---

[2] Cecilia L. Ridgeway and Lynn Smith-Lovin, "The Gender System and Interaction," *Annual Review of Sociology* 25, no. 1 (1999): 191, doi:10.1146/annurev.soc.25.1.191.

[3] Merry, *Gender Violence*, 11.

[4] Liz Kelly, *Surviving Sexual Violence* (Oxford: Polity Press, 1988); bell hooks, "Violence in Intimate Relationships: A Feminist Perspective," in *Gender Violence: Interdisciplinary Perspectives*, ed. Laura L. O'Toole, Jessica R. Schiffman, and Margie L. Kiter Edwards, 2nd ed. (New York: New York University Press, 2007), 269–75; Adrien K. Wing, introduction to *Critical Race Feminism: A Reader*, ed. Adrien K. Wing (New York: New York University Press, 2003), 1–19; Joanne Belknap, *The Invisible Woman: Gender, Crime, and Justice*, 4th ed. (Stamford, CT: Cengage Learning, 2014), 289.

forms of discrimination, and sometimes act as precursors to more direct forms of violence. In addition to microaggressions, gender violence can involve manipulation, unwanted attention, coercion, control, deceit, verbal attacks, harassment, threats to self or others, financial exploitation, invasion of privacy, manipulation, physical abuse, or assault. Gender violence can cause short- and long-term discomfort, fear, emotional distress, economic instability, severe psychological trauma, and physical injury. It can send threatening messages to the community to which an individual belongs (like girls in a school, the transgender population in a particular city, or anyone expressing femininity). It can also be fatal.

The overlap of acts of gender violence with other systems of power and privilege based on race, class, age, nationality, ethnicity, language, religion, and other categories of identity has several implications. First, it means that gender roles and expectations differ depending on a variety of cultural factors and contribute to the perpetration and acceptance of gender violence in different ways. Second, this overlap influences how someone experiences an act of gender violence against them, why certain individuals may be targeted within specific contexts, and the challenges one might face seeking support, help, or justice after experiencing gender violence. Third, a variety of cultural factors impact how people who commit acts of gender violence are viewed and how others respond to their actions. Fourth, acts of gender violence fortify existing systems of oppression by further marginalizing groups with less power and privilege.[5]

Gender violence is a complex social issue characterized by violent power dynamics and various degrees of harm and force and overlap with intersecting systems of oppression. Gender violence is also *violent* in the sense that its pervasiveness influences the ways that people move through the world and interact with others—whether or not they have directly experienced severe physical or psychological effects. People may quit jobs in response to rumors of pay inequity, compulsively use risk-reduction techniques to keep themselves safe when alone at night, withdraw from deepening intimate

---

[5] Crenshaw, "Mapping the Margins;" Hill Collins, *Black Feminist Thought*; Rubin, "Thinking Sex"; Patterson, introduction to *Queering Sexual Violence*; Vazquez, "Spirit and Passion."

partnerships, or hide parts of their identities that might make them vulnerable to attack. The *fear* of gender violence contributes to ways individuals learn gender in societies, making it a component of how we express ourselves and communicate with one another.

Due to the gendered cultural context in which it occurs, an argument could be made that most of men's and boys' violence against anyone—when motivated by the societal pressures associated with manhood and the performance of traditional masculinity—is gender violence. Gender roles and expectations may psychologically harm all people subjected to a rigid system of gender, including men. In fact, much of men's violence against one another (including bullying, hazing, physical assault, murder, gun violence, bombings, war-related violence, and acts of violent extremism) may be motivated by gendered assumptions. In addition to also being the recipients of other men's psychological and sexual violence, men are subjected to the pressures of being perceived as traditionally masculine in a system that all genders of people may participate in upholding. This can lead to men's decreased self-esteem, self-destructive behavior, and self-harm.

Gender violence, as a whole, can be categorized based on specific actions involved in how it is committed (see table 2.1). I prefer to describe the six main types of gender violence as gender-based discrimination, sexual violence, partner violence, stalking, ideologically motivated gender violence, and gender-based hate crime. The actions included in each category share specific dynamics of power and control and often overlap with one another, have a symbiotic relationship with other forms of gender violence, and can occur simultaneously against a person or in a given situation— making them far more complicated than the distinct types presented here. In addition, since the study of gender violence is an evolving field, these categorizations, definitions, and examples are constantly subject to change.

Gender-Based Discrimination

Discrimination is unfair treatment based on prejudiced perceptions of someone's identity or group membership. Discrimination functions to limit, restrict, or exclude members of certain populations

TABLE 2.1. **Types of Gender Violence**

Type	Gender-Based Discrimination	Sexual Violence	Partner Violence	Stalking	Ideologically Motivated Gender Violence	Gender-Based Hate Crime
Description	Unfair treatment based on prejudiced beliefs about gender and sexuality	Nonconsensual sexual conduct or sexual touching	Pattern of abusive behavior by a dating or romantic partner for power and control	Pattern of harassing and monitoring that causes someone to feel discomfort, fear, or distress	Acts of gender violence allowed and encouraged by ideological beliefs in specific cultural contexts	Psychological, physical, or sexual attacks motivated by prejudiced beliefs about gender and sexuality
Examples	Institutional discrimination, organizational discrimination, public/online discrimination, obstetric violence, period poverty, criminalization of sexual orientation and gender identity	Sexual assault, nonconsensual condom removal/use resistance, genital exposure, drug-facilitated sexual assault, sex trafficking, sexual exploitation, sexual harassment, street harassment, voyeurism, nonconsensual distribution of sexual content, sextortion	Intimate partner violence, dating violence, domestic violence, reproductive coercion, coercive control	Online harassment, bullying/cyberbullying, slut shaming	Forced/child marriage, bride kidnapping, acid attacks, dowry violence, genital cutting, breast ironing, forced sterilization, forced contraception/abortion, gendercide, gender-selective abortion/infanticide, institutionally sanctioned abuse	Homophobic hate crime, transphobic hate crime, aphobic hate crime, hate-motivated murder

Additional Information

LGBTIQA+ Terminology

Language used to describe people who identify across the LGBTIQA+ spectrum is constantly evolving. In general, the initialism *LGBTIQA* (or groups of similar letters, sometimes ordered differently, and sometimes with an added plus sign) is used as a unifying descriptor of people who identify themselves as outside of the assumed heterosexual, cisgender norm.

Lesbian refers to women who are physically, romantically, or emotionally attracted to other women. Individuals who are nonbinary or gender nonconforming may or may not use this term to describe themselves.

Gay describes people who are physically, romantically, or emotionally attracted to people of the same gender. People of all genders use this term to self-identify.

Bisexual refers to people who are physically, romantically, or emotionally attracted to people of the same or different gender. *Pansexual* is a similar term describing someone who experiences attraction to others regardless of gender identity. Some individuals may prefer one term or use both terms interchangeably.

Transgender describes someone whose gender identity is different from their gender designated at birth. Since a person's gender identity (their innate sense of who they are) is different from their gender expression (how they outwardly express themselves to others), a person may identify as transgender and express themselves in a variety of ways. Someone who is trans may identify or express themselves as any gender with or without the transgender label. *Gender nonconforming* has emerged as an umbrella term for transgender, agender or androgynous (being gender neutral or both man and woman), genderqueer or nonbinary (rejecting the limiting categories of man or woman in their expression), and related identities.

Intersex describes someone who has biological traits like genitals, chromosomes, and internal reproductive hormones that don't match what is typically identified with one gender. Individuals may be designated intersex as infants, not realize they are intersex until puberty or later in life, or may live their entire lives not knowing they are intersex. They can have a variety of different sexual orientations, gender identities, and gender expressions.

Queer is an umbrella term that refers to people who do not identify as heterosexual or *cisgender* (people whose gender designated at birth matches their gender identity). Individuals may self-describe as queer when they feel other labels are too limiting, or as a rejection of those labels. Though *queer* has historically been used as a pejorative slur against LGBTIQA+ people, it has been reclaimed by many to describe themselves. Since it is not a universally accepted term, it is best not to use it unless someone has self-identified as queer.

A-spectrum is an umbrella term used to describe identities across the asexuality and aromantic spectrums. *Aspecs* (people on one or both of these spectrums) may use a variety of terms to self-identify. *Asexual* is a term that describes individuals who experience little or no sexual attraction to others as opposed to being *allosexual* (experiencing sexual attraction to others). Some *aces* (people who are asexual) experience a small degree of sexual attraction (*greysexual*) or sexual attraction when a strong emotional or romantic connection is made with someone (*demisexual*). In contrast to being *alloromantic* (experiencing romantic attraction to others), people who are *aromantic* (or *aro*) experience little or no romantic attraction—or they may experience some (*greyromantic*) or conditional romantic desire (*demiromantic*) for others.

+ Other Identities: The *LGBTIQA* initialism is limited and does not represent all queer or nonnormative identities. As language evolves and LGBTIQA+ activism becomes more inclusive, the initialism will likely evolve. It has become common in Canada, for example, to use *LGBTQ2S* to include two-spirit Indigenous people. *Two-spirit* is an English term that refers to Indigenous individuals who have both masculine and feminine energies or spirits, or an umbrella term for Indigenous people who identify outside the cisgender norm.

Be careful not to assume someone's sexual orientation or gender identity. Unsure of what term or pronoun to use? Always defer to whatever someone has used to describe themselves. If you are unsure, asking may be appropriate—or better yet, wait for that person to share about their identities and labels with you voluntarily.

from receiving the same rights, recognition, benefits, opportunities, or inclusion as those in dominant groups. This can lead to the creation of uncomfortable, offensive, hostile, or unsafe environments for people in nondominant groups. *Gender-based discrimination* involves actions motivated by biased attitudes related to perceived gender, gender identity and expression, sexual orientation, or sexual behavior. Biased attitudes might include those related to gender roles, sexuality, relationship status, appearance, pregnancy status, parental status, or biological functions like breastfeeding or menstruation. Discrimination may involve sexism (individual or institutional prejudice based on gender), homophobia (based on sexual orientation), transphobia (based on gender identity), or aphobia (based on perception of asexual or aromantic identity).

Often punishable through antidiscrimination laws, gender-based discrimination may occur within institutions (like education, health care, or the criminal system), workplaces, organizations (like professional, hobby-related, or religious groups), public spaces (like shopping centers, restaurants, concert venues, restrooms, or transportation services), and online spaces (like websites and social media platforms). In education, it may involve lack of access or barriers to learning or extracurricular activities. Sexist and racist stereotypes may limit girls' confidence and opportunities to excel in the classroom, and restrictive dress codes may lead to unfair discipline for violations. Lack of menstrual products and limited time between classes presents challenges for menstruation management. Schools may prohibit students from wearing clothing, using the restroom or locker room, or joining the athletic team that aligns with their gender identity. *Misgendering* (using pronouns that don't align with how a person wants to be identified) and *deadnaming* (referring to someone using an old name that does not represent their current gender identity) by teachers, administrators, or students may make educational environments hostile for gender nonconforming individuals.

In the workplace, people may experience unfair recruitment and hiring practices, unfair evaluation, pay inequity, exclusion from events or activities, restrictions on leadership, gendered (and racialized) dress codes, idea censorship, misgendering, deadnaming, or refusal to acknowledge or address their complaints. Employees may experience silencing, bullying, or intimidating verbal, nonverbal, or physical behaviors by supervisors or coworkers. Employers may avoid acknowledgment of certain gender identities or sexual orientations. Workplaces may not be accommodating to people who are pregnant, recovering from childbirth or loss of a pregnancy, or breastfeeding.

Gender-based discrimination in health care may occur in hospitals, doctor's offices, and other medical establishments. Physicians, nurses, mental health professionals, emergency medical technicians, and other staff may disregard needs and questions based on a patient's gender or refuse care based on perceived sexual orientation or gender expression. Individuals may lack access to contraception, safe abortions, and choice over their reproductive decisions. *Obstetric violence* occurs when medical professionals treat people who are pregnant or giving birth in disrespectful or harmful ways that may include verbal abuse, failure to gain informed consent for procedures, refusal to provide pain medication, and other forms of abuse and neglect[6] that contribute to birth complications and pregnancy-related deaths. Insurance policies may not cover expenses for reproductive care, hormone treatment, or gender-affirming surgeries, and laws may prohibit doctors from providing them. Many individuals experience *period poverty*, or lack of access to adequate menstrual hygiene management products, facilities, or education.[7] People who are incarcerated may face gender-based discrimination in their reproductive care and lack access to sufficient and good-quality menstrual products in prison.[8] Incarcerated people also face limitations in navigating pregnancy and parenting[9] as well as being able to access gender-affirming health care. The combination of these issues makes the conditions of most women's prisons in the United States worse than men's prisons.[10]

In criminal systems around the world, same-gender romantic and sexual relationships—or sexual acts associated with same-gender interactions, even when consensual—may be criminalized.

---

[6] Nicole Hill, "Understanding Obstetric Violence as Violence against Mothers through the Lens of Matricentric Feminism," *Journal of the Motherhood Initiative for Research & Community Involvement* 10, no. 1/2 (2019): 233–43, https://jarm.journals.yorku.ca/index.php/jarm/article/view/40566.

[7] Janet Michel, Annette Mettler, Silvia Schönenberger, and Daniela Gunz, "Period Poverty: Why It Should Be Everybody's Business," *Journal of Global Health Reports* 6 (2022): 1–4, doi:10.29392/001c.32436.

[8] Mitchell O'Shea Carney, "Cycles of Punishment: The Constitutionality of Restricting Access to Menstrual Health Products in Prisons," *Boston College Law Review* 61, no. 7 (2020): 2541–94, https://lira.bc.edu/work/sc/6b45a9df-7cf8-4ad3-9725-0a78874b69e9.

[9] Belknap, *Invisible Woman*, 270.

[10] Ibid., 269.

Laws may fail to protect people who identify as other than cisgender and heterosexual. Same-gender couples in committed relationships may lack access to marriage or civil unions that offer the same recognition and financial benefits as heterosexual marriages. Transgender and gender nonconforming individuals may struggle to obtain birth certificates, passports, driver's licenses, and other legal documents that affirm their gender identities. Obtaining, providing, or assisting someone with getting an abortion may be illegal and result in severe penalties. Police, attorneys, judges, and other criminal system professionals may fail to believe, protect, or assist people whom they perceive as other than cisgender and heterosexual—especially when they are Indigenous or people of color. Law enforcement officers often use unnecessary and lethal force when interacting with these populations.

In public spaces, people may be denied service or entrance at restaurants, stores, or other establishments. They may be charged more for products, closely monitored, or photographed or filmed without their consent. Individuals may be forcibly removed from businesses for being perceived as looking out of place or using the washroom that matches their gender identity. Online, social media platforms may use policies or algorithms that censor or *shadowban* (when a platform partially or fully blocks a user's content to others without the user's knowledge) people based on their LBGTIQA+ identity, ethnicity, race, size, or discussion of related issues.

Depending on the context, gender-based discrimination may or may not have legal or institutional repercussions. In workplaces, Title VII of the Civil Rights Act prohibits unfair treatment by employers based on gender, sexual orientation, gender identity, pregnancy, and decisions based on gender stereotypes, and the Equal Pay Act requires that men and women be given equal pay for equal work.[11] In educational institutions, Title IX prohibits discrimination related to gender, sexual orientation, gender identity, and pregnancy by any education program or activity receiving

---

[11] US Equal Employment Opportunity Commission, "Sex Discrimination," https://www.eeoc.gov/youth/sex-discrimination.

federal financial support.[12] Unfortunately, asexuality is not mentioned in most state and federal antidiscrimination laws.[13]

Abuse committed by medical staff or police may result in criminal charges or civil lawsuits, but because gendered, racial, and class-based biases are common in those systems, it can be difficult to hold institutions accountable. Discrimination in public and online spaces can be difficult to negotiate when authorities are used as a tool for discrimination (like alerting a bouncer to someone's restroom choice, or calling the police to remove someone for breastfeeding in a store) or when online platforms censor their own users for calling attention to discrimination (like stealth-banning comments on a blog critical of the hosting website's practices).

Sexual Violence

Gender violence that involves sexual contact, behavior, or exploitation is known as *sexual violence*. Often an umbrella term for all forms of nonconsensual sexual conduct or touching, sexual violence is premised on the absence of consent and the use of sexualized actions to exert power and control. Consent is freely and explicitly expressed permission without coercion, manipulation, fraud, or force of any kind. It cannot be requested or gained from a person who is asleep, unconscious, or incapacitated by drugs. Consent cannot exist when someone submits in the midst of being manipulated or pressured, or when they have far less power than their initiator (like a teenager to an adult or an employee to their supervisor).

Sexual assault involves nonconsensual external touching of an area of the body, penetration of a part of the body by a part of someone's else's body or with an object, or sexual exposure of one person's body to someone else. In many situations, sexual assault involves sexualized parts of the body (like genitals, buttocks, breasts, chest, or thighs), but less conspicuous behaviors like inappropriate hugging, sexualized gestures or movements,

---

[12] US Department of Health and Human Services, "Title IX of the Education Amendments of 1972," 2021, https://www.hhs.gov/civil-rights/for-individuals/sex-discrimination/title-ix-education-amendments/index.html.

[13] Lihi Yona, "Identity at Work," *Berkeley Journal of Employment & Labor Law* 43, no. 1 (2022): 139–201, doi:10.15779/Z38JQ0SWZD.

or unnecessary touch anywhere on the body could be considered sexual assault. Legal definitions vary from state to state and use different terms to define and describe sexual assault, including rape, attempted rape, forcible rape, attempted sexual assault, forcible sexual offense, sexual exploitation, unlawful sexual conduct, criminal sexual misconduct, unlawful sexual penetration, sexual abuse, sexual coercion, sexual battery, sexual imposition, importuning, statutory rape, molestation, carnal knowledge, oral copulation by force or fear, sexual torture, and others.

Nonconsensual condom removal, also known as *stealthing*, occurs when a sexual partner removes or purposefully misuses a condom without the other person's consent. There are currently no laws against stealthing though many experts consider it a form of sexual assault.[14] *Coercive condom use resistance* involves the use of manipulative strategies to avoid using a condom with someone who wants to use one.[15]

Genital exposure is showing someone's genitals to another person without their consent. *Indecent exposure* might also include breasts or buttocks and apply to public nudity or sex acts (alone or with others) that are done in public. These could qualify as sexual violence if they cause distress or fear, are done in conjunction with another form of gender violence (such as stalking), or occur in the presence of a minor. *Drug-facilitated sexual assault* involves the use of a drug to commit sexual violence through consensual or nonconsensual intake. In some drug-facilitated sexual assaults, attackers drug victims without their knowledge to make them incapacitated. In others, attackers groom victims by offering a series of beverages, hits, or pills to make them vulnerable to attack. Perpetrators might also target individuals already under the influence of alcohol or other drugs in their efforts to assault someone they perceive as less defensive or capable of fighting back.

Sex trafficking is the use of force, fraud, or coercion to make someone engage in commercial sex acts against their will. According

---

[14] Mikaela Shapiro, "Yes, 'Stealthing' Is Sexual Assault . . . and We Need to Address It," *Touro Law Review* 37, no. 3 (2021): 1–30, https://digitalcommons.tourolaw.edu/lawreview/vol37/iss3/16.

[15] Allira Boadle, Catherine Gierer, and Simone Buzwell, "Young Women Subjected to Nonconsensual Condom Removal: Prevalence, Risk Factors, and Sexual Self-Perceptions," *Violence against Women* 27, no. 10 (2021): 1696–1715, doi:10.1177/1077801220947165.

to federal law, sex trafficking involves recruiting, harboring, transporting, providing, obtaining, patronizing, or soliciting someone for a commercial sex act using force (like physical abuse, sexual assault, or confinement), fraud (making false promises related to work or living conditions, wage withholding, or using false or misleading contracts), or coercion (threats of harm to self or others, debt bondage, document confiscation, or psychological manipulation).[16] *Commercial* means sexual activities exchanged for value, like money, goods, favors, or other benefits. Sex trafficking also applies when the person made to provide the commercial sex act is under the age of eighteen—even if force, fraud, or coercion is not involved.[17] Most sex trafficking business is conducted online, but it may also occur in residential brothels, strip clubs, escort services, massage parlors, pornography production companies, and street prostitution.[18]

State-level sex and labor trafficking laws may differ somewhat from federal law and vary from state to state. *Labor trafficking* has similar dynamics but involves force, fraud, or coercion for involuntary servitude, debt bondage, or slavery.[19] *Sexual exploitation* or *commercial sexual exploitation* involves exploiting someone sexually for material gain, or forcing labor through sexual services. This could include sex trafficking and could occur in pornography, escort services, phone sex, exotic dance, or other industries. Sometimes, sexual exploitation may be carried out through implicit rules about clothing or behaviors to which a person must adhere to meet the demands of a job, role, or opportunity (like wearing tight-fitting clothing, posing in sexual ways, or flirting with customers).

Sexual harassment is usually described in one of two forms—quid pro quo and hostile environment—and often describes gender-based violence in the workplace or within educational institutions. Quid pro quo harassment occurs when a supervisor, teacher, or other individual in a position of power asks for or uses sexual

---

[16] Human Trafficking Hotline, "Federal Law," https://humantraffickinghotline.org/what-human-trafficking/federal-law.

[17] U.S. Department of Justice, "Citizen's Guide to U.S. Federal Law on Child Sex," May 28, 2020, https://www.justice.gov/criminal-ceos/citizens-guide-us-federal-law-child-sex-trafficking.

[18] Polaris, "The Action Means Purpose 'A-M-P' Model," 2012, https://traffickingresourcecenter.org/sites/default/files/AMP%20Model.pdf.

[19] Human Trafficking Hotline, "Federal Law."

favors in exchange for benefits (*quid pro quo* means "this for that") for the person in the lower power position (like an employee, student, or team member). Hostile environment harassment is when a student or employee experiences communication or environment-specific messaging (like disparaging jokes, posted flyers, or comments on an online message board) or another form of gender violence like assault or stalking that makes them feel unwelcome. Depending on the behaviors involved with the harassment, these kinds of violations may fall under Title IX, employment discrimination, or criminal sexual assault laws.

Street harassment in the context of sexual violence involves verbal and nonverbal behaviors that make someone feel uncomfortable or threatened in a public space. Whether sexual or gender-based, street harassment could include unwelcome sexual or gender-based comments, yelling, staring, nonconsensual flirting, pushing, cornering, following, or various forms of sexual assault. Street harassment occurs in public spaces such as streets, sidewalks, parks, buses, trains, or subways; the term is also used to refer more generally to various forms of verbal and nonverbal harassment that occur outside of private or institutionalized spaces like businesses, places of employment, or schools. Gender-based street harassment is often committed by strangers toward people they target based on perceived gender and sexual orientation; street harassment can also lead to stalking or more invasive or injurious forms of physical or sexual assault. Around the world, few laws prohibit street harassment unless it involves other forms of gender violence.

Voyeurism involves watching someone without their permission in environments with presumed privacy—such as restrooms, hotel rooms, or private residences—in which someone may undress or engage in sexual behaviors. Voyeurism may include photography or video used for commercial sale or blackmail, sometimes referred to as *nonconsensual pornography*. *Nonconsensual distribution of sexual content* occurs when consensually filmed or photographed material is shared with others without permission. Sometimes called *image-based abuse*, this may occur when a person obtains content consensually, then sells or distributes that content to others without permission. This type of abuse can also involve digitally altered images or deepfakes. *Sextortion* involves using blackmail to coerce sexual acts or demand money from someone, often via threats to share sexual images or video online or elsewhere.

A lover, committed partner, family member, friend, classmate, coworker, acquaintance, or stranger can commit sexual violence. Motivated by a desire to exert control over someone, sexual violence is less about sex and more about power. It often involves one or more of the following behaviors: identifying and targeting someone; presuming entitlement to another's body or attention; grooming someone to increase trust and comfort; exploiting a person's real or perceived vulnerabilities; circumventing negotiation of consent; violating personal boundaries through manipulation, coercion, or force; and attempting to control the way someone views the assault through intimidation, threats, or manipulation. Sexual violence may occur in the form of child abuse or elder abuse, though gender may not always play an explicit role. Even so, sexual violence in these contexts often involves dynamics of power and control by a member of a dominant group (like adults, able-bodied family members, or caretakers) toward a member of a nondominant or more vulnerable group (like children, elderly individuals, or people with disabilities).

In the context of gender, similar power dynamics may be present when someone from any dominant group (based on race, class, sexual orientation, citizenship, religion, etc.) uses sexual violence to assert power over a person from a nondominant group. An individual act of sexual violence may involve sending a threatening message to people of a particular community and be used to attempt to control the sexuality of specific groups of people. A heterosexual man might rape a lesbian as a form of homophobic dominance. A group of heterosexual men might assault a bisexual woman as a warning to others who identify across the LGBTIQA+ spectrum. Sexual violence may play a role in gang initiation, organizational hazing, and bullying; it has also been used as a tool of oppression in cultural conflict and colonization as well as a mechanism of prisoner torture and interrogation.

Partner Violence

Partner violence is a pattern of behavior in which a dating or romantic partner seeks to gain and maintain power and control over another person. This type of violence can be verbal and emotional, involving language and actions that hurt a person's self-esteem or sense of well-being. Psychological forms may occur through deceit, manipulation, blaming, minimizing feelings, *gaslighting* (manipulating someone into questioning their own reality or sanity; also known as *crazymaking*), or destroying personal property. Physical forms involve pinching, punching, hitting, kicking, throwing, burning, strangling, and holding someone down. One-time or repeated sexual violence may also be a part of the abuse. Abusive partners may use isolation to separate a partner from their support system or stalking to monitor their partner's life. They may use economic forms of abuse to prevent a partner from gaining or keeping a job, require a partner to work one or multiple jobs, limit their access to finances, or control their income. They may use *cultural abuse*—tactics that target specific parts of someone's identity or membership in a cultural group, like threatening to out someone's sexual orientation, using someone's citizenship status as leverage, or attacking someone's religious beliefs to demean them. Abusers may also use children or pets to exert power and control over a partner.[20]

Partner violence may involve *reproductive coercion*, or behaviors meant to control or manipulate someone's sexual and reproductive health. A partner may engage in sexually coercive behaviors like intentionally exposing someone to sexually transmitted infections, sabotaging their contraceptive method, or pressuring them to get pregnant or continue a pregnancy they do not want.[21] Partner violence may involve acts of infidelity, cheating, or engaging in intimate or romantic interactions without the knowledge or permission of the other partner(s) involved in the relationship. This should not be confused with *consensual nonmonogamy* (when people have romantic or sexual relationships with a partner outside the pair or group; also known as ethical or responsible nonmonogamy) or *polyamory* (when more than two people are part of one intimate

[20] Domestic Abuse Intervention Programs, "Power and Control Wheel," 2017, https://www.theduluthmodel.org/wheels/.

[21] WomensLaw.org, "Reproductive Abuse and Coercion," January 13, 2020, https://www.womenslaw.org/about-abuse/forms-abuse/reproductive-abuse-and-coercion.

or sexual relationship) that involves the consent of everyone involved.[22]

It is important to note that partner violence is a *pattern* of abusive behavior that may begin with verbal or psychological forms of violence that escalate into more physical forms. Abusers often use a variety of behaviors to gain and maintain power and control, and their tactics may or may not be known or obvious to people outside the relationship. In situations involving partner violence, there is a clear abuser and victim(s). Partner violence is not used to describe situations that are unhealthy in which both or all parties may occasionally harm, deceive, verbally attack, or manipulate one another.

While *intimate partner violence* often refers to abuse against someone in a long-term or committed relationship, *dating violence* is used to describe abuse in a shorter-term or more casual scenario, such as relationships between teenagers and between young adults. Though it is often assumed that any intimate relationship is romantic or sexual in nature, gendered patterns of abuse can also occur among nonsexual companions or people who identify as asexual or aromantic. *Domestic violence* is a legal term usually used to describe a pattern of abuse that occurs among people who are cohabitating, related, married or civilly unionized, or who share children. Though it is used in most state laws and campus policies as a synonym for intimate partner violence, it legally may include abuse among family members or roommates. This means that domestic violence may apply in situations of elder abuse, child abuse, sibling abuse, or physical altercations between any household member—but may *not* legally apply in long- or short-term dating relationships in which partners are not married or cohabitating. Domestic violence laws usually only apply to physical abuse in relationships, although some countries and US states have *coercive control* laws that recognize emotional and psychological forms of abuse. Dating violence between partners who don't live together, aren't married, or don't share children is not usually illegal, but it may be a punishable offense if it involves another form of gender violence or occurs within institutions like college campuses.

---

[22] The Network/La Red, "Partner Abuse in Poly Communities," 2018, https://www.tnlr.org/en/partner-abuse-in-poly-communities/.

Stalking

Stalking is a pattern of harassing and monitoring behavior that causes someone to feel discomfort, distress, or fear. It typically involves repeated, unwelcome attempts to contact someone, watch them, or track their whereabouts. Unwanted communication through phone calls, texts, emails, social media posts, or instant messages may be a part of this pattern. A stalker may monitor a person's schedule, communicate they know this schedule to incite discomfort or fear, or use this knowledge to appear at a person's school, workplace, home, or favorite locations. They may use technology to track a person's movement on- or offline; they may leave notes or objects for a person to find. Stalkers may repeatedly call and hang up, drive or walk by a person's home, or use a third party to attempt to communicate with the victim. They may make implicit or explicit threats to someone or the people closest to them, like family, friends, significant others, or children. They may also engage in other behaviors that violate a person's privacy, like pretending to be a victim's significant other in order to obtain information about them from family members, or stealing an object from someone's home to communicate a message they were there without the victim realizing it at the time.

Whether unwelcome repeated actions to contact, observe, or threaten someone are subtle or blatantly violent, behaviors can still be characterized as stalking if the recipient of those actions views them as distressing or terrorizing. The same may be true whether the person engaging in the behavior is a current or former romantic partner, friend, family member, coworker, classmate, acquaintance, or stranger. Stalking may intersect with other forms of gender violence: harassers may repeatedly threaten someone to dissuade them from reporting what is happening to an employer, and abusive partners may monitor whereabouts as part of larger patterns of manipulative control. Traffickers may hunt down victims who escape. Perpetrators of sexual assaults, hate crimes, acid attacks, or honor killings may stalk someone in the days or weeks leading up to or after premeditated physical violence.

Online harassment may meet the definition of stalking if the behavior occurs repetitively in online environments and causes a person to feel threatened or distressed, whether in virtual or physical spaces. Online harassment can include hateful or threatening private messages, public posts, or suggestions to others that provoke similar behavior targeting a particular person. Online harassment could include hacking, character defamation, impersonation, identity theft, using someone's likeness in images or video, or outing someone's identity. It could include *doxing*, or *dropping docs*: finding and then sharing someone's private information to enable others' harassing behavior. Online harassment might also take the form of DoS (denial-of-service) attacks in which harassers disrupt host services (often through message-bombing to intentionally flood someone's account) to make a network or resources unavailable to the target user. *Swatting* in online environments occurs when someone obtains a person's physical address and makes false emergency reports in which police or medical services are dispatched to the location. *Cyber-mob attacks* involve groups of people who engage in any or all of these behaviors. In gaming, players may engage in *griefing*, or disrupting play in multiplayer environments through trolling, destruction, and other forms of harassment. Some griefing may be overtly gendered and violent in nature, like players who inflict virtual rape on other players and NPCs (nonplayer characters).

Bullying and *cyberbullying* are terms often used to describe various forms of physical and online harassment directed toward children, adolescents, and young adults. Though bullying usually connotes more casual or less serious kinds of offenses, if the behaviors are repetitive, distressing, or involve threats, it is likely more accurate to describe them as stalking or harassment—even if they occur among younger populations. If the bullying involves a component of gender, labels of sexual harassment or gender-based discrimination may apply.

Stalking in electronic and online environments may involve aspects of sexual violence, like nonconsensual image sharing, using someone's likeness in sexualized images, sexting, and slut shaming. *Sexting* involves sending or forwarding sexual images, photographs, and videos through email or instant messages. If the sexting is unwelcome or images are shared with others without permission, it may qualify as stalking or nonconsensual distribution of images. If sexting occurs in a workplace or educational environment, it may legally qualify as sexual harassment. If it includes sharing images or video of minors, the sexts may meet the legal definition of child pornography.

Slut shaming occurs when people use derogatory sexual labels toward those they target (often women or girls) as a comment on their perceived sexual behavior, sexual or gender expression, or violation of expected gender norms. Slut shaming may be used by someone to retaliate against claims of harassment, abuse, or assault. A stalker may use slut shaming as an attempt to instill a sense of fear, embarrassment, or shame in someone. It is especially common in online harassment and bullying among teens and young adults.

Stalking laws differ across states, territories, and countries and use language like *menacing*, *criminal harassment*, and *telecommunications harassment*. Some US states only consider situations stalking if victims experience fear as a result of the behavior; in other states, repetitively causing distress is enough to meet the legal definition. Though it is considered a federal crime in the United States to travel across states or Indian territories to stalk someone,[23] online stalking or harassment may or may not meet the definition of state or federal laws depending on the device used, especially if it is a new technology. Many social media and gaming platforms have policies against stalking; in workplaces and educational environments, stalking and harassing behaviors may violate institutional policies.

Ideologically Motivated Gender Violence

Ideologically motivated gender violence describes acts of gender violence that are allowed and encouraged within specific cultural contexts. Influenced by systemic, widespread sanctioning of particular ideological attitudes—whether political, religious, economic, legal, or organization specific—this type of violence occurs at the intersection of gender and accepted cultural norms or practices. Certain acts of gender violence may be deemed culturally acceptable or necessary by specific communities when justified by political

---

[23] Crimes and Criminal Procedure Part I—CRIMES (§§ 1–2725), Chapter 110A—Domestic Violence and Stalking (§§ 2261–2266), Section 2261A—Stalking, U.S.C. 18 Ch. 110A (2022).

or religious beliefs, economic philosophy, law (or lack of law), or historical tradition. Groups with the power to dictate the rules of acceptable and unacceptable behavior—such as governments, religious institutions, spiritual groups, political organizations, military establishments, and community groups—set standards for compliance to whatever is deemed "normal," "traditional," or "legal." Many acts of ideologically motivated gender violence become normalized through these implicit or explicit rules. In one sense, all acts of gender violence could be considered culturally sanctioned. What distinguishes ideologically motivated gender violence from other forms is their explicit connection to institutional or community-wide ideological attitudes and values.

Types of ideologically motivated gender violence are constantly emerging and evolving. *Forced marriage* involves wedding someone to another without their consent—often girls and women to men. Different from arranged marriage, in which families play a role in choosing partners, forced marriages occur when individuals are denied the choice of whether and when to marry.[24] When girls are minors or below a legal age of consent, these situations might be more aptly named *child marriage*. Forced marriages are sometimes negotiated to alleviate economic hardship for a family who gives their daughter to another family in marriage; others may occur as a way to manage disputes, repay debts, reunite family members, or negotiate economic, social, or political alliances.[25] They can also happen in areas of armed conflict. Forced marriages may involve *bride kidnapping* (also known as *wife theft* or *marriage by capture*), in which a groom or his relatives, friends, or community members abduct a woman or girl and use physical or psychological coercion to force her to marry. Bride kidnappings may be especially common in situations in which the groom or his family has a low socioeconomic standing that hurts his ability to attract a wife, or he has been pressured or forced by his community to marry in order to

---

[24] US Citizenship and Immigration Services, "Forced Marriage," https://www.uscis.gov/humanitarian/forced-marriage.

[25] Girls Not Brides, "Why It Happens," 2024, https://www.girlsnotbrides.org/about-child-marriage/why-child-marriage-happens/.

avoid the social stigma of being an unsuccessful man.[26] Sometimes men may abduct women from one another—a practice called *wife-raiding* or *wife theft*—which usually involves the groom's family apologizing and compensating the bride's family after the kidnapping in order to move a marriage forward.[27] In the United States, there is no federal law addressing forced marriage, although some states have forced marriage laws and nonconsensual marriage in many contexts could be considered illegal via sex trafficking laws. Child marriage is limited or banned in some US states, but in many others, there are no statutes banning marriage at any age.[28] Bride kidnapping is illegal in countries with a large history of the practice, but it is often defended as consensual elopement and can be difficult to distinguish from *mock bride theft* or *ceremonial capture*, in which the bride, groom, and their families consensually participate in a ritualized version of the tradition.[29]

Girls and women attempting to escape forced marriage may be victims of *acid attacks* or *corrosive violence*, in which a person is targeted and physically assaulted with acid or corrosive chemicals that cause massive burns and skin deformities, often on the face. Acid attacks may also be committed against someone for their real or perceived violation of gender stereotypes, engagement in premarital sex, rejection of heterosexuality, or as a form of partner or domestic violence. Though acid attacks may be used in other forms of violent activity like gang conflict, they are most commonly committed against women and girls. In the United States, acid attacks may legally fall under physical assault, domestic violence, or stalking laws. In some areas of the world, laws have been passed to limit access to purchasing chemicals commonly used in these attacks.

Honor killings are murders of individuals—usually women—often planned and committed by family members who believe the targeted individual has brought dishonor on the family. Within

26 Alexandria McKenna Lundberg, "Prosecuting Bride Kidnapping: The Law Isn't Enough; Aligning Cultural Norms with the Law," *Case Western Reserve Journal of International Law* 53, no. 1 (2021): 475–522, https://scholarlycommons.law.case.edu/cgi/viewcontent.cgi?article=2607&context=jil.

27 Human Rights Watch, "Bride-Kidnapping," September 2006, https://www.hrw.org/reports/2006/kyrgyzstan0906/3.htm.

28 Fraidy Reiss, "Child Marriage in the United States: Prevalence and Implications," *Journal of Adolescent Health* 69, no. 6 (2021): S8–S10, doi:10.1016/j.jadohealth.2021.07.001.

29 Lundberg, "Prosecuting Bride Kidnapping."

specific cultural contexts, an individual may be believed to shame their family by dressing inappropriately, being in a relationship not approved by their family, having sex outside of marriage, engaging in nonheterosexual sex, refusing an arranged marriage, resisting a bridal kidnapping, seeking divorce, committing adultery, renouncing faith, experiencing rape, or speaking out against abuse by a partner. In an honor killing, a family views death as a path to rid them of the shame associated with their family member's actions and restore their honorable reputation in a community. Honor killings may be carried out in a variety of forms, including lethal acid attack, stoning, shooting, beating, strangulation, stabbing, beheading, or forced suicide. They may take place in public places as warnings to other community members about the consequences of engaging in behavior believed to be inappropriate. In some areas of the world, it is legal for a man to kill his wife if he witnesses her in sexual contact with another man, or for a father to kill his own child.[30]

Dowry deaths are murders or suicides of women caused by dowry disputes. In places in which dowries (property, money, or gifts usually transferred from the bride's to the groom's family in heterosexual marriage) are still the norm, the husband and his family may harass the bride and her family in an attempt to extort them financially. As a result, a bride's family may be pressured to take out high-interest loans and sacrifice their standard of living in order to pay.[31] A bride may be physically abused or murdered by hanging or poisoning; in *bride burnings*, a woman is murdered using flammable liquids and fire. Dowry deaths may occur in the form of suicide when a woman feels no longer able to bear the torture and harassment of a dowry dispute. Though dowries are illegal in many countries of the world, they are still a common practice in many places and contribute to child labor, trafficking, and the murder or neglect of infant girls.[32]

[30] Fariba Parsa, "Iranian Women Campaign to Stop the Rise in 'Honor Killings,'" August 26, 2021, Middle East Institute, https://www.mei.edu/publications/iranian-women-campaign-stop-rise-honor-killings.

[31] Milli Singh, "Effect of Dowry on the Familial, Education, Psychological and Social Areas in Bride and Her Parents Lives," *International Journal of Social Impact* 1, no. 4 (2016): 60–70, https://oaji.net/articles/2016/1170-1479315888.pdf.

[32] Ibid.

Genital cutting or *genital mutilation* refers to the nonconsensual cutting or removal of parts of external genitalia. Ritual cutting or scraping of the clitoris or labia is often known as *female genital mutilation*, or FGM, and performed on girls because of cultural attitudes about girls' sexuality, modesty, beauty, and purity. This type of genital cutting may result in painful sex and a variety of physical health problems, including painful urination, pregnancy and childbirth complications, infections, chronic bleeding, and death. *Nonconsensual circumcision*, or removal of penis foreskin without consent or medical necessity, may be performed on infant or pubescent boys as part of health or ritual practices associated with hygiene, disease prevention, sexual behavior, aesthetics, or religious tradition. In these situations, cutting may reduce sensitivity, increase risk for urethral complications, and have negative psychological effects. Though circumcision of infants and children is still widely debated as a form of gender violence, there are a growing number of researchers and leaders who acknowledge the practice as unnecessary, potentially harmful, or involving a lack of consent and bodily autonomy,[33] with some asserting nonconsensual circumcision is a human rights violation.[34] *Forced circumcision* on adult men has been used as a form of ethnic cleansing (attempts to remove ethnic or religious groups from geographic areas using coercion, force, and violence)[35] and genocide; research documents the use of forced circumcision in Turkey during the Armenian genocide of 1915 and in Indonesia as a form of religious extremism against Christian men in 2001.[36]

---

[33] Hossein Dabbagh, "Is Circumcision 'Necessary' in Islam? A Philosophical Argument Based on Peer Disagreement," *Journal of Religion and Health* 61, no. 6 (2022): 4871–86, doi:10.1007/s10943-022-01635-0; Michela Fusaschi, "Gendered Genital Modifications in Critical Anthropology: From Discourses on FGM/C to New Technologies in the Sex/Gender System," *International Journal of Impotence Research* 35, no. 1 (2023): 6–15, doi:10.1038/s41443-022-00542-y; Peter W. Adler, Robert Van Howe, Travis Wisdom, and Felix Daase, "Is Circumcision a Fraud?," *Cornell Journal of Law & Public Policy* 30, no. 1 (2020): 45–107, https://ww3.lawschool.cornell.edu/research/JLPP/upload/Adler-et-al-final.pdf; Max Buckler, "Be Honest about the Bris: A Jewish Call for Greater Integrity," *Evolve*, February 2, 2022, https://evolve.reconstructingjudaism.org/be-honest-about-the-bris-a-jewish-call-for-greater-integrity/.

[34] Geoff Hinchley, "Is Infant Male Circumcision an Abuse of the Rights of the Child? Yes," *BMJ* 335 (2007): 1180, doi:10.1136/bmj.39406.520498; Steven J. Svoboda, "Circumcision of Male Infants as a Human Rights Violation," *Journal of Medical Ethics* 39, no. 7 (2013): 469–74, doi:10.1136/medethics-2012-101229.

[35] United Nations, "Ethnic Cleansing," Office on Genocide Prevention and the Responsibility to Protect, https://www.un.org/en/genocideprevention/ethnic-cleansing.shtml.

[36] Michael Glass, "Forced Circumcision of Men (Abridged)," *Journal of Medical Ethics* 40, no. 8 (2014): 567–71, doi:10.1136/medethics-2013-101626.

Case Example

From Vacation Cutting Abroad to Activism in the United States

Mariya Taher is an American-born Muslim woman, writer, researcher, and award-winning gender violence expert in the area of female genital cutting, or FGC. At seven years old, she underwent vacation cutting—when a child is taken abroad to have FGC performed—during a family trip to India.[a] She didn't question what happened to her until high school, and even then, she had a difficult time finding information about the practice in cultural contexts beyond Africa and African diasporic communities.[b] After years of activist work and providing services for women affected by gender violence, she and four women began discussing their strong feelings about the practice of *khatna* (cutting) within the Bohra community. Together, they cofounded Sahiyo, a transnational organization that works to empower Asian and other communities to end FGC.[c] Mariya has led successful efforts to pass legislation on genital cutting in multiple states in the United States, and she speaks openly about her experience to help others. Because FGC is a practice often done in secret, Mariya believes storytelling is key for shattering silence and isolation.[d] This has even been true for her own family: after she spoke at the United Nations in 2016, her aunts revealed to her they had chosen not to have FGC done to their daughters; they had only pretended they had to avoid being shamed by their community.[e]

[a] Sahiyo, "Shattered Silences by Mariya Taher," April 26, 2018, YouTube video, from a StoryCenter workshop, funded by the Women's Foundation of California, https://www.youtube.com/watch?v=nxdr8TJm8AM&ab_channel=Sahiyo.

[b] Women Who Win News Desk, "The Power of a Story: Mariya Taher Shares the Story behind Her Powerful Fight to End Gender-Based Violence and the Founding of Sahiyo," Women Who Win, December 12, 2020, https://www.womenwhowin100.com/blog/the-power-of-a -story-mariya-taher-shares-the-story-being-sahiyo-and-her-powerful-fight-to-end-gender -based-violence.

[c] Sahiyo, "Our Story," 2024, https://sahiyo.org/about/our-story.html.

[d] Sahiyo, "Shattered Silences."

[e] Ibid.

In the United States and other countries, circumcisions are usually legal if parental consent is given and the action is performed by a hospital or for religious, community, or family reasons.[37] Genital cutting on women and girls is internationally recognized as a human rights violation and against federal law in the United States. Genital cutting on girls—and moving girls across borders to obtain such procedures—is also illegal in many other countries around the world. Though genital cutting on girls is usually performed by community practitioners, there has been a shift in some areas toward medicalization. The World Health Organization suggests that health-care providers who perform the procedure may do so because they don't want to go against social norms, believe it reduces risk of complications if carried out by a physician, may be financially incentivized, or believe that medicalization is a first step toward fully abandoning the practice.[38]

Medically unnecessary surgeries used to change the anatomy of intersex children are also a form of genital cutting. Similar abuses might include irreversible medical interventions, unnecessarily invasive exams, and pressure from physicians to undergo surgery.[39] These procedures on intersex children may cause incontinence, scarring, loss of sexual sensation and function, sterilization, need for lifelong hormonal therapy, psychological trauma, and other health problems. For these reasons, the United Nations condemns medically unnecessary surgeries on intersex infants, and when nonconsensual sterilization occurs as a result of such surgeries, it is typically considered a violation of reproductive freedom.[40] As of 2024, there is no concrete legislation in the United States that protects intersex children from medically unnecessary and nonconsensual surgeries.[41]

Breast ironing, also known as breast flattening, is a practice that involves the repetitive pounding, pressing, rubbing, or burning

---

[37] British Medical Association, "The Law and Ethics of Male Circumcision: Guidance for Doctors," *Journal of Medical Ethics* 30, no. 3 (2004): 259–63, http://dx.doi.org/10.1136/jme.2004.008540.

[38] World Health Organization, "Female Genital Mutilation," February 5, 2024, https://www.who.int/news-room/fact-sheets/detail/female-genital-mutilation.

[39] Human Rights Watch, "'I Want to Be Like Nature Made Me': Medically Unnecessary Surgeries on Intersex Children in the US," July 25, 2017, https://www.hrw.org/report/2017/07/25/i-want-be-nature-made-me/medically-unnecessary-surgeries-intersex-children-us.

[40] Ibid.

[41] ILGA, "Intersex Legal Mapping Report: Global Survey on Legal Protections for People Born with Variations in Sex Characteristics," December 2023, https://ilga.org/wp-content/uploads/2024/02/ILGA_World_Intersex_Legal_Mapping_Report_2023.pdf, 89.

of girls' breasts in puberty in order to delay growth or make them disappear. Women relatives, midwives, or healers who perform breast ironing are motivated by their belief that it deters attention from men and protects young women and girls from forms of gender violence like sexual harassment, exploitation, sexual assault, and child marriage.[42] Breast ironing can cause long-term health risks, including severe pain, tissue damage, deformities, and emotional harm. Though there is not a lot of research on the practice and it is not explicitly outlawed anywhere in the world, it is generally considered a violation of human rights.[43]

Forced sterilization, also known as compulsory, coerced, or involuntary sterilization, is a form of violence in which individuals are forced or manipulated into undergoing procedures to prevent reproduction without their full, free, and informed consent.[44] Coercive pressure may involve misleading information; offers of food, money, land, and housing; and threats, fines, or punishments. Forced sterilization disproportionately affects women and girls in marginalized populations and is closely related to other reproductive abuses like *forced contraception* or *forced abortion.* Historically, forced sterilization around the world was informed by eugenics—beliefs and practices aimed at improving the human population based on certain exclusionary qualities—and encouraged through laws and governmental programs that targeted racial and ethnic minorities, poor people, immigrants, and people with disabilities.[45] The United States was an international leader in eugenics during the twentieth century whose state-sanctioned sterilizations were most common between the 1920s and 1970s, especially as a way to control Black, Latina, and Indigenous women's reproduction.[46] More recently, institutions have used forced sterilization as a tool of discriminatory public health and population control

---

[42] Fikrejesus Amahazion, "Breast Ironing: A Brief Overview of an Underreported Harmful Practice," *Journal of Global Health* no. 11 (2021): 1–4, https://jogh.org/documents/2021/jogh-11-03055.pdf.

[43] Ibid.

[44] World Health Organization, "Eliminating Forced, Coercive, and Otherwise Involuntary Sterilization: An Interagency Statement," 2014, http://apps.who.int/iris/bitstream/handle/10665/112848/9789241507325_eng.pdf.

[45] Alexandra Minna Stern, "US Targeted Minorities and Those with Disabilities—and Lasted into the 21st Century," *Conversation*, August 26, 2020, https://theconversation.com/forced-sterilization-policies-in-the-us-targeted-minorities-and-those-with-disabilities-and-lasted-into-the-21st-century-143144.

[46] Ibid.

targeting Indigenous individuals, people living in poverty, people with HIV or mental illness, people who are incarcerated, and marginalized ethnic and racial groups. Forced sterilization continues to be part of legal and medical transition requirements for people who identify as transgender in some areas of the world,[47] and involuntary sterilization may occur as a result of medically unnecessary surgeries performed on intersex infants.

Gendercide is the intentional and often systemic mass killing of people of a particular gender. *Femicide* refers to the systemic murder of women and girls, often through gender-selective *infanticide* (intentional killing or neglect of infants) or death as a result of gender violence, including acid attacks, rape, physical assault, or genital cutting. Femicide can involve honor killings, serial or mass murder of women or girls, *lesbicide* (murder of lesbians), or racial femicide (racially motivated murder of women). *Gender-selective abortion* is the systemic termination of pregnancies in which a fetus is designated female before birth, and *gender-selective infanticide* (often called female infanticide) is the killing or neglect of babies because they are girls. Gender-selective infanticide may also occur when a baby is born with identifiable intersex characteristics. Cultural and ideological beliefs, legal imperatives, and economic conditions contribute to femicide and infanticide in various forms. *Androcide* is the systemic murder of men and boys; though far less common than femicide, warring nations have used androcide as a tactic meant to decrease an enemy's military or soldier pool through the murder of men considered battle aged.[48]

In addition to the specific types of gender violence explained above, *institutionally sanctioned abuses* occur when an organization or governing body normalizes, ritualizes, or hides continued gender violence in the interest of preserving its power and influence. Such abuses may be difficult to expose because they often function to support and maintain hierarchies of power and control within the group. In addition, these abuses may occur in spaces shielded from public access or knowledge. The workings of an institution itself may be built on cycles of abuse, and groups may use particular

---

[47] Blas Radi, "Reproductive Injustice, Trans Rights, and Eugenics," *Sexual and Reproductive Health Matters* 28, no. 1 (2020): 396–407, https://www.jstor.org/stable/48617639.
[48] David Buchanan, "Gendercide and Human Rights," *Journal of Genocide Research* 4, no. 1 (2002): 95–108, doi:10.1080/14623520120113919.

ideological beliefs to justify or excuse their actions. This is why institutionally sanctioned abuse is often an open secret to members of the companies, organizations, governments, industries, or communities in which they occur. People may experience the abuse themselves, participate in abusing others, or know about the abuse but fear a variety of consequences (like loss of their job or community, or violence by others) for speaking up about what is happening.

Examples of institutionally sanctioned abuse include sex trafficking rings that provide the financial backing for an organization, ritualized sexual abuse by leaders of a cult, or cycles of harassment considered rites of passage for moving up in an industry. It is common for these types of situations to only become publicly known after individuals report the abuse, speak publicly about it, or grant journalists and filmmakers access to their stories. High-profile examples in the United States include the sexual harassment of models in the fashion industry, sexual abuse of men athletes at The Ohio State University, sexual harassment of women workers at Mitsubishi Motors, sexual assault in the Bikram and Kundalini yoga communities, sexual abuse by clergy in the Catholic Church, and sex trafficking and exploitation by Jeffrey Epstein and a circle of unknown others.

Gender-Based Hate Crime

Hate crimes are psychological, physical, or sexual attacks motivated by prejudicial beliefs about particular groups of people. Someone who commits a hate crime targets an individual based on their membership or perceived membership in a social group related to race, religion, ability, nationality, ethnicity, size, or other aspect of identity. Hate crimes may include harassment, stalking, hate messages, threats, destruction of property, sexual assault, physical assault, or murder. *Gender-based hate crimes* are attacks that target individuals because of their real or perceived gender identity, gender expression or performance, sexual or romantic orientation, or sexual behavior. People most often targeted by gender-based hate crimes are members of LGBTIQA+ communities.

Gender-based hate crime may begin with or intersect with street harassment by strangers in public spaces when impromptu verbal abuse becomes physical. It can be premeditated and target acquaintances, coworkers, classmates, or family members. *Homophobic hate crime* involves actions motivated by prejudicial attitudes about sexuality and sexual identity toward people who identify as lesbian, gay, bisexual, pansexual, or queer. *Transphobic hate crime* involves prejudicial attitudes about gender identity and people who identify as or are perceived as being transgender or gender nonconforming. *Aphobic* (or acephobic) *hate crime* involves violent actions against people who identify or are perceived as asexual or aromantic.

Homophobic, transphobic, and aphobic hate crimes and other gender-based attacks (such as those targeting people who identify as polyamorous) may be carried out by individuals or groups to communicate hate, intolerance, or revenge for perceived betrayal to an individual or community. Perpetrators of these crimes often target or exploit the aspects of an individual they find unacceptable through biased language and explicit actions meant to humiliate, threaten, or injure someone. Examples of gender-based hate crime might include a group who steals clothing or medicine from a person who identifies as transgender and depends on those items for their gender expression; an online community that doxes and stalks someone who outs themselves as aromantic; a group of college students who vandalize a queer-friendly office on campus; or a man who targets women employees in a mass shooting where he works.

Gender-based hate crimes may result in murder. When normalized in a particular cultural context or sanctioned by a powerful group, such attacks may take the form of gendercide, femicide, or lesbicide—which are all complicated further by power dynamics related to race, class, religion, citizenship, and other aspects of identity. In regions of the world in which same-gender sex acts are considered crimes, punishments for being openly gay or having consensual sex include fines, incarceration, corporal punishment, or the death penalty. Over sixty-five countries have laws that criminalize having sex with someone of the same gender or expressing gender identity different from culture or tradition; in addition, people who express nonnormative or nonconforming gender expressions are often targeted for arrest in many areas even when laws don't criminalize their self-expression.[49] State-sanctioned violence and lack of legal protections for LGBTIQA+ individuals enable gender-based hate crime on individual and institutional levels.

---

[49] Kellyn Botha, "Our Identities under Arrest: A Global Overview on the Enforcement of Laws Criminalising Consensual Same-Sex Sexual Acts between Adults and Diverse Gender Expressions," ILGA World, December 2021, https://ilga.org/our-identities-under-arrest-prosecutions-lgbt-gender-diverse-persons.

Case Example

#SeLlamabaAlexa

Her name was Alexa Negrón Luciano.[a] Alexa was soft-spoken and believed to have struggled with depression. She lived on the street in Toa Baja, Puerto Rico, and carried a broken rearview mirror with her to watch out for people who might attack her. On her twenty-ninth birthday in 2020, Alexa used the women's restroom at a McDonald's restaurant. After someone called the police and accused her of using her mirror to spy on people in the stalls, she was questioned by a police officer and a photo of their interaction was posted with transphobic language on social media. Since the accusation made against her was unsubstantiated, police did not arrest her or file any charges—but the social media post went viral, catalyzing hateful and vulgar comments about Alexa across the internet.[b] Less than twelve hours later, Alexa was hunted down and shot by a group of men who filmed the murder and posted it online. Despite the governor's announcement that what happened would be investigated as a hate crime, no one was arrested for her murder.[c] Alexa was one of six transgender or gender nonconforming individuals known to be murdered in Puerto Rico in 2020. Another known thirty-eight transgender or gender nonconforming people were murdered in other parts of the United States that same year, and most of the people killed were people of color.[d]

[a] Susanne Ramirez de Arellano, "Trans Justice Now: Violent Murder of Alexa Negrón Luciano Draws Outrage in Puerto Rico," *BeLatina*, March 17, 2020, https://belatina.com/alexa-negron-luciano-murder-awaits-justice/.

[b] David Begnaud (@DavidBegnaud), "Horrific: Transgender woman murdered today in Puerto Rico by killers who recorded the crime Before the murder, the victim was accused on social media of peeping in a public restroom; there was no proof of that, police say. 9hrs after those accusations were posted, she was killed.," Twitter, February 24, 2020, video, 9:40, https://twitter.com/DavidBegnaud/status/1232066389055279105.

[c] Anagha Srikanth, "Transgender Woman Murdered after Using Women's Restroom in Puerto Rico," *Hill*, February 25, 2020, https://thehill.com/changing-america/respect/diversity-inclusion/484704-a-transgender-woman-was-killed-after-using; Ramirez de Arellano, "Trans Justice Now."

[d] Human Rights Campaign, "Fatal Violence against the Transgender and Gender Non-Conforming Community in 2020," https://www.hrc.org/resources/violence-against-the-trans-and-gender-expansive-community-in-2020.

In the United States, hate crimes are considered a distinct category of violent and property crimes that have an added element of bias. A criminal offense qualifies as a hate crime when it is "motivated in whole or in part by an offender's bias,"[50] including perceived gender, sexual orientation, or gender identity,[51] and convictions result in harsher punishments for these crimes. In US states and territories, hate crime definitions vary. In either case, the prosecution of hate crimes requires evidence of biased motivation, usually in the form of *hate speech* (pejorative verbal language, gestures, symbols, objects, images, and other forms of expression). Because explicit hate speech may or may not be used when a crime is committed, hate crime prosecutions are rare.[52] Hate speech itself is considered legal in the United States under the First Amendment unless it directly incites criminal activity or involves specific threats of violence against a person or group;[53] institutions and organizations often have their own polices for responding to hate speech. Worldwide, hate speech is considered a threat to social peace, but its relationship to nondiscrimination and equality is widely debated.[54]

Overlaps and Intersections

As I mentioned at the beginning of this chapter, it is difficult to examine the dynamics of one type of gender violence without recognizing its overlap with other types and intersections with other systems of oppression. As you continue reading this book, I recommend returning to this chapter for clarity on definitions—but try not to get stuck in the terminology. Definitions, laws, and language are constantly shifting, but the massive volume of all forms of gender violence in the United States and around the world is undeniable.

---

[50] Federal Bureau of Investigation, "Hate Crimes," https://www.fbi.gov/investigate/civil-rights/hate-crimes#Definition.

[51] US Department of Justice, "Laws and Policies," December 13, 2023, https://www.justice.gov/hatecrimes/laws-and-policies.

[52] Michael Lieberman, "Hate Crimes, Explained," October 27, 2021, Southern Poverty Law Center, https://www.splcenter.org/hate-crimes-explained.

[53] Stephen J. Wermiel, "The Ongoing Challenge to Define Free Speech," *Human Rights* 43, no. 4 (2024), https://www.americanbar.org/groups/crsj/publications/human_rights_magazine_home/the-ongoing-challenge-to-define-free-speech/the-ongoing-challenge-to-define-free-speech/.

[54] United Nations, "Hate Speech," https://www.un.org/en/hate-speech/understanding-hate-speech/what-is-hate-speech.

CHAPTER 3

Prevalence of Gender Violence

Gender violence is one of the largest problems facing our global community. The World Health Organization estimates that one-third of women worldwide have experienced sexual violence or intimate partner violence,[1] but this widely cited statistic only scrapes the surface of the massive prevalence of gender violence for all genders of people everywhere. It supports what we already know about gender violence—that most of its direct victims are women—but it fails to account for the millions of men, transgender, and gender nonconforming individuals who have experienced gender violence. Its scope is too narrow to include individuals affected by stalking, trafficking, harassment, adolescent dating violence, street harassment, genital cutting, acid burnings, honor killings, and hate crimes. It cannot begin to highlight the interconnectedness of gender violence with other forms of oppression. In this chapter, I provide a statistical overview of what we know about rates of gender violence based on quantitative (numbers-based) social scientific research and data from government and institutional reports. I discuss prevalence across all types of gender violence as it affects various groups based on gender, sexual orientation and gender identity, race and ethnicity, age and ability, socioeconomic class and nationality, disasters and biological hazards, and migration, displacement, and genocide—though all these issues overlap much more than these distinctions suggest. As much as possible, I draw from academic journal articles that have undergone rigorous peer review; some numbers, however, are only available from organizational reports that have not undergone the same process.

---

[1] World Health Organization, "Violence against Women Prevalence Estimates, 2018—Executive Summary," 2021, https://www.who.int/publications/i/item/9789240026681, ix.

The quantitative data that follows tell an important story about the scope of the problem of gender violence and the groups of people impacted by it most. You may find it difficult to learn that rates are incredibly high for some populations, and you may feel particularly unsettled if you are a member of one or more of these groups. As you read, keep in mind that belonging to a group that is at higher risk of experiencing gender violence does not mean that experiencing it is inevitable, or that any individual or group is *inherently* more vulnerable. Instead, higher risk of experiencing gender violence is the result of numerous intersecting power dynamics that reveal massive inequalities in the ways groups of people may be treated in particular cultural contexts. Some groups are at higher risk because they lack access, resources, and privileges available to other groups. I will return to this discussion at the end of the chapter, but keep these things in mind now as you proceed. Consider taking breaks as you read. Process this information with others, and be extra mindful about taking care of yourself as needed.

Gender

One-third of the world's women tells one powerful piece of the larger and much more complicated story of gender violence. It suggests its enormity, its broad reach, its commonality across geographic regions and cultures around the world, and its severe impact on women. In the United States alone, researchers estimate that one in five women experiences rape, one in three experiences violence by an intimate partner, and one in six experiences stalking.[2] Women between the ages of eighteen and twenty-four may be at higher risk for sexual assault and rape than women in other age-groups,[3] and preliminary research suggests that women in this age-group experience the most severe forms of online harassment.[4] There are an estimated thirty-five incidents of rape for every one

---

[2] Michele C. Black et al., "The National Intimate Partner and Sexual Violence Survey: 2010 Summary Report," National Center for Injury Prevention and Control, 2011, https://www.ojp.gov/ncjrs/virtual-library/abstracts/national-intimate-partner-and-sexual-violence-survey, 2.

[3] Sofi Sinozich and Lynn Langton, "Rape and Sexual Assault Victimization among College-Aged Females, 1993–2013," U.S. Department of Justice, December 2014, https://bjs.ojp.gov/content/pub/pdf/rsavcaf9513.pdf.

[4] Maeve Duggan, "Online Harassment," October 22, 2014, Pew Research Center, https://www.pewresearch.org/internet/2014/10/22/online-harassment/.

thousand women on a college campus,[5] and in one study of young women, 10 percent of participants had experienced nonconsensual condom removal.[6] Women are also likely to experience higher rates of nonconsensual pornography distribution than men: one study found that 9.2 percent of women participants versus 6.6 percent of men had been victims.[7]

Among women in the United States, 65 percent have experienced street harassment,[8] and 85 percent of this group experienced it before turning seventeen years old.[9] Internationally, over 50 percent of women in twenty-two countries have reported being fondled or groped by street harassers, and 71 percent of women who responded to a global street harassment survey reported being followed.[10] Depending on how harassing behaviors are defined in studies, researchers estimate that a range of 25 to 85 percent of women experience sexual harassment in the workplace.[11]

The global estimate of individuals trapped in forced labor is 27.6 million—11.8 million of which are women and girls—and 6.3 million people worldwide are victims of forced sexual exploitation including sex trafficking.[12] Four out of five commercial sexual exploitation victims are thought to be women or girls.[13] Numbers in the United States are difficult to pinpoint, but the most extensive data reveals that a majority of the 82,000 human trafficking cases

---

[5] Bonnie S. Fischer, Francis T. Cullen, and Michael G. Turner, "The Sexual Victimization of College Women," U.S. Department of Justice Office of Justice Programs Bureau of Justice Statistics, December 2000, https://www.ncjrs.gov/pdffiles1/nij/182369.pdf.

[6] Boadle, Gierer, and Buzwell, "Young Women Subjected to Nonconsensual Condom Removal."

[7] Yanet Ruvalcaba and Asia A. Eaton, "Nonconsensual Pornography among US Adults: A Sexual Scripts Framework on Victimization, Perpetration, and Health Correlates for Women and Men," *Psychology of Violence* 10, no. 1 (2020): 68–78, doi:10.1037/vio0000233.

[8] Stop Street Harassment, "Unsafe and Harassed in Public Spaces: A National Street Harassment Report," 2014, https://www.stopstreetharassment.org/wp-content/uploads/2012/08/2014-National-SSH-Street-Harassment-Report.pdf.

[9] Beth A. Livingston, "Hollaback! International Street Harassment Survey Project," 2015, https://righttobe.org/research/cornell-international-survey-on-street-harassment/.

[10] Ibid.

[11] Chai R. Feldblum and Victoria A. Lipnic, "Select Task Force on the Study of Harassment in the Workplace," Equal Employment Opportunity Commission, June 2016, https://www.eeoc.gov/select-task-force-study-harassment-workplace.

[12] International Labour Organization, Walk Free, and International Organization for Migration, "Global Estimates of Modern Slavery: Forced Labour and Forced Marriage," 2022, https://www.ilo.org/publications/major-publications/global-estimates-modern-slavery-forced-labour-and-forced-marriage, 2–4.

[13] Ibid.

identified by the National Human Trafficking Hotline between 2007 and 2021 involved women who were victimized by sex trafficking.[14]

Experts estimate that around 230 million girls and young women have experienced genital cutting.[15] In a study of English- and Spanish-speaking women and girls between the ages of sixteen and twenty-nine in one US state, 19.1 percent had experienced pregnancy coercion and 15 percent had experienced birth control sabotage.[16] Prevalence of obstetric violence is underresearched, but one US study found that over 17 percent of women surveyed had experienced it.[17] Young women may experience higher rates of obstetric abuse: in one study, one in four birthing mothers twenty-four years old or younger reported mistreatment by service providers compared to one in seven women over thirty.[18] There is little information on current rates of forced sterilization, but some data specific to the United States estimates that more than 60,000 people were sterilized between the early 1900s and 1970 due to eugenics laws.[19] In the 1970s, around 100,000 to 150,000 US women from low economic backgrounds were sterilized through federally funded programs.[20]

More than one-third of homicides of women worldwide are perpetrated by an intimate partner.[21] The United Nations found that in 2017, 58 percent of the 87,000 women who were intentionally killed around the world were killed by intimate partners

---

[14] National Human Trafficking Hotline, "Hotline Statistics," 2024, https://humantraffickin ghotline.org/states.

[15] UNICEF, "Female Genital Mutilation: A Global Concern (2024 Update)," 2024, https:// data.unicef.org/resources/female-genital-mutilation-a-global-concern-2024/.

[16] Elizabeth Miller et al., "Pregnancy Coercion, Intimate Partner Violence and Unintended Pregnancy," *Contraception* 81, no. 4 (2010): 316–22, https://doi.org/10.1016/j.contra ception.2009.12.004.

[17] Saraswathi Vedam et al., "The Giving Voice to Mothers Study: Inequity and Mistreatment during Pregnancy and Childbirth in the United States," *Reproductive Health* 16, no. 1 (2019): 1–18, doi:10.1186/s12978-019-0729-2.

[18] Ibid.

[19] Alexandra Minna Stern, "That Time the United States Sterilized 60,000 of Its Citizens," *HuffPost*, January 7, 2016, https://www.huffingtonpost.com/entry/sterilization-united -states_us_568f35f2e4b0c8beacf68713.

[20] Southern Poverty Law Center, "Relf V. Weinberger," https://www.splcenter.org/seeking -justice/case-docket/relf-v-weinberger.

[21] Heidi Stöckl, Karen Devries, Alexandra Rotstein, Naeemah Abrahams, Jacquelyn Campbell, Charlotte Watts, and Claudia Garcia Moreno, "The Global Prevalence of Intimate Partner Homicide: A Systematic Review," *Lancet* 382, no. 9895 (2013): 859–65, doi:10.1016/ S0140-6736(13)61030-2.

or other family members.[22] Women are the most likely victims of the thousands of acid attacks that occur annually,[23] and around five thousand women are victims of honor killings every year.[24] A reported 14.9 million women and girls experience forced marriage worldwide, making up over two-thirds of the international total.[25] It is unknown how many deaths occur due to dowry-related abuse every year worldwide, but in some countries, documented cases are in the thousands and actual incidences are believed to be much higher.[26]

Gender violence experienced by men is often underacknowledged and underresearched. Men and boys are thought to comprise 4 percent of sex trafficking victims worldwide,[27] and 115 million boys and men across the globe were married before they turned eighteen.[28] Research shows that among men in the United States, one in thirty-three has been a victim of attempted or completed rape,[29] and one in nine has experienced contact sexual violence, physical violence, or stalking by an intimate partner.[30] About 9 percent of sexual assaults involve men as victims,[31] and 2 percent of American men have been stalked at some point in their lives.[32] Twenty-five percent of men experience street harassment, and they

---

[22] United Nations Office on Drugs and Crime, "Global Study on Homicide: Gender-Related Killing of Women and Girls," 2019, https://www.unodc.org/documents/data-and-analysis/gsh/Booklet_5.pdf.

[23] Acid Survivors Trust International, "Systemic Harm Based on Gender," 2024, https://www.asti.org.uk/learn/gender-based-violence.

[24] United Nations Populations Fund, "The State of the World Population," 2000, https://www.unfpa.org/sites/default/files/pub-pdf/swp2000_eng.pdf.

[25] International Labour Organization, Walk Free, and International Organization for Migration, "Global Estimates," 5.

[26] Singh, "Effect of Dowry"; Navpreet Kaur and Roger W. Byard, "Bride Burning: A Unique and Ongoing Form of Gender-Based Violence," *Journal of Forensic and Legal Medicine* 75 (2020): 1–4, https://doi.org/10.1016/j.jflm.2020.102035.

[27] International Labour Organization, "Global Estimates of Modern Slavery," 27.

[28] UNICEF, "Child Marriage," June 2023, https://data.unicef.org/topic/child-protection/child-marriage/#status.

[29] Patricia Tjaden and Nancy Thoennes, "Full Report of the Prevalence, Incidence, and Consequences of Violence against Women," U.S. Department of Justice, 2000, https://www.ojp.gov/pdffiles1/nij/183781.pdf, 13.

[30] Sharon G. Smith, Kathleen C. Basile, Leah K. Gilbert, Melissa T. Merrick, Nimesh Patel, Margie Walling, and Anurag Jain, "The National Intimate Partner and Sexual Violence Survey (NISVS): 2010–2012 State Report," National Center for Injury Prevention and Control, 2017, https://stacks.cdc.gov/view/cdc/46305.

[31] Michael Planty, Lynn Langton, Christopher Krebs, Marcus Berzofsky, and Hope Smiley-McDonald, "Female Victims of Sexual Violence, 1994–2010," 2013, U.S. Department of Justice, https://bjs.ojp.gov/content/pub/pdf/fvsv9410.pdf, 3.

[32] Tjaden and Thoennes, "Stalking in America," 2.

Case Example

Sexual Violence in Specific Contexts

Rates of sexual violence against all genders of people may be higher in specific cultural contexts. Sexual assault may happen more in the university Greek system: a study of college students found that sorority women reported nonconsensual sexual contact and unwanted attention twice as much as nonsorority women, and attempted or completed rape three times as much as nonsorority women.[a] Fraternity men reported nonconsensual sexual contact and unwanted sexual attention three times more than men not in fraternities.[b] Prisons are another context in which sexual assaults occur at higher rates. A US study of prisons in the Midwest found that 6 to 27 percent of incarcerated women in some facilities had experienced sexual coercion while incarcerated;[c] 21 percent of men in seven midwestern prisons had experienced at least one instance of pressured or forced sexual contact while serving time.[d]

Sexual violence may be more rampant in certain vocations. Sexual harassment is common among women who are farmworkers, many of whom are Latina immigrants. One study of Mexican immigrant farmworking women in California revealed that 97 percent of its 150 respondents had experienced sexual harassment from coworkers and superiors.[e] US military service members may be at higher risk of experiencing harassment and sexual assault than civilians; an analysis of nearly seventy studies revealed that between 13.9 and 31.2 percent of military personnel and veterans have experienced military sexual trauma, and prevalence was especially high among women.[f] Gender violence is also believed to happen more in the sex work industry. A review of research revealed that 45 to 75 percent of sex workers around the world had experienced sexual or physical violence at some point in their lives.[g] The criminalization of sex work—and police arrests connected to those laws—are associated with increased violence against sex workers. Unfortunately, most of the research available on sex work focuses on women; very little exists on men and transgender individuals.[h]

[a]   Melissa L. Barnes, Alexis Adams-Clark, Marina N. Rosenthal, Carly P. Smith, and Jennifer J. Freyd, "Pledged into Harm: Sorority and Fraternity Members Face Increased Risk of Sexual Assault and Sexual Harassment," *Dignity: A Journal of Exploitation and Violence* 6, no. 1 (2021): 1–30, doi:10.23860/dignity.2021.06.01.09.

b Ibid.

c Cindy Struckman-Johnson and David Struckman-Johnson, "Sexual Coercion Reported by Women in Three Midwestern Prisons," *Journal of Sex Research* 39, no. 3 (2002): 217–27, https://www.jstor.org/stable/3813617.

d Cindy Struckman-Johnson and David Struckman-Johnson, "Sexual Coercion Rates in Seven Midwestern Prison Facilities for Men," *Prison Journal* 80, no. 4 (2000): 379–90, doi: 10.1177/0032885500080004004.

e Irma Morales Waugh, "Examining the Sexual Harassment Experiences of Mexican Immigrant Farmworking Women," *Violence against Women* 16, no. 3 (2010): 237–61, doi:10.1177/1077801209360857.

f Laura C. Wilson, "The Prevalence of Military Sexual Trauma: A Meta-analysis," *Trauma, Violence, & Abuse* 19, no. 5 (2018): 584–97, doi:10.1177/1524838016683459.

g Kathleen N. Deering et al., "A Systematic Review of the Correlates of Violence against Sex Workers," *American Journal of Public Health* 104, no. 5 (2014): e42–e54, doi:10.2105/AJPH.2014.301909.

h Ibid.

are more likely to experience it if they don't identify as heterosexual.[33] One study on US adolescents found that twelve- to seventeen-year-old boys were more likely to be victims of sextortion than girls (5.8 percent versus 4.1 percent).[34] Though researchers estimate that 71.2 percent of boys and men age fifteen and older in the United States and 37 to 39 percent worldwide are circumcised,[35] the prevalence of nonconsensual and forced circumcision among boys and men worldwide is unknown.

Sexual Orientation and Gender Identity

LGBTIQA+ individuals in the United States and around the world experience discrimination based on their sexual orientation and gender identity in various areas of their personal and professional lives: one study suggests that over 25 percent of lesbian, gay, and bisexual individuals experience workplace harassment, and around

33 Stop Street Harassment, "Unsafe and Harassed."
34 Justin W. Patchin and Sameer Hinduja, "Sextortion among Adolescents: Results from a National Survey of US Youth," *Sexual Abuse: Journal of Research and Treatment* 32, no. 1 (2020): 30–54, doi:10.1177/1079063218800469.
35 Brian J. Morris, Richard G. Wamai, Esther B. Henebeng, Aaron A. R. Tobian, Jeffrey D. Klausner, Joya Banerjee, and Catherine A. Hankins, "Estimation of Country-Specific and Global Prevalence of Male Circumcision," *Population Health Metrics* 14, no. 4 (2016), doi:10.1186/s12963-016-0073-5.

75 percent of transgender individuals experience mistreatment, discrimination, or harassment at work.[36] Another study reported that 20 percent of LGBTQ individuals surveyed were discriminated against when it came to equal pay or promotion, and 22 percent encountered mistreatment when trying to buy or rent housing. Fifty-seven percent reported experiencing slurs, and 53 percent received insensitive or offensive comments from others.[37] Based on data gathered from 2004 to 2015, there were an estimated 250,000 US residents who experienced hate crimes every year; 30 percent of victims believed they were targeted based on gender, and 22 percent believed it was because of their sexual orientation.[38] A survey focused on hate violence experienced by LGBTQ and HIV-affected individuals found that 20 percent of hate crimes over one year took the form of verbal harassment, 17 percent were threats or intimidation, and 11 percent were physical assaults.[39]

People across the LGBTIQA+ spectrum likely experience higher discrimination and manipulation in online environments than their heterosexual peers. A study of adolescent girls in Belgium found that slut shaming is far more common against girls who are attracted to other girls (57 percent) than heterosexual girls (12 percent).[40] A study of adolescents in Spain revealed that 41 percent of LGBTIQA+ youth had experienced online discrimination in comparison to only 3 percent of heterosexual youth; in addition, LGBTIQA+ youth experienced twice the amount of unwanted sexual attention compared to heterosexual youth and almost three times the amount

[36] Brad Sears and Christy Mallory, "Documented Evidence of Employment Discrimination & Its Effects on LGBT People," Williams Institute, University of California School of Law, 2011, http://williamsinstitute.law.ucla.edu/wp-content/uploads/Sears-Mallory-Discrimination-July-20111.pdf.

[37] Harvard T.H. Chan School of Public Health, Robert Wood Johnson Foundation, and National Public Radio, "Discrimination in America: Experiences and Views of LGBTQ Americans," 2017, https://repository.gheli.harvard.edu/repository/12301/.

[38] Madeline Masucci and Lynn Langton, "Hate Crime Victimization, 2004–2015" U.S. Department of Justice Bureau of Justice Statistics, June 2017, https://bjs.ojp.gov/library/publications/hate-crime-victimization-2004-2015.

[39] National Coalition of Anti-violence Programs, "Lesbian, Gay, Bisexual, Transgender, Queer, and HIV-Affected Hate Violence in 2016," New York City Gay and Lesbian Anti-violence Project, 2017, https://avp.org/wp-content/uploads/2017/06/NCAVP_2016Hate Violence_REPORT.pdf.

[40] Margot Goblet and Fabienne Glowacz, "Slut Shaming in Adolescence: A Violence against Girls and Its Impact on Their Health," *International Journal of Environmental Research and Public Health* 18, no. 6657 (2021): 1–15, doi:10.3390/ijerph18126657.

of victimization through sextortion.[41] In a study of twelve- to seventeen-year-old students in the United States, researchers found that nonheterosexual youth were more than twice as likely to experience sextortion as heterosexual youth (10.9 percent versus 4.5 percent).[42] Bisexual women may be the most at-risk group in the United States for experiencing nonconsensual distribution of sexual images; among participants in one study, rates among bisexual women were the highest (17.2 percent), followed by bisexual men (12.8 percent) and gay men (10.2 percent), versus heterosexual women (6.7 percent) and heterosexual men (5.6 percent).[43] In the US military, people who are gay, lesbian, or bisexual are thought to be at especially high risk for experiencing sexual assault: in one organization's analysis of data, sexual assaults against service members who did not describe themselves as heterosexual accounted for half of the sexual assaults committed in 2016 and 2018.[44]

Rates of partner violence and sexual assault are estimated be higher among traditionally marginalized populations, especially when sexual orientation is taken into account. Research suggests that 25 percent of all relationships—regardless of the gender identities or sexual orientations of all partners—are abusive, though lesbian, gay, and bisexual individuals experience higher incidences of partner violence.[45] Forty-three percent of lesbian women and 61 percent of bisexual women may experience violence by an intimate partner in their lifetime.[46] Bisexual women are thought to have a higher lifetime prevalence of rape and sexual violence than heterosexual women—more than 46 percent—by a perpetrator of any gender.[47] An estimated 74.9 percent of bisexual women, 47 percent

[41] Manuel Gámez-Guadix and Daniel Incera, "Homophobia Is Online: Sexual Victimization and Risks on the Internet and Mental Health among Bisexual, Homosexual, Pansexual, Asexual, and Queer Adolescents," *Computers in Human Behavior* 119 (2021), doi:10.1016/j.chb.2021.106728.

[42] Patchin and Hinduja, "Sextortion among Adolescents."

[43] Ruvalcaba and Eaton, "Nonconsensual Pornography."

[44] Andrew R. Morral and Terry L. Schell, "Sexual Assault of Sexual Minorities in the U.S. Military," Rand Corporation, June 1, 2021, https://www.rand.org/pubs/research_reports/RRA1390-1.html.

[45] Forge, "Transgender Rates of Violence," 2012, https://forge-forward.org/resource/rates-of-violence/.

[46] Mikel L. Walters, Jieru Chen, and Matthew J. Breiding, "The National Intimate Partner and Sexual Violence Survey (NISVS): 2010 Findings on Victimization by Sexual Orientation," National Center for Injury Prevention and Control, 2013, https://stacks.cdc.gov/view/cdc/12362.

[47] Ibid.

of bisexual men, 46 percent of lesbian women, and 40 percent of
gay men experience forms of sexual violence *other* than rape in
their lifetime.[48]

In addition to research that suggests 63 percent of transgender
individuals in the United States have experienced a serious act
of discrimination that may include bullying, harassment, physical assault, or denial of medical care,[49] multiple studies indicate
that around 50 percent of transgender people have experienced
sexual violence.[50] Fifty-four percent of transgender individuals are
estimated to experience some form of intimate partner violence
in their lifetimes.[51] National surveys reveal that 77–78 percent of
individuals who were out or perceived as transgender or gender
nonconforming reported experiencing harassment in the K–12
education system, and 12–13 percent reported experiencing sexual
violence as a K–12 student.[52] Twenty-four percent reported being
verbally, physically, or sexually harassed at a college or vocational
school.[53] Research also suggests that transgender individuals commonly experience gender-based discrimination in the workplace;
in a national survey on the experiences of transgender people in
the United States, 30 percent of respondents reported being fired,
denied a promotion, or experiencing other mistreatment such as
physical or sexual assault.[54] Twenty-nine percent of transgender
individuals were living in poverty at the time of the survey, and 30
percent had experienced homelessness at some point in their lives.[55]
These numbers help to provide perspective on why transgender
individuals may participate in the underground economy through
sex work, drug sales, and other kinds of work that are criminalized;

[48] Ibid.
[49] Jaime M. Grant, Lisa A. Mottet, J. D. Justin Tanis, Jack Harrison, Jody L. Herman,
and Mara Keisling, "Injustice at Every Turn: A Report of the National Transgender
Discrimination Survey," National Center for Transgender Equality and the National Gay
and Lesbian Task Force, 2011, https://transequality.org/sites/default/files/docs/resources/
NTDS_Report.pdf, 8.
[50] Forge, "Transgender Rates of Violence."
[51] Sandy E. James, Jody L. Herman, Susan Rankin, Mara Keisling, Lisa Mottet, and
Ma'ayan Anaf, "The Report of the 2015 U.S. Transgender Survey," National Center for
Transgender Equality, 2016, https://ustranssurvey.org/download-reports/, 207.
[52] Ibid., 11; Grant, Mottet, Tanis, Harrison, Herman, and Keisling, "Transgender Discrimination Survey," 3.
[53] James, Herman, Rankin, Keisling, Mottet, and Anaf, "Report of the 2015 U.S. Transgender Survey," 11.
[54] Ibid., 4.
[55] Ibid., 5.

in this survey, one in five respondents earned money this way, and numbers were even higher for undocumented residents, transgender women of color, and people who lost their job because of their gender identity or expression.[56] Fifty-eight percent of respondents indicated they had experienced mistreatment by police in the past year.[57]

Access to public services and restrooms is often a problem: one survey of transgender individuals found that one in ten respondents experienced someone denying them access to a restroom in the past year, and 59 percent avoided using a public restroom in the past year because they were afraid of confrontations or other problems they might experience. Thirty-two percent limited what they ate and drank to avoid using the restroom, and 8 percent reported having urinary tract infections and kidney-related problems as a result of avoiding public bathrooms.[58] Thirty-one percent of respondents experienced at least one type of mistreatment in the past year in public spaces like retail stores, government offices, and hotels. Twenty percent did not use at least one type of public accommodation in the past year for fear of being mistreated due to their transgender identity.[59] Transgender and gender nonconforming individuals also experience challenges in accessing health care, including hormones, mental health counseling, and surgeries due to documentation challenges, insurance exclusions, and discrimination within health-care systems, especially if they have low socioeconomic status;[60] health discrimination is even more likely for LGBT individuals who are also people of color.[61]

Despite the lifelong effects of medically unnecessary surgeries and abusive treatment of intersex infants and children, the prevalence of these procedures in the United States and around the world is unknown. Because they have historically been viewed as

---

[56] Ibid., 158.
[57] Ibid., 14.
[58] Ibid., 17.
[59] Ibid., 213.
[60] Julie Koch, Christine McLachlan, Cornelius J. Victor, Jess Westcott, and Christina Yager, "The Cost of Being Transgender: Where Socio-economic Status, Global Health Care Systems, and Gender Identity Intersect," *Psychology & Sexuality*, 11, nos. 1–2 (2019): 103–19, https://doi.org/10.1080/19419899.2019.1660705.
[61] Center for American Progress and Movement Advancement Project, "Paying an Unfair Price: The Financial Penalty for LGBT People of Color in America," April 2015, https://www.lgbtmap.org/policy-and-issue-analysis/unfair-price-lgbt-people-of-color, 17.

commonplace and surgeons are not required to report numbers and types of surgeries,[62] this form of violence is often invisible and unacknowledged by the medical community and broader public. There is also a drastic lack of quantitative data on the criminalization of consensual same-gender sex and nonconforming gender expression worldwide. Preliminary data gathered by one organization suggests that in 2021 there were at least nine hundred instances of criminal enforcement against LGBTIQ individuals around the world.[63]

Studies including rates of gender violence experienced by aspecs are virtually nonexistent, though acephobia is becoming more well known and recent research has begun to document evidence of anti-asexual bias.[64] One study on stigma and discrimination found that asexual individuals reported feeling stigmatized more than men and women who did not identify as asexual; aces also reported more everyday discrimination.[65] Nonscientific data collected by the Asexual Community Census suggest that rates of sexual violence may be high among asexual individuals and even higher for aces who identify as nonbinary. Many aces have experienced excessive and inappropriate personal questions about their asexual identity, verbal and online harassment, and attempts by people trying to "fix" or "cure" them of their asexual identity.[66]

Race and Ethnicity

When race and ethnicity are taken into account, women of color in the United States are found to experience sexual violence, stalking, and intimate partner violence at rates sometimes 10 to 20 percent

---

[62] Human Rights Watch, "'I Want to Be Like Nature Made Me.'"

[63] Kellyn Botha, "Our Identities under Arrest: A Global Overview on the Enforcement of Laws Criminalising Consensual Same-Sex Sexual Acts between Adults and Diverse Gender Expressions," ILGA, December 2021, https://ilga.org/wp-content/uploads/2024/02/Our_Identities_Under_Arrest_2021-1.pdf.

[64] Cara C. MacInnis and Gordon Hodson, "Intergroup Bias toward 'Group X': Evidence of Prejudice, Dehumanization, Avoidance, and Discrimination against Asexuals," *Group Processes and Intergroup Relations* 15, no. 6 (2012): 725–43, doi:10.1177/1368430212442419.

[65] Esther D. Rothblum, Evan A. Krueger, Krystal R. Kittle, and Ilan H. Meyer, "Asexual and Non-asexual Respondents from a U.S. Population-Based Study of Sexual Minorities," *Archives of Sexual Behavior* 49, no. 2 (2020): 757–67. doi:10.1007/s10508-019-01485-0.

[66] Robin Weis et al., "2019 Asexual Community Survey Summary Report," Ace Community Survey Team, October 24, 2021, https://asexualcensus.wordpress.com/2019-asexual-community-survey-summary-report/.

Additional Information

Indigenous women and women of color in the United States often experience higher levels of

- Sexual violence
- Stalking
- Partner violence
- Period poverty
- Obstetric violence
- Maternal mortality
- Educational discrimination
- Wage discrimination
- Hate violence

higher than White women.[67] Indigenous women and women of color are also more impacted by period poverty, obstetric violence, and maternal mortality. In one US study, researchers found that Latina women were most likely to have experienced period poverty in the past year (24.5 percent), followed by Black women (19 percent) and White women (11.7 percent).[68] A study of US women who gave birth between 2010 and 2016 found that of the Indigenous women surveyed, 32.8 percent experienced at least one type of mistreatment by health-care professionals, followed by 25 percent of Hispanic women, 22.5 percent of Black women, 21.1 percent of Asian women, and 14.1 percent of White women.[69] Between 2016 and 2021, the maternal mortality rate for Black women was 2.6 to 3.5 times the rate for White women.[70] Research also shows

---

[67] Smith, Basile, Gilbert, Merrick, Patel, Walling, and Jain, "National Intimate Partner and Sexual Violence Survey."

[68] Lauren F. Cardoso, Anna M. Scolese, Alzahra Hamidaddin, and Jhumka Gupta, "Period Poverty and Mental Health Implications among College-Aged Women in the United States," *BMC Women's Health* 21, no. 1 (2021): 1–7, doi:10.1186/s12905-020-01149-5.

[69] Vedam et al., "Giving Voice to Mothers."

[70] Marian F. MacDorman, Marie Thoma, Eugene Declcerq, and Elizabeth A. Howell, "Racial and Ethnic Disparities in Maternal Mortality in the United States Using Enhanced Vital Records, 2016–2017," *American Journal of Public Health* 111, no. 9 (2021): 1673–81, doi:10.2105/AJPH.2021.306375; Donna L. Hoyert, "Maternal Mortality Rates in the United States, 2021," National Center for Health Statistics, March 2023, https://www.cdc.gov/nchs/data/hestat/maternal-mortality/2021/maternal-mortality-rates-2021.pdf.

that from 2007 to 2016, Black and American Indian/Alaska Native women at least thirty years old were nearly four to five times more likely to die from pregnancy-related causes than all other racial and ethnic groups.[71]

These populations experience more educational, work, and criminal system discrimination. According to the US Department of Education, Black girls are suspended at much higher rates (12 percent) than girls of any other race or ethnicity as well as most boys. The school suspension rate for American Indian and Native Alaskan girls is 7 percent; the rate for White boys is 6 percent and for White girls 2 percent.[72] One study found that during one school year, suspension and expulsion rates for Black girls in some US cities were ten to fifty-three times greater than rates for White girls.[73] In the workplace, Black and Latina women are much more likely to experience wage discrimination. Though the average wage gap based on gender alone (not accounting for differences in race) is 20.88 cents, the gap is an average of 36.89 cents for African American women and 45.90 cents for Latinas.[74] In the United States, Black women are more likely to be incarcerated than White women: between 1983 and 2008, Black women were imprisoned at seven times the rate of White women,[75] most likely because they are incarcerated for drug-related crimes at a significantly higher rate.[76]

Research suggests that transgender and gender nonconforming Indigenous people and people of color were over three times more likely to experience hate violence in 2016.[77] Among transgender

[71] Emily E. Petersen et al., "Racial/Ethnic Disparities in Pregnancy-Related Deaths—United States, 2007–2016," *Morbidity and Mortality Weekly Report* 68, no. 35 (2019): 762–65, https://www.cdc.gov/mmwr/volumes/68/wr/mm6835a3.htm.

[72] U.S. Department of Education Office for Civil Rights, "Civil Rights Data Collection Data Snapshot: School Discipline," March 2014, https://civilrightsdata.ed.gov/assets/downloads/CRDC-School-Discipline-Snapshot.pdf.

[73] Kimberlé W. Crenshaw, "Black Girls Matter: Pushed Out, Overpoliced and Underprotected," with Priscilla Ocen and Jyoti Nanda, African American Policy Forum and Center for Intersectionality and Social Policy Studies, 2015, https://www.atlanticphilanthropies.org/wp-content/uploads/2015/09/BlackGirlsMatter_Report.pdf.

[74] Stephen J. Chapman and Nicole Benis, "Ceteris Non Paribus: The Intersectionality of Gender, Race, and Region in the Gender Wage Gap," *Women's Studies International Forum* 65 (2017): 78–86, doi:10.1016/j.wsif.2017.10.001.

[75] Mark G. Harmon and Breanna Boppre, "Women of Color and the War on Crime: An Explanation for the Rise in Black Female Imprisonment," *Journal of Ethnicity in Criminal Justice* 16, no. 4 (2018): 309–32, doi:10.1080/15377938.2015.1052173.

[76] Ibid., 328.

[77] National Coalition of Anti-violence Programs, "Lesbian, Gay, Bisexual, Transgender, Queer, and HIV-Affected Hate Violence."

Americans, individuals who also identify as Black, multiracial, Middle Eastern, or American Indian tend to experience sexual assault at some point in their lives an average of 6 to 18 percent more than people in other racial and ethnic groups.[78] Perhaps most striking, 84 percent of American Indian or Alaska Native women and 81 percent of American Indian or Alaska Native men have experienced sexual violence, stalking, or intimate partner violence in their lifetime; 97 percent of women and 90 percent of men in these instances reported that they were victimized by non-Native individuals.[79]

Age and Ability

People who are dependent on others to meet daily financial, health, or other needs—due to youth, old age, or disability—may experience higher rates of some forms of gender violence like sexual abuse, sexual exploitation, or sex trafficking. One study focused on US boys and girls between the ages of ten and eighteen revealed that 15 percent of participants had experienced online harassment of a sexual nature, and 37 percent were victims of cyberbullying.[80] In another study, 15.6 percent of twelve- to fifteen-year-old girls and 9.3 percent of twelve- to fifteen-year-old boys reported experiencing online sexual solicitation by adults.[81] One study reveals that US adults who were the victims of nonconsensual distribution of sexual material had experienced it for the first time between the ages of fourteen and twenty.[82]

It is estimated that 51 percent of the 3.3 million children in situations of forced labor worldwide are in commercial sexual exploitation.[83] One in three girls is thought to experience sexual violence

---

[78] James, Herman, Rankin, Keisling, Mottet, and Anaf, "Report of the 2015 U.S. Transgender Survey."

[79] Andre B. Rosay, "Violence against American Indian and Alaska Native Women and Men: 2010 Findings from the National Intimate Partner and Sexual Violence Survey," U.S. Department of Justice, May 2016, https://www.ncjrs.gov/pdffiles1/nij/249736.pdf.

[80] Jennifer E. Copp, Elizabeth A. Mumford, and Bruce G. Taylor, "Online Sexual Harassment and Cyberbullying in a Nationally Representative Sample of Teens: Prevalence, Predictors, and Consequences," *Journal of Adolescence* 93 (2021): 202–11, doi:10.1016/j.adolescence.2021.10.003.

[81] Patricia de Santisteban and Manuel Gámez-Guadix, "Prevalence and Risk Factors among Minors for Online Sexual Solicitations and Interactions with Adults," *Journal of Sex Research* 55, no. 7 (2018): 939–50, doi:10.1080/00224499.2017.1386763.

[82] Ruvalcaba and Eaton, "Nonconsensual Pornography."

[83] International Labour Organization, Walk Free, and International Organization for Migration, "Global Estimates," 46.

by the time they are eighteen years old,[84] and one in five adolescent girls is physically or sexually abused by a dating partner.[85] More than one in three girls worldwide enter marriage unions before the age of fifteen,[86] and between 2000 and 2018 in the United States, an estimated 297,000 children were married before they were eighteen, 78 percent of whom were girls wed to adult men.[87] At least sixty million girls are thought to be missing from various populations around the world due to gender-selective abortions, infanticide, or neglect.[88] In the United States, the percentage of newborns circumcised during birth hospitalization was 58.3 percent in 2010.[89] Among adult men in the United States, one in six are estimated to have experienced childhood sexual abuse.[90]

Elder populations may be at higher risk for sexual violence due to old age or disability. Though an estimated 10 percent of older adults experience *elder abuse*—which can include sexual violence[91]—there has been little quantitative research on its gendered aspects. People with disabilities tend to experience higher rates of sexual and other abuse: women with disabilities may be four times more likely to experience sexual assault than those without them.[92] Especially vulnerable to abuse from personal attendants, health providers, and caregivers, women with physical disabilities tend to experience emotional, physical, or sexual abuse for longer

[84] David Finkelhor, Gerald Hotaling, I. A. Lewis, and Christine Smith, "Sexual Abuse in a National Survey of Adult Men and Women: Prevalence, Characteristics, and Risk Factors," *Child Abuse & Neglect* 14, no. 1 (1990): 1–28, doi:10.1016/0145-2134(90)90077-7.
[85] Jay G. Silverman, Anita Raj, Lorelei A. Mucci, and Jeanne E. Hathaway, "Dating Violence against Adolescent Girls and Associated Substance Use, Unhealthy Weight Control, Sexual Risk Behavior, Pregnancy, and Suicidality," *JAMA* 286, no. 5 (2001): 572–79, doi:10.1001/jama.286.5.572.
[86] UNICEF, "Ending Child Marriage: Progress and Prospects," 2013, https://data.unicef.org/resources/ending-child-marriage-progress-and-prospects/.
[87] Reiss, "Child Marriage."
[88] UNICEF, "Child Marriage."
[89] Centers for Disease Control and Prevention, "Trends in Circumcision for Male Newborns in U.S. Hospitals: 1979–2010," August 2013, https://www.cdc.gov/nchs/data/hestat/circumcision_2013/circumcision_2013.pdf.
[90] Finkelhor, Hotaling, Lewis, and Smith, "Sexual Abuse."
[91] Mark S. Lachs and Karl A. Pillemer, "Elder Abuse," *New England Journal of Medicine* 373, no. 20 (2015): 1947–56, doi:10.1056/NEJMra1404688.
[92] Sandra L Martin et al., "Physical and Sexual Assault of Women with Disabilities," *Violence against Women* 12, no. 9 (2006): 823–37, doi:10.1177/1077801206292672.

durations of time than women without disabilities.[93] Women with disabilities who are also women of color and those with less education and financial resources may experience even higher rates.[94] Transgender individuals are more likely to face challenges that intersect with having a disability: in a 2015 survey, 24 percent of transgender respondents with disabilities were unemployed and 45 percent were living in poverty; 59 percent reported experiencing serious psychological distress, 54 percent had attempted suicide at some point in their life, and 42 percent had been mistreated by health-care providers.[95]

Socioeconomic Class and Geography

Though poverty and a region's lack of economic development may increase an individual's risk factors for experiencing a variety of forms of gender violence, the statistical correlation is unclear. Reports do reveal locations where rates of certain types may be more prevalent, but research is limited. Forced sexual exploitation of both adults and children is thought to be highest in Asia and the Pacific region (around 70 percent), followed by Europe and Central Asia (14 percent) and Africa (8 percent).[96] The highest levels of child marriage among girls are thought to be in West and Central Africa, Eastern and Southern Africa, South Asia, and Arab states; the highest rates for boys are in Belize, Suriname, Nicaragua, and Central African Republic.[97] In the United States, states with the highest per capita rates of marriage before age eighteen between 2000 and 2018 were Nevada, Idaho, Arkansas, Kentucky, Wyoming, and Utah.[98] Bride kidnapping is still practiced in Armenia, Ethiopia, Kazakhstan, and South Africa, but it is unclear how often

[93] Mary Ellen Young, Margaret A. Nosek, Carol Howland, Gail Chanpong, and Diana H. Rintala, "Prevalence of Abuse of Women with Physical Disabilities," *Archives of Physical Medicine and Rehabilitation* 78, no. 12 (1997): S34–S38, doi:10.1016/s0003-9993(97)90219-7.
[94] Ibid.
[95] James, Herman, Rankin, Keisling, Mottet, and Anaf, "Report of the 2015 U.S. Transgender Survey."
[96] International Labour Office, "Global Estimates of Modern Slavery: Forced Labour and Forced Marriage," 2017, http://www.ilo.org/wcmsp5/groups/public/---dgreports/---dcomm/documents/publication/wcms_575479.pdf.
[97] UNICEF, "Child Marriage"; International Labour Organization, Walk Free, and International Organization for Migration, "Global Estimates," 5.
[98] Reiss, "Child Marriage."

abductions are consensual.[99] Dowries are still common in parts of India, Bangladesh, Pakistan, and Sri Lanka,[100] with dowry deaths thought to be most common in India, Pakistan, and Bangladesh.[101]

The United Nations believes that the largest number of women and girls killed by intimate partners or other family members live in Asia. When population rates are factored in, however, African women and girls are at the highest risk of being killed by an intimate partner or other family member.[102] Researchers assert that honor killings happen most frequently in the Middle East (Iraq, Syria, Jordan, Iran, and Yemen), South Asia (India and Pakistan), and the Mediterranean (especially Turkey).[103] Though estimates are not available, acid attacks against women are especially prevalent in India, Columbia, Cambodia, Pakistan, Nepal, Uganda, and Bangladesh—though acid attacks against men are currently rising in the UK.[104] Genital cutting on women and girls occurs most in some areas of Africa, Asia, and the Middle East, with more than half of instances thought to be concentrated in Indonesia, Egypt, and Ethiopia.[105] The highest rates of breast ironing are likely in parts of Africa south of the Sahara, with Cameroon thought to have especially high levels.[106]

Maternal death rates are affected by class and geography. In 2017, almost 94 percent of maternal deaths could have been prevented if the regions in which they occurred had more resources available; rates were highest in Sub-Saharan Africa and South Asia, accounting for 86 percent of estimated numbers worldwide.[107] Menstrual hygiene management may have a severe impact on adolescent girls in low- and middle-income countries, though numbers

[99] Charles M. Becker, Bakhrom Mirkasimov, and Susan Steiner, "Forced Marriage and Birth Outcomes," *Demography* 54, no. 4 (2017): 1401–23, doi:10.1007/s13524-017-0591-1.

[100] Siwan Anderson, "The Economics of Dowry and Brideprice," *Journal of Economic Perspectives* 21, no. 4 (2007): 151–74, doi:10.1257/jep.21.4.151.

[101] Kaur and Byard, "Bride Burning."

[102] United Nations Office on Drugs and Crime, "Global Study on Homicide."

[103] Arash Heydari, Ali Teymoori, and Rose Trappes, "Honor Killing as a Dark Side of Modernity: Prevalence, Common Discourses, and a Critical View," *Social Science Information* 60, no. 1 (2021): 86–106, doi:10.1177/0539018421994777.

[104] Acid Survivors Trust International, "A Worldwide Problem," 2024, https://www.asti.org.uk/a-worldwide-problem.html.

[105] UNICEF, "Female Genital Mutilation."

[106] Amahazion, "Breast Ironing."

[107] Sampriti Debnath and Nitish Mondal, "Maternal Mortality—an Ongoing Epidemic," *Anthrocom Journal of Anthropology* 18, no. 1 (2022): 489–96, https://antrocom.net/archives/2022/volume-18-number-1/maternal-mortality-an-ongoing-epidemic/.

Additional Information

Factors that lead to higher risk of maternal death include

- Being younger than thirty years old
- Getting mistreated or neglected by medical professionals due to race or ethnicity
- Living somewhere without adequate pregnancy resources

are not available.[108] Contemporary forced sterilization rates are difficult to determine: in Puerto Rico, about one-third of mothers between the ages of twenty and forty-nine were sterilized in 1965,[109] and by 1980, Puerto Rico had the highest rate of women's sterilization globally.[110] Nonconsensual and forced circumcision rates are difficult to determine. The estimated prevalence of circumcision is above 90 percent in some areas of East Asia, the South Pacific, Central Asia, the Middle East, and many central, eastern, and northern countries in Africa—but these numbers largely exclude infant circumcision, do not include details about medical necessity or consent, or differentiate circumcision performed in childhood, adolescence, or adulthood. [111]

The intersection of geography, political ideology, race, and socioeconomic class plays a role in employment discrimination and incarceration. In the United States, one study found that the average gender wage gap was highest in the Southwest and lowest in the Northeast.[112] Sexual violence, wage theft, and workplace hazards are widespread among women farmworkers, and of the estimated 630,000 women who are engaged in farmwork in the United States, many are Latina and face challenges including poverty, fear, shame,

---

[108] Jaseela Majeed, Prerna Sharma, Puneeta Ajmera, and Koustuv Dalal, "Menstrual Hygiene Practices and Associated Factors among Indian Adolescent Girls: A Meta-analysis," *Reproductive Health* 19, no. 1 (2022): 148, doi:10.1186/s12978-022-01453-3.

[109] Harriet B. Presser, "The Role of Sterilization in Controlling Puerto Rican Fertility," *Population Studies* 23, no. 3 (1969): 343–61, doi:10.2307/2172875.

[110] Elena R. Gutiérrez and Liza Fuentes, "Population Control by Sterilization: The Cases of Puerto Rican Women and Mexican-Origin Women in the United States," *Latino(a) Research Review* 7, no. 3 (2009): 85–100.

[111] Brian J. Morris, Wamai, Heneheng, Tobian, Klausner, Banerjee, and Hankins, "Male Circumcision."

[112] Chapman and Benis, "Ceteris Non Paribus."

It Happens at Home

College students in my classes—especially if they grew up in the United States—are often shocked to learn about the prevalence of gender violence. They knew it was a problem, they tell me, but not that rates are so high. Many of them have never heard of acid attacks, honor killings, or dowry deaths, and their exposure to issues of sex trafficking, forced marriage, and genital cutting is often limited to problems they have heard about in other countries. I certainly don't blame students: in US culture, we tend to frame gender oppression as something that happens to people who aren't like us, or to people "over there." We tend to think of our culture as evolved, socially conscious, even "postfeminist." This can lead to dangerous comparisons that minimize the realities of gender violence in the United States and sensationalize it in other parts of the world. Though it is true that some types of gender violence are more common in certain regions like those with less financial resources, it is often easier to critique others than process the incredible discomfort of knowing these things are happening in schools, workplaces, college campuses, public spaces, and homes across the United States. Every semester, I boldly but carefully lead students into this knowledge. I am continuously reminded of how much work we have to do as well as how powerful it is to witness students use this new understanding of gender violence to work against it, support one another, and propose creative solutions.

language access, lack of resources for assistance, undocumented status, and lack of information about their rights.[113] Some US-owned maquiladoras in Mexico not bound to US discrimination laws pregnancy-test their women employees and fire them when they become pregnant.[114] LGBTIQA+ individuals around the world may have a harder time avoiding imprisonment in areas where police corruption

---

[113] Southern Poverty Law Center, "Injustice on Our Plates," November 8, 2010, https://www.splcenter.org/20101107/injustice-our-plates#exploitation.

[114] Elvia R. Arriola, "Voices from the Barbed Wires of Despair: Women in the Maquiladoras, Latina Critical Legal Theory, and Gender at the U.S.-Mexico Border," in *Critical Race Feminism: A Reader*, ed. Adrien K. Wing (New York: New York University Press, 2003), 406–14.

is more prevalent and fewer support networks are available; this is especially true of people without the financial means to pay bail costs or bribe corrupt law enforcement officials.[115]

Disasters and Biological Hazards

Weather-related disasters and biological hazards may increase rates of gender violence and make it more difficult for people to receive assistance and support. According to a review of research, women and girls are disproportionately impacted by disasters and experience more partner violence, sexual assault, genital cutting, honor killing, and trafficking after they occur.[116] Analysis of the Mount Saint Helens eruption in 1980, Loma Prieta earthquake in 1989, Indian Ocean earthquake and tsunami in 2004, and Hurricane Katrina in 2005 demonstrates that women are far more likely than men to die during and after a natural disaster, and reports of sexual and partner violence tend to skyrocket.[117] These events can cause disruptive stress, mental health issues, housing and job insecurity, economic strain, loss of community support, and trauma that can exacerbate already unsafe family environments—and make it more difficult for someone to leave or access help.[118] In addition, men may vent their emotional suffering through violence, and opportunistic perpetrators may take advantage of turmoil to commit abuse.[119] Women's traditional responsibilities involving the care of children, sick individuals, and the elderly also become more difficult following a disaster.[120] Because it is challenging to conduct social scientific studies in crisis situations, accurate quantitative data on gender violence in the aftermath of natural disasters is not available.

---

[115] Botha, "Our Identities under Arrest."

[116] Alyssa M. Thurston, Heidi Stöckl, and Meghna Ranganathan, "Natural Hazards, Disasters and Violence against Women and Girls: A Global Mixed-Methods Systematic Review," *BMJ Global Health* 6, no. 4 (2021): 1–21, doi:10.1136/bmjgh-2020-004377.

[117] Lin Chew and Kavita N. Ramdas, "Caught in the Storm: The Impact of Natural Disasters on Women," December 2005, Global Fund for Women, https://www.ncdsv.org/uploads/1/4/2/2/142238266/gfw_caughtinthestormimpactnaturaldisasterswomen_12-2005.pdf, 2; Alisa Klein, "Preventing and Responding to Sexual Violence in Disasters," Louisiana Foundation Against Sexual Assault & National Sexual Violence Resource Center, https://www.nsvrc.org/resource/2500/sexual-violence-disasters, 11.

[118] Sarah Fisher, "Violence against Women and Natural Disasters: Findings from Post-tsunami Sri Lanka," in *Companion Reader on Violence against Women*, ed. Clarie M. Renzetti, Jeffrey L. Edleson, and Raquel K. Bergen (Thousand Oaks, CA: Sage, 2012), 138.

[119] Ibid., 144.

[120] Ibid., 137.

Biological hazards like pandemic viruses and disease outbreaks can exacerbate already existing challenges for people who experience gender violence and contribute to a lack of resources and support. Homophobic discrimination against gay and bisexual men, for example, hindered adequate US media coverage and response to the AIDS epidemic in the 1980s and 1990s—and financial resources that could have focused on prevention were spent on legislative efforts to punish and further stigmatize people with HIV and AIDS.[121] Since the 1990s, AIDS has impacted Black men more than any other racial group in the United States. According to one study, Black men who have sex with men experience the highest prevalence of HIV, the highest rates of unrecognized HIV infection, and the highest AIDS mortality rates.[122] In 2021, known rates of HIV diagnosis among people in the United States over the age of thirteen were highest among men (79 percent) and most often transmitted through sexual contact between men.[123] Black/African American individuals in the United States were 7.9 times more likely than White individuals to be diagnosed with HIV; rates were also 3.8 times higher for Hispanic/Latino individuals, 3.7 times higher for multiracial individuals, 2.8 times higher for Native Hawaiian/Pacific Islanders, and 2.0 times higher for American Indian/Alaska Natives than for White individuals.[124]

AIDS continues to be a problem globally as well. According to the UN, there are five main populations that are especially vulnerable to HIV who also frequently lack adequate access to services: gay men and other men who have sex with men, transgender individuals, sex workers, incarcerated individuals, and people who inject drugs.[125] Even though an increased awareness of these issues around the world led to a 23 percent decline in new HIV infections between 2010 and 2019, rates still increased an estimated 25 percent among gay men and other men who have sex with men—and

[121] Gregory M. Herek, "AIDS and Stigma," *American Behavioral Scientist* 42, no. 7 (1999): 1106–16, doi:10.1177/00027649921954787.
[122] Gregorio A. Millett and John L. Peterson, "The Known Hidden Epidemic: HIV/AIDS among Black Men Who Have Sex with Men in the United States," *American Journal of Preventive Medicine* 32, no. 4 (2007): S31–S33, doi:10.1016/j.amepre.2006.12.028.
[123] Centers for Disease Control and Prevention, "HIV Surveillance Report, 2021," vol. 34, May 2023, https://stacks.cdc.gov/view/cdc/149071.
[124] Ibid.
[125] UNAIDS, "Key Populations," 2024, https://www.unaids.org/en/topic/key-populations.

HIV rates have not decreased among transgender women and sex workers.[126]

The global COVID-19 pandemic that began in 2019 intensified gender violence, especially against women and girls. Though it is difficult to accurately estimate changes in rates of gender violence, one review of research suggests that worldwide nearly one in three women experienced partner violence during the COVID-19 pandemic, and partner violence service providers reported a 25 to 50 percent increase in hotline calls and up to a 150 percent increase in website traffic during this time.[127] Multiple countries around the world reported increases in gender violence cases and higher demand for emergency shelter,[128] and there were widespread reports of forced labor linked to the COVID-19 crisis.[129] Many international, national, and regional organizations suggest that increases in experiences of gender violence and their severity were likely due to the disruption of crisis services, mobility restrictions, higher unemployment rates, and economic insecurity during the height of the pandemic—and these challenges had a particularly harmful impact on groups that already faced limited access to services and less financial resources like people who identify across the LGBTIQA+ spectrum, people with migrant status, older women, people with disabilities, and people who are low income.[130]

Migration, Conflict, and Displacement

Little is known about the prevalence of sexual assault, trafficking, partner violence, or other issues faced by migrants in comparison to citizens of a particular country. Some research shows higher

[126] UNAIDS, "Update: New HIV Infections among Gay Men and Other Men Who Have Sex with Men Increasing," December 7, 2020, https://www.unaids.org/en/resources/presscentre/featurestories/2020/december/20201207_new-hiv-infections-increasing.

[127] Mearg E. Kifle, Setognal B. Aychiluhm, and Etsay W. Anbesu, "Global Prevalence of Intimate Partner Violence during the COVID-19 Pandemic among Women: Systematic Review and Meta-analysis," *BMC Women's Health* 24, no. 1 (2024): 1–14, doi:10.1186/s12905-023-02845-8.

[128] Nobuhle J. Dlamini, "Gender-Based Violence, Twin Pandemic to COVID-19," *Critical Sociology* 47, no. 4/5 (2021): 583–90, doi:10.1177/0896920520975465.

[129] International Labour Organization, Walk Free, and International Organization for Migration, "Global Estimates," 2.

[130] UNFPA, UN Women, and Quilt.AI, "Covid-19 and Violence against Women: The Evidence Behind the Talk," 2021, https://asiapacific.unfpa.org/en/publications/covid-19-and-violence-against-women-evidence-behind-talk; Dlamini, "Gender-Based Violence."

intimate partner homicide rates against immigrant and refugee women,[131] and other reports suggest migrant women face increased risk of sexual violence.[132] Immigrants who are trapped in sex trafficking may have low education levels, lack of formal job skills, and limited language proficiency that make escaping much harder.[133]

In armed conflict, natural disasters, and other humanitarian emergencies, experts believe that rates of sexual violence against displaced and refugee women increase because of the disruption of housing and community resources. Though some reports show high numbers of sexual violence in refugee camps (between 66 and 80 percent of women and girls in camps in Liberia and Sierra Leone, for example), widespread numbers are less available.[134] It is common for relief agencies to give less food and medical attention to women refugees than to men, resulting in malnourishment; in addition, governments often ignore or allow unequal treatment and violence against women in these contexts.[135] Sexual slavery, rape as a weapon of war or ethnic cleansing, and sexual exploitation by those providing basic needs or safe passage may be more common in these settings,[136] as well as forced pregnancy to replace dwindling numbers of a population.[137] In areas of armed conflict, sexual violence may be used to consolidate control of territory and resources, such as the kidnapping of women and girls to exploit for ransoms or forced marriage to decrease girls' educational and economic opportunities; abduction and sexual assault may also be used as a

---

[131] Mieko Yoshihama, "Literature on Intimate Partner Violence in Immigrant and Refugee Communities: Review and Recommendations," in *Intimate Partner Violence in Immigrant and Refugee Communities: Challenges, Promising Practices and Recommendations*, ed. Family Violence Prevention Fund (Princeton, NJ: Robert Wood Johnson Foundation, 2009), 34–64, https://www.rwjf.org/en/library/research/2009/03/intimate-partner-violence-in-immigrant-and-refugee-communities.html.

[132] Amnesty International, "Invisible Victims: Migrants on the Move in Mexico," 2010, https://www.amnestyusa.org/wp-content/uploads/2017/04/amr410142010eng.pdf, 15.

[133] Sahnah Lim, Seunggun Lee, Lori Cohen, John J. Chin, Chau Trinh-Shevrin, and Nadia S. Islam, "Factors Influencing Recovering and Well-Being among Asian Survivors of International Criminal Sex Trafficking in an Urban U.S. City," *Journal of Interpersonal Violence* 38, nos. 3–4 (2023): 2360–86, doi:10.1177/08862605221101187.

[134] British Refugee Council, "The Vulnerable Women's Project Refugee and Asylum Seeking Women Affected by Rape or Sexual Violence," 2009, https://documentation.lastradainternational.org/lsidocs/RC%20VWP-report-web.pdf.

[135] Merry, *Gender Violence*, 171–72.

[136] World Health Organization, "WHO Ethical and Safety Recommendations for Researching, Documenting and Monitoring Sexual Violence in Emergencies," 2007, https://www.who.int/publications/i/item/9789241595681.

[137] Merry, *Gender Violence*, 172.

means of collective punishment against enemies or as reward for men engaged in fighting.[138] Men also experience conflict-related sexual violence: since the onset of the South Sudan conflict in 2013, for example, South Sudanese men experienced a variety of forms of sexual violence while in South Sudan, in transit as refugees to resettlement communities, and within resettlement communities in Uganda. Violence included exposure of their genitals, genital mutilation and beating, rape, forced rape of others, forced witnessing of the rape of women in their lives, forced performance of "wife" roles involving domestic and sexual labor, and being forced to exchange sex for favors.[139]

Rape, assault, and the killing of women is a common feature of war and ethnic conflict, as documented in India, Darfur, the Sudan, and Rwanda.[140] A review of data suggests high numbers of sexual violence in the Democratic Republic of Congo amid armed conflict and in Sri Lanka during its civil war. Sexual violence with genocidal intent occurred in the 1990s in the Bosnia-Herzegovina conflict, where experts estimate that 25,000 to 50,000 Bosnian women were raped during the war—often in groups, designated camps, and on the front line of battle. In the 1994 genocide in Rwanda, an estimated 500,000 Tutsi women and girls were raped by members of the Hutu ethnic majority.[141] More recently, Uyghur women in China have experienced mass sterilization, coerced interracial marriage, separation from their children and homes to concentration camps and prisons, forced labor, rape, and sexual torture.[142]

Androcide and forced circumcision may happen more in times of war and genocide. During the Kosovo War and events leading up to it in the mid- to late 1990s, Serbian police and Yugoslav soldiers selectively targeted thousands of Albanian men in Kosovo

---

[138] United Nations, "Sexual Violence in Conflict: Report of the United Nations Secretary-General," July 6, 2023, https://www.un.org/sexualviolenceinconflict/wp-content/uploads/2023/07/SG-REPORT-2023SPREAD-1.pdf, 10–14.

[139] Tosin Olaluwoye, Elizabeth Hoban, and Joanne Williams, "Forms of Sexual Violence Perpetrated in Conflict and Post-conflict Settings against South Sudanese Men Resettled in Two Communities in Uganda: An Exploratory Qualitative Study," *Conflict and Health* 17 (2023): 1–9, doi:10.1186/s13031-023-00544-7.

[140] Merry, *Gender Violence*, 156.

[141] Ibid.

[142] Rukiye Turdush and Magnus Fiskesjö, "Dossier: Uyghur Women in China's Genocide," *Genocide Studies and Prevention: An International Journal* 15, no. 1 (2021): 22–43, doi:10.5038/1911-9933.15.1.1834.

considered to be fighting age for torture, execution, and detainment in labor facilities and prisons.[143] Evidence of mass events involving the forced circumcision of men between 2000 and 2013—often in the midst of military conflict, genocide, or tribal rule—has also been documented in India, Nepal, Indonesia, Iraq, South Africa, Pakistan, Sudan, Turkey, Uganda, and Yugoslavia.[144]

Statistical Limitations

Considered holistically, these numbers provide a foundation for understanding the individual and collective impact of gender violence nationally and around the world. It is important to note, however, the limitations of quantitative research. Differences in how researchers define certain types of gender violence—as well as how they select samples, gather data, and do their analysis—may mean more or less generalizable findings, skewed results, or inconsistent conclusions across studies.[145] Statistics generated from reports and academic studies should be used with caution; even well-intentioned researchers sometimes misrepresent findings when citing quantitative data.

I gathered information for this chapter directly from studies and reports. I took extra care to evaluate this research carefully[146] and avoid misrepresentation of findings, which made it necessary to omit many studies due to their narrow research scope, small sample size, or lack of validity or reliability. At times, I chose not to include research that found no significant differences among demographic groups. In my search for data, I discovered that statistics simply do not exist that might provide a fuller and more accurate picture of the prevalence of gender violence in some contexts and among certain populations. Though the information included in this chapter addresses gender violence broadly and includes many intersections of identity and culture, historical biases have meant that most

---

[143] Buchanan, "Gendercide."

[144] Glass, "Forced Circumcision."

[145] Walter S. DeKeseredy and Martin D. Schwartz, "Theoretical and Definitional Issues in Violence against Women," in *Sourcebook on Violence against Women*, ed. Claire M. Renzetti, Jeffrey L. Edleson, and Raquel K. Bergen, 2nd ed. (Thousand Oaks, CA: Sage, 2001), 3–22.

[146] Diane R. Follingstad, "The Challenges of Measuring Violence against Women," in *Sourcebook on Violence against Women*, ed. Claire M. Renzetti, Jeffrey L. Edleson, and Raquel Kennedy Bergen, 4th ed. (Thousand Oaks, CA: Sage, 2018), 57–77, 57–58.

formalized research on gender violence in the United States has focused on White, cisgender, heterosexual, middle-class women. In addition, many scholarly studies draw from participant samples limited to college students—a population to which researchers often have access but that might not provide results generalizable to the larger public. Some populations remain largely invisible and underacknowledged; this is especially true of groups that may face multiple intersecting forms of oppression due to identity differences, language barriers, food or housing insecurity, incarceration, and other factors. Funding limitations, strict institutional review board policies, ethical concerns with disclosures about trauma, and challenges in participant recruitment can also make gathering and publishing data on gender violence and the individuals affected by it very difficult. Even when quality studies do exist, research that has become an agreed-upon standard in a particular field—some of which is provided here—can sometimes be challenged or disproven. It is likely that over time our understanding of these numbers will continue to shift as researchers address gaps and ask new questions.

The Dynamics of Higher Risk

One advantage of comprehensively considering quantitative data on gender violence is our ability to identify many of the groups affected by it most. As I mentioned at the beginning of this chapter, higher risk of experiencing gender violence should not be conflated with inherent vulnerability. People aren't at higher risk because of differences in their gender, gender expression, sexual orientation, race, class, or other aspects of identity—they are at higher risk because of the bias, discrimination, and lack of equality based on these differences in the cultural contexts in which they exist. In other words, things like race and class do not cause higher risk, but racism and classism do. People who commit gender violence may target individuals they perceive as members of more vulnerable groups as a way to exert power and control over them. Acts of gender violence may be committed with the knowledge that members of some groups may have a harder time seeking justice, accountability, safety, or assistance—and use someone's lack of access, resources, or privileges against them. People may also commit gender violence as a direct expression of hate, intolerance, or superiority.

Whatever specific dynamics are involved, the problem of gender violence is shaped by social and cultural attitudes that can shift over time. We don't have to accept gender violence and higher rates of it against certain populations as normal or inevitable. It is, however, important for us to acknowledge how cultural difference and other factors affect rates, and to use this lens when we consider its overall impact. Though succinct statistics with a super narrow scope (like *one-third of the world's women*) may be the easiest way to raise awareness of gender violence, they oversimplify the problem and minimize its effects on many of the people harmed by it most. This is why I encourage educators and activists to be diligent in presenting this bigger picture any time they seek to make a persuasive case about gender violence using quantitative data. Even then, prevalence research only gives us one piece of the picture. We must also consider *how* gender violence dynamics impact the individuals who experience it.

CHAPTER 4

Individual Impact of Gender Violence

A comprehensive approach to understanding the effects of gender violence begins with prevalence and extends to its impact on the lives of the individuals who live that statistical reality. People respond to experiences of gender violence in various ways depending on a lot of contextual and intersecting factors. From the trauma at the time of an incident, to the obstacles one might face in accessing immediate assistance, to the many years of coping that may follow, the physical and psychological effects are incalculable.

Descriptive data from qualitative research and information gathered by crisis workers over the last fifty years yield many insights into the individual impact of gender violence, especially in how it may manifest as trauma and the factors that may influence someone's experience. In this chapter, I explain common responses to gender violence and focus special attention on the effects of single and compound trauma. I explore factors that influence how someone experiences gender violence and how they may move forward. I identify challenges people may encounter in seeking and receiving assistance and support. I highlight the impact of cultural difference for how people experience, make sense of, and move forward after gender violence.

Whether you are new to learning about gender violence or someone who witnesses disclosures on the daily, this chapter will help you understand common responses to gender violence in a deeper way. If you have experienced gender violence yourself, you may be able to make greater sense of how you reacted to what happened; even so, this chapter may be especially difficult to read if you are reflecting on something for the first time or negotiating a situation that is still fresh. Take breaks to breathe and seek support, and know that whatever you are feeling is okay. It might be help-ful to remember that you are not alone (think of how many others have experienced something similar to what you went through, as demonstrated in chapter 3), and this content—though challenging to take in—is an avenue for people to better understand what you experienced and improve how they respond to situations like yours in the future.

Common Reactions

There is no one normal way to respond to gender violence. People who experience it respond in a variety of ways, and the following list represents the breadth of possible common reactions. Individu-als may experience any, all, or none of these feelings, behaviors, or symptoms. Depending on the type of incident and a variety of other factors, people's experiences before, during, and after gender violence may vary significantly from one another. Even so, the con-nection between gender violence and trauma is undeniable when considering the potential individual impact of these actions on the bodies and lives of real people.

Responses to gender violence may manifest on physical, psycho-logical, and emotional levels. First, it is important to acknowledge that the physical effects of gender violence may be fatal. Individu-als often die from extensive injuries after sexual abuse, physical assault, acid attacks, or targeted homicide. People may experience life-threatening bodily trauma. Even without severe physical injury, an individual's reaction to the trauma of an event may manifest physically through nausea, vomiting, headache, changes in blood pressure, diminished alertness or exaggerated startle reflex, extreme stress, memory loss, lack of concentration, disordered eating, or inability to sleep.

After gender violence, a person may experience psychological responses including fear, anxiety, frustration, confusion, anger, shock, numbness, embarrassment, shame, isolation, hostility, rage, sadness, dissociation, or apathy. Individuals may experience feelings of vulnerability, distrust, and lack of safety, and relive incidents through disturbing thoughts, memories, nightmares, and flashbacks. Mood swings, drastic changes in attitude, hypervigi-lance, depression and anxiety, reduced ability to express emotions, social withdrawal, and intense desire for revenge may occur. Some individuals may fear being blamed or not believed for what happened or shamed about their decisions preceding incidents. They may fear retribution or other negative consequences that might result from reporting or disclosing the abuse to others. They may engage in relationships with others differently, or pretend nothing happened. Especially after incidents involving sexual violence, it is common for individuals to experience a sudden loss of interest in sex or drastic changes in sexual activity.

Individuals may have diagnosable symptoms of traumatic response. *Posttraumatic stress disorder* (PTSD) involves long-term symptoms that have a significant effect on at least one major area of a person's life.[1] An individual may have intense and disturbing thoughts and feelings about a traumatic event for more than a month after it has ended; this can involve intrusive thoughts through dreams, involuntary memories, and flashbacks; avoidance of reminders of the event, including associated people, places, objects, activities, or locations; ongoing negative thoughts and feelings that include detachment from others; and arousal and reactive symptoms such as irritability, anger, recklessness, self-destructive behaviors, being startled easily, or difficulty focusing or sleeping.[2] *Acute stress disorder* is similar to PTSD but typically occurs in the short term—a few days to a month—after a traumatic event occurs. Acute stress may lead to longer-term PTSD depending on coping behaviors, psychological support, and treatment after trauma.[3] Research suggests a correlation between gender violence and increased risk of PTSD; one study suggests that women are twice as likely to develop PTSD than men, most likely due to higher rates of sexual victimization.[4]

PTSD and acute stress disorder are closely related to *rape trauma syndrome* (or RTS), the common descriptor for traumatic response after sexual assault or attempted sexual assault.

[1] Lilia M. Cortina and Sheryl Pimlott Kubiak, "Gender and Posttraumatic Stress: Sexual Violence as an Explanation for Women's Increased Risk," *Journal of Abnormal Psychology* 115, no. 4 (2006): 753–59, doi:10.1037/0021-843X.115.4.753.
[2] American Psychiatric Association, "What Is Posttraumatic Stress Disorder?," 2017, https://www.psychiatry.org/patients-families/ptsd/what-is-ptsd.
[3] Ibid.
[4] Cortina and Kubiak, "Gender and Posttraumatic Stress."

Introduced by researchers in the 1970s,[5] RTS is usually described as involving five phases. The first, pre-assault discomfort, is only experienced by some and involves an intuitive sense that something bad is about to happen. The remaining phases are more common: the second phase is the assault itself, during which an individual may experience shock, dissociation, a sense of paralysis, fight-or-flight responses, or memorization of all details in the moment of violence. In the third phase, acute crisis, an individual may struggle with a variety of common physical and emotional reactions (like those described earlier). This can last for several days, weeks, or months. Outward adjustment is the fourth phase and involves attempts to regain a sense of normalcy after acute crisis has sub-sided. In this stage, an individual may move back and forth or cycle through various emotions, coping behaviors, suppression, denial, and flashbacks or reliving of trauma for a number of months or years. The fifth phase—originally called resolution—is now more commonly described as reorganization or reintegration. It involves integrating the experience of gender violence into one's life by facing it head-on, identifying healthy ways of coping so the event eventually loses power over major aspects of a person's life, and examining values, priorities, life choices, and relationships in its aftermath. Though a total resolution of the experience may never occur, this phase typically represents an individual's successful, though imperfect, ability to decentralize the experience of gender violence in comparison to other parts of their life as they move forward. An individual may not experience a linear progression through each phase of RTS. It is also normal for individuals to skip or never experience some phases (especially pre-assault discomfort or reintegration) depending on the situation.

In addition to being a useful tool for understanding the impact of single-event trauma for many victims of sexual violence, the basic principles of RTS can be applied to other forms of gender violence like one-time or short-term situations involving harassment, stalk-ing, exploitation, kidnapping, or physical assault. Situations involv-ing ongoing or repeated abuse may affect a person differently than one-time incidents. *Complex trauma* describes the compounded

[5] Ann W. Burgess and Lynda L. Holmstrom, "Rape Trauma Syndrome," *American Journal of Psychiatry* 131, no. 9 (1974): 981–86, doi:10.1176/ajp.131.9.981.

traumatic response that may result from multiple-event or prolonged partner violence, sexual abuse, dating violence, stalking, sexual harassment, dowry violence, or sex trafficking victimization. Complex trauma can involve difficulties in emotion regulation, changes in consciousness (such as regression, dissociation, or flashbacks), somatization (unexplained physical pain or medical problems), spiritual alienation (loss of hope or feeling distanced from divinity), empathic attachment to the desires of abusers, changes in expectations of personal relationships, trouble establishing healthy boundaries, unconscious habits of obedience, difficulty making accurate assessments of danger, prolonged feelings of unsafety in one's own body, and increased vulnerability to further abuse.[6] Complex trauma in relationship to gender violence has been called different things: for example, the term *battered women's syndrome*[7] emerged in the 1970s to explain why many women stayed in physically abusive relationships—especially in the long term—and why some would kill their abusers. Though the term was successful in beginning to theorize the impact of ongoing partner abuse, it is no longer useful because it is gender-specific, excludes types of abuse beyond physical assault, and does not depict the experiences of all individuals who experience partner violence. *Stockholm syndrome* and *traumatic bonding* are other terms used interchangeably to describe various aspects of complex trauma that may result from severe or long-duration gender violence.

Psychological trauma can change the composition of the brain. One analysis of multiple studies concluded that trauma exposure is linked to size decreases in the hippocampus,[8] a part of the brain that plays a big role in learning, memory, and emotional response.[9] This is why people who experience trauma may remember all or no parts of what happened, or may remember

---

[6] Debi S. Edmund and Patricia J. Bland, "Real Tools: Responding to Multi-abuse Trauma," Alaska Network on Domestic Violence & Sexual Assault, 2011, https://andvsa.org/realtoolsprint/.

[7] Lenore Walker, *The Battered Woman* (New York: Harper & Row, 1979).

[8] Fu Lye Woon, Shabnam Sood, and Dawson W. Hedges, "Hippocampal Volume Deficits Associated with Exposure to Psychological Trauma and Posttraumatic Stress Disorder in Adults: A Meta-analysis," *Progress in Neuro-psychopharmacology & Biological Psychiatry* 34, no. 7 (2010): 1181–88, doi:10.1016/j.pnpbp.2010.06.016.

[9] Kuljeet Singh Anand and Vikas Dhikav, "Hippocampus in Health and Disease: An Overview," *Annals of Indian Academy of Neurology* 15, no. 4 (2012): 239–46, doi:10.4103/0972-2327.104323.

bits and pieces of what happened out of order. Other long-term physical effects might involve pregnancy, contraction of sexually transmitted infection, physical disability, or stress-related medical issues like heart problems. Psychological effects in the long term might include development of low self-esteem, substance abuse, disordered eating, addiction, mental illness, self-destructive behavior, or self-harm. As direct or indirect results of gender violence, individuals may encounter a variety of additional difficulties that change their quality of life, including decreased job performance, loss of pets, financial hardship, lost access to personal records, child custody issues, or job loss. These challenges make an individual more prone to experiencing severe health problems, housing insecurity, poverty, incarceration, severe mental illness, and premature death.

Case Example

One Man's Reaction to Sexual Violence

When I give trainings for hotline workers and hospital advocates, I often share the story of a young man I assisted early in my career. One morning, he walked into the crisis services office where I worked, proclaimed to everyone in a seemingly nonchalant way that he had been raped, and awaited our response. After we sat down in a more private room, he told me what happened. His details of the assault were intermingled with jokes and incredulousness about the whole thing. It turns out he had shared his story with various authorities over the previous several hours and hadn't slept since the day before. He had only visited my office because he was told it was the next thing he should do; it was clear he was exhausted and likely in a state of shock. I'll never know exactly why he made his proclamation to my office the way he did or made so many jokes during our conversation. Perhaps he was nervous and wanted to alleviate tension or hide embarrassment, or maybe this was his way of dealing with trauma. Whatever the reasons, I knew enough at the time to know his response was normal given the circumstances and that he was coping in his own way.

Factors That Influence Reactions

Reactions to gender violence are unique and influenced by many factors. Much depends on the type of violence and its duration and frequency, perceived level of threat and personal violation, environmental specifics, personal characteristics, relationship with those who committed the abuse, and how and when others responded to the situation. Because gender violence encompasses a broad range of actions that individuals may experience very differently from one another, it is impossible to predict a certain type of response. Even two individuals who experience almost identical forms of gender violence may react in profoundly different ways. It is important to neither assume certain reactions based on the type of violence experienced, nor dismiss the possibility of any particular response for a given situation. Weighing or comparing instances of gender violence to one another may minimize someone's experience, unfairly value the legitimacy of some responses over others, or place unreasonable expectations on individuals to respond in certain ways in order to prove gender violence occurred.

The type of violence and its duration and frequency play a primary role in how an individual responds. Since gender violence can involve various levels of physical and sexual contact and verbal and nonverbal behaviors, there are a wide range of ways individuals may experience what happened or deal with its aftermath. Reactions may be dependent on whether the event happened once or multiple times, and how long each event lasted (several minutes, days, or years). One person who experiences stalking may cry and express feelings of shame, anger, and fear; another may seem disengaged and numb. A woman who is raped by a kidnapper over a period of days will most likely react differently than a teenager verbally harassed on the street every day on their way to work; an aromantic man psychologically abused by his spouse for several months may exhibit similar posttraumatic stress symptoms as a girl coping with years of abuse in a sex trafficking ring. Responses may not always be predictable: it is possible for a person who experienced a nonpenetrative sexual assault to exhibit more severe reactions than someone who experienced a more invasive form, or that a person experiencing partner violence might perceive the verbal abuse from their partner as more harmful than the physical abuse.

An individual's perception of threat and personal violation matters a lot in how they respond. Explicit or implied threats to their body, safety, life, job, well-being, social life, success, privacy, personal autonomy, loved ones, pets, or property may have been part of the abuse. A sex trafficker may have controlled someone's money and citizenship documents; a professor could have coerced a student not to report by threatening lower grades. A harasser may have damaged an individual's vehicle in the parking lot of their workplace; a girl's family may have been threatened when she didn't acquiesce to a man's demand for marriage. The level of personal violation or boundary crossing can also influence response: a sexual assault over clothing might be experienced differently than one under clothing, and the way someone is assaulted—and the body parts or specifics involved—may provoke different reactions. This might be especially significant for violence committed against transgender, gender nonconforming, aspec, or intersex individuals.

The environmental specifics of gender violence are important to consider. The location of the incident(s), whether at home, school, work, a place of religious worship, or elsewhere—and how often a person must return to that location—may contribute to how they respond. The time of the day, part of the week, season of the year, or co-occurrence with a holiday, day of significance, or other difficult life event may have an effect. A person's perception of safety and control at particular locations or times felt before the event, and the degree to which these are established or regained afterward, are important. A man may have trouble coping with sexual harassment at work if he has to return there every day and interact with the supervisor who continues to make comments about his body; a teenager may experience posttraumatic response every year during the winter holiday season when returning to the relative's home where their abuse occurred.

The relationship between the group or person who committed gender violence and the victim of that violence—whether they are strangers, acquaintances, family members, spouses, coworkers, or dating partners—can influence how someone reacts to what happened. A woman sexually assaulted by a stranger may feel increased hypervigilance, decreased feelings of safety, and extreme fear in situations where she is alone; a man may only experience flashbacks in the specific place in which his abuse occurred. A college student may have prolonged anxiety if forced to remain in a professor's course after making a report of harassment; a spouse may engage in denial that their significant other, whom they love, is an abuser.

Identity, personal characteristics, and circumstances play a role in reactions to gender violence. Aspects of social identity that individuals might use to justify violence against someone—like their sexual orientation, gender identity, race, size, class, ability, age, religion, and citizenship status—also make a difference for how that harm is experienced and how a person moves forward. An Asian American woman who endures a sexist and racist physical attack may attribute her experience to anti-Asian violence in the wake of COVID-19, increasing her fear of being in White-dominant spaces. A young nonbinary preteen who endures continuous fatphobic harassment while gaming online may view what is happening as normal or routine but become especially self-conscious of their body size in ways they carry through adolescence. Personality, neurodiversity, health, developmental stage at the time of the incident(s), or prior experience add additional layers of complexity to someone's response. A person on the autism spectrum, for example, may misinterpret a trusted friend's harmful intentions or be particularly prone to internalize an abuser's gaslighting.[10] A person with a history of anxiety and depression may react more severely to being stalked; a child may be too young to understand the implications of genital cutting and be much more resilient than expected. An outgoing individual might throw themselves into work as a way to cope with what happened; a person with health problems connected to breast ironing or acid violence may never reveal to others why they avoid physical intimacy. Circumstances—what is happening in a person's life or in their family, community, or country—during or after gender violence add even more layers: a parent may not be able to afford missing work to emotionally process their pregnancy discrimination. A woman in a refugee camp may experience compounded levels of trauma when she is sexually assaulted after being displaced from her home. People may feel they need to

---

[10] Sarah Douglas and Felicity Sedgewick, "Experiences of Interpersonal Victimization and Abuse among Autistic People," *Autism* 28(7): 1732–45, doi:10.1177/13623613231205630.

keep what happened a secret due to fear of further violence—like an honor killing or hate crime—being carried out against them. All of the above factors make a difference for how an individual makes sense of their experience and the ways they cope, heal, or negotiate long-term recovery. Individuals who engage in self-blame, perceive they cannot control PTSD symptoms, or cope using maladaptive strategies (distraction, denial, and disengagement) may experience increased levels of posttraumatic distress.[11]

How and when others outside the situation respond before, during, and after the incident can also have an impact. This can apply to friends, family members, coworkers, or first responders who may learn about what happened by witnessing it firsthand or through personal disclosure. An individual's response to their situation may be heavily determined by whether or not others are aware of what happened, how others respond when they do become aware, and how and when others intervene if the situation is ongoing. If a student reports a bullying incident to a school but is blamed for what happened to them, they may distrust all others who promise to provide assistance. If an athlete tells a coach about being touched inappropriately by other staff and they are believed, they are more empowered to seek additional help, use healthy coping methods, and stay in the sport they love rather than leave out of hopelessness that the situation will improve. To emphasize this even more: it is a common belief among the crisis services community that the response received after someone's first disclosure of gender violence has the biggest influence on how that individual moves forward. People who are blamed, disbelieved, or treated poorly may endure a variety of physical and psychological effects that extend or add to those already experienced from the initial event. This is because an individual may feel victimized all over again if they share then experience blame and insensitive treatment;[12] this is why experts in the crisis field often describe

---

[11] Cynthia J. Najdowski and Sarah E. Ullman, "PTSD Symptoms and Self-Rated Recovery among Adult Sexual Assault Survivors: The Effects of Traumatic Life Events and Psychosocial Variables," *Psychology of Women Quarterly* 33, no. 1 (2009): 43–53, doi:10.1111/j.1471-6402.2008.01473.x.

[12] Rebecca Campbell, Sharon M. Wasco, Courtney E. Ahrens, Tracy Sefl, and Holly E. Barnes, "Preventing the 'Second Rape': Rape Survivors' Experiences with Community Service Providers," *Journal of Interpersonal Violence* 16, no. 12 (2001): 1239–59, doi:10.1177/088626001016012002.

Case Example

Viewed with Suspicion after Partner Violence

A woman I know was stuck in an emotionally, physically, and sexually abusive relationship with her boyfriend for years. After a physical attack, her boyfriend was arrested and a judge instituted an order of protection requiring that he stay away from her. He violated the order over and over, using threats of further violence. He was especially upset that a domestic violence charge against him could ruin his career, and his threats intensified until she agreed to recant her story to the police. She signed official papers suggesting she had exaggerated the situation, which resulted in the county prosecutor dropping charges. Using manipulation and physical violence, her boyfriend forced her to pay his legal fees that resulted from the monthslong process following his arrest. Despite the harrowing abuse that continued after that time, many of their friends and family viewed her with suspicion after the incident. When they married, the abuse was minimized by people around her to the point that they didn't think it had really happened, and she coped by pretending things were okay as the abuse continued.

this experience as a *secondary victimization*, a *second assault*, or a *second rape*. Regardless of the type of gender violence involved or the label used, the frequency and severity of traumatic events are magnified by negative responses to initial disclosures. A religious person's physical health may worsen after they work up the courage to share with a trusted clergy member only to be blamed for the abuse committed against them. A woman may feel especially anxious if she reports her dowry-related abuse to authorities and is not believed.

The combination of factors described above illuminate the wide array of individual responses to gender violence. A woman may experience discomfort after a coworker grabs her butt in a bar, but she might not perceive the situation as particularly troubling. Someone in an abusive relationship may never experience an end to their partner's manipulation, but outwardly normalize the situation as a coping mechanism. A gay man may experience permanent alienation after his family learns of his sexual orientation after a hate crime, but find healthy ways of moving forward with the support of his chosen family. Individuals may feel devastated by an experience but never recognize or acknowledge it as gender violence; others may experience posttraumatic symptoms for decades. People may replay the moments of an attack for their entire lives, or flourish once they have the resources to leave a situation. Because identity and experience are complex, these and any number of additional factors make all experiences of gender violence unique.

Barriers to Seeking and Receiving Support

The obstacles individuals may encounter when deciding whether or not to seek help after experiencing gender violence, as well the challenges they may encounter in getting help, are important to recognize as part of the widespread impact of these issues. In addition to how they individually respond to the incident(s), people may or may not seek help based on the availability and ease of accessing assistance, their perception of service providers or first responders, and intersecting issues based on membership in underserved populations.

Despite the strides that have been made in gender violence crisis service provision, there are still communities across the United States with limited access to assistance. In rural areas of the country, one rape crisis center may be responsible for filling the needs of seven counties. In urban areas, many shelters lack the capacity to accommodate all individuals trying to escape their abusers and have long waiting lists. Hospitals and law enforcement agencies do not always contact or provide a crisis advocate to provide trauma-centered support. College campuses may not have a dedicated crisis response office where students can get confidential assistance without campus authorities being notified of their situation, and K–12 schools often lack the resources to train their staff. Grant requirements limit the types of services that can be provided through non-profit organizations, which means that some victims get referred rather than immediately supported. Partner violence shelters that house men or individuals who do not identify or pass as women are still uncommon. Agencies may not be perceived as available or committed to serving particular populations because they lack a diverse staff, don't provide language translators, or only reference women victims of men's violence in their promotional materials or intake processes.

Unfortunately, lack of access and culturally specific training means that many people who experience gender violence can't get help from the places that, at least in theory, exist to support them. Even well-intentioned service providers and other organizations may fail to provide effective support or launch successful programs if they are unaware of the impact of power, privilege, and the specific challenges associated with identity and group membership. Without this understanding, organizations are more likely to contribute to an individual's perceived invisibility, alienation, or secondary victimization. One can imagine how difficult it might be for a person of color to seek services from an office employed by an all-White staff, or how terrible it could be for an individual to be turned away from a shelter because they are gender nonconforming. Or, how ineffectively a staff member might communicate over a hotline if they assume a caller is heterosexual, or for someone's religious community to be disparaged when a therapist learns they aren't Christian. At best, staff unaware of these issues may not be able to provide the kind of assistance an individual needs. At worst, someone seeking help may feel dismissed, isolated, or further traumatized. Service providers and first responders need to understand how cultural bias may influence reporting and other institutional processes and the decisions that individuals make about how to navigate or avoid systems that might treat them unfairly. With this awareness, they can empathize more with an elderly woman who is repeatedly dismissed by her employer as senile when she reports harassment to her employer, or a Latina woman who refuses to tell police about her experience of stalking because she does not want a Latino man to be subjected to a racist criminal system. Advocates can get more creative with brainstorming how to help a man with a disability navigate being abused by his caretaker and conservator in charge of all of his medical and financial decisions. They can improve their programs to better address housing insecurity, unemployment, and citizenship status issues important for meeting an individual's basic needs after escaping a sex trafficking ring.

Widespread Individual Impact

To summarize, when an individual experiences gender violence, they may be affected in physical, emotional, and psychological ways. They negotiate the unique dynamics of their situation based on a variety of individual and contextual factors, including barriers to receiving support. Consider this in the context of our comprehensive framework: if we were able to multiply the statistical prevalence of gender violence (from chapter 3) by its direct impact on people who experience it (from this chapter), imagine what that would reveal (see figure 4.1). The estimated breadth of impact would be massive. It wouldn't even take into account the fact that many people experience multiple forms of gender violence throughout their lifetimes. And it still couldn't offer us the full picture on these issues because we don't yet have the research necessary to estimate and fully understand effects on certain groups.

This is why it is critical for crisis workers, first responders, and anyone witnessing a disclosure of gender violence to gain a better understanding of what people may go through and how to help them. What I offer in this chapter is just a starting place. If you are interested in learning more, I recommend checking out the wealth of online information offered by experts and organizations across the country who specialize in either assisting people who have experienced gender violence or advocating for members of marginalized groups. Better yet, seek in-person and educational trainings and events that such organizations offer to grow in your understanding. The more all of us know about individual impact, the more we increase our collective empathy for those directly affected by gender violence. Together, we can provide the kind of support that makes the aftermath far less daunting for people in our families, social circles, and communities.

Statistical Prevalence × Individual Impact =

MASSIVE DIRECT IMPACT ON LARGE NUMBERS OF THE POPULATION

Figure 4.1. Imagining the Widespread Individual Impact of Gender Violence
Note: Based on higher rates of statistical prevalence, the large-scale impact of gender violence is likely more severe for marginalized populations—especially Indigenous people, women of color, people living in low-income areas, LGBTIQA+ individuals, women with disabilities, and other groups that face the most barriers to receiving assistance and support after experiencing gender violence.

CHAPTER 5

Collective Impact of Gender Violence

The full effects of gender violence do not stop at its prevalence and individual impact. Gender violence causes ripples that sweep through some of the biggest systems integral to our daily lives, like our jobs, schools, and health care. Without a big-picture perspective, these waves might feel subtle, even undetectable. We might not realize how gender violence is connected to unemployment or housing instability. We wouldn't consider how much money is spent to arrest, charge, and jail individuals who commit gender violence, or the resources required for governments to sufficiently respond to these issues. We would fail to imagine the wide-ranging impact of gender violence across the globe.

In my work, I have witnessed partners and parents, family members and friends suffer the difficult and sometimes devastating aftershocks of gender violence. I have observed the stress and burnout experienced by first responders and fellow service providers. I have seen gender violence wreak havoc in communities and cause splits across social media platforms. One act of gender violence—especially when reported on by corporate news or amplified by high-profile people—can incite fear among an entire population. This is because gender violence is neither an individual problem nor an epidemic endured by just one community or region. It is a pandemic-sized catastrophe with cataclysmic consequences.

This chapter helps us visualize this wide-ranging impact. Using published research and my experience in the field, I discuss the effects of gender violence at each level of society from the people closest to the individuals who directly experience it to our global community. Together, these waves of impact—on close relationships, first responders, communities, major institutions, and state and national economies—create a deluge of collective repercussions that affect everyone across the globe (see figure 5.1).

Global

National

Statewide

Institutional

Community

Family Members

Partners

Friends

Coworkers

Individual

Witnesses

Classmates

First Responders

Crisis Service Providers

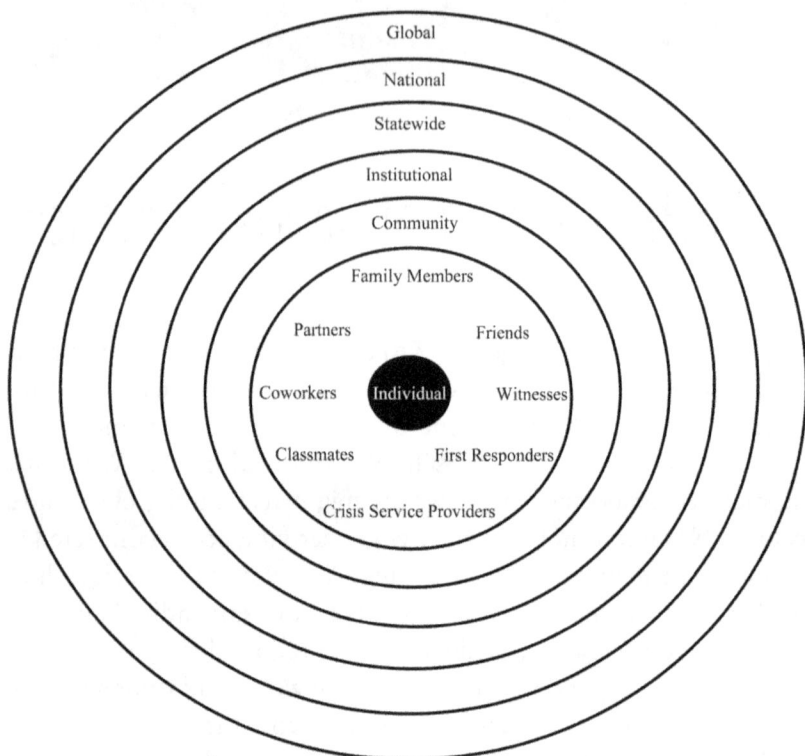

Figure 5.1. Gender Violence: Waves of Impact

Close Relationships

As firsthand witnesses to the aftermath of gender violence experienced by those close to them, family members, friends, significant others, and close acquaintances may experience a variety of responses similar to directly experiencing gender violence (what we explored in chapter 4). These can happen whether they were present at the initial event, observers of abuse over a length of time, or told about the situation years after it occurred. Perhaps they are a long-standing confidant to an individual experiencing harassment at their job, the coworker who took them to the hospital after being targeted for an acid attack, or the dating partner who learns about their history of medically unnecessary genital surgeries before they are sexually intimate for the first time.

There is no one normal way for a person to respond when they learn someone they know or love has been harmed. On a psychological level, reactions may initially include confusion, shock, anger, fear, frustration, anxiety, guilt, and denial. Immediate physical effects could include increased heart rate, nausea, inability to eat or sleep, and fatigue. Someone's unique response is influenced by when and where the violence occurred, its duration and frequency, the level of threat and personal violation involved, the perceived severity of harm, their relationship to the person who committed the violence, their relationship to the individual who experienced it, and their perception of how others responded to the situation. A relative may engage in denial when he is first told his friend has been the victim of an honor killing. Family members may simultaneously feel angry and guilty after years of witnessing a woman's abuse, then murder, by her husband. A dating partner may feel distraught after learning about her girlfriend's nonconsensual pornography victimization, even though it occurred years ago. Students in an LGBTIQA+ club on a college campus may experience fear and hypervigilance after learning that one of their current members is in a coma as a result of a homophobic hate crime.

Though relational impact is difficult to measure, a survey of victim service providers in the United States at nonprofit organizations, in justice systems, and within health-care settings offers some perspective. When they were asked which people were most impacted by a crime victim's experience, 92 percent of providers believed that children are always or often negatively affected.[1] Seventy-nine percent believed this to be true about spouses or partners, and 76 percent felt that other family members are always or often negatively affected. Thirty-eight percent perceived a victim's experiences to often negatively impact friends, 26 percent believed this about coworkers and classmates, and 19 percent believed neighbors were often negatively affected.[2]

People are likely to experience psychological and physical effects as long as the individual who experienced the gender violence exhibits signs of acute or long-term traumatic response. This can cause stress and hardship in their relationship, result in lost

---

[1] Kristina Lugo and Roger Przybylski, "Estimating the Financial Costs of Crime Victimization," National Institute of Justice, 2018, https://www.ojp.gov/pdffiles1/nij/grants/254010 .pdf, 52.

[2] Ibid.

work hours, derail educational success, contribute to health problems, and potentially affect them for the rest of their lives. Even
individuals *not* aware of the gender violence that occurred may be
impacted by shifts in someone's behavior or experience loss of their
relationship.

First Responders and Service Providers

First responders, crisis advocates, hotline workers, medical staff,
and others closely involved with regularly providing emotional support, documenting the details of what happened, collecting forensic
evidence, or assisting victims through medical or legal processes
may experience stress and traumatic effects. Sometimes referred
to as compassion fatigue, helper fatigue, or vicarious trauma, a
trauma exposure response involves a shift in attitude and behavior
after exposure to others' suffering over a significant period of time.[3]
Signs of trauma exposure response may include someone feeling
helpless or hopeless, being hypervigilant, minimizing, dissociating,
feeling like they can never do enough, being angry and cynical,
being fearful, feeling guilty, experiencing chronic exhaustion and
physical ailments, being unable to embrace complexity, losing
creativity, being unable to listen, deliberate avoidance, feeling per-
secuted, feeling numb or unable to empathize, and clinging to gran-
diosity or an inflated sense of importance related to their work.[4]

First responders and service providers may show signs of
trauma exposure response in cycles or continuously in their work.
The stressful nature of crisis-oriented situations, strict confiden-
tiality and privacy guidelines, long overnight and on-call hours,
and underpaid labor can intensify these challenges. Trauma exposure response can alter physical and psychological health, affect
relationships with others, make the job of responding to trauma
unbearable, and perhaps most importantly for people affected
by gender violence, diminish their effectiveness in helping others.
Without strong skills in *trauma stewardship*—the development and
maintenance of long-term strategies to remain helpful through the

---

[3] Laura van Dernoot Lipsky, *Trauma Stewardship* (San Francisco: Berrett-Koehler, 2009).
[4] Ibid.

Case Example

Working in the Burnout Zone

I didn't fully understand the challenges of doing crisis response work until I did it as a full-time job. The hours were long and I was often on-call overnight and on weekends, sometimes dispatched to hospitals for several hours at a time after which I'd return home at dawn. I couldn't talk details about what I did with dating partners and friends even though I was struggling to process knowing the reality of someone's experience and exactly where it had occurred in my community. I hated encountering the limits of my position and often found myself awake at night stressing over how to help a specific individual when there weren't local resources available for their situation. And then there was the pay. At one nonprofit, my yearly salary was less than $25,000 even with an advanced degree. It was no wonder that most of my coworkers were exhausted and burnt out. Though doing this work was incredibly rewarding, it was difficult to learn how undervalued it often is in US culture.

challenges of witnessing suffering[5]—the very issues that necessitate their work may make staying with it incredibly difficult. Burnout from trauma exposure response often leads to high staff and volunteer turnover rates that create even more challenges for crisis centers related to hiring, training, and providing services.

Communities

Gender violence also effects the communities to which an individual belongs. These could include social circles, schools or college campuses, places of employment, religious or spiritual groups, geographical neighborhoods, towns or cities, or other groups. A community may experience a variety of acute reactions or long-term effects depending on their relationship to the individual who experienced the gender violence as well as to who committed it, the perceived severity of the event, where it occurred, if the event

---

[5] Ibid., 6.

targeted a particular group, and the extent to which they have previous knowledge about the impact of gender violence. To put this last factor into perspective, 69 percent of victim service providers in a study believed that gender-based crimes like partner and sexual violence are particularly misunderstood by the general public compared to other crimes.[6]

In the short term, a community may experience a sense of collective confusion, fear, shock, discomfort, anger, loss, anxiety, or shame when they learn about an act of gender violence committed against one of their members. Students may be afraid to walk near an area of campus where street harassment is rampant; aces in a massively multiplayer online role-playing game may be nervous they will experience death threats like a fellow gamer who spoke out about his experiences. Employees of a company may be shocked to learn one of their most trusted supervisors enforced sexist and racist dress codes; a neighborhood may mourn the loss of an individual down the street who was killed as part of dowry abuse.

After the initial shock of the incident has passed, communities may cope with what happened in ways that may be productive or harmful for the situation and the person that directly experienced it. On the positive side, a school may institute new policies to protect students from similar events, a city may hold a meeting to discuss improving community response, a neighborhood may host a candlelight vigil to support a family after their mother goes missing. On the negative side, employers may penalize people who ask for accountability, an organization may refuse to take any public responsibility for what happened, and a university may ignore the situation altogether. Concerned about damage to their reputation, a spiritual center may deny that its leaders committed abuse for years against its members. Hoping for things to quickly return to business as usual, an employer may remove a worker for harassing others but take no further action to prevent future inappropriate behavior. Stuck in disbelief that a trusted coach could be capable of abusing their children, community members might launch a smear

---

[6] Lugo and Przybylski, "Estimating the Financial Costs."

campaign on social media to discredit the teens who made accusations of indecent exposure against him.

Even when victims of violence are supported by their communities, a group's lack of knowledge or resources may lead to an inadequate response that leaves ongoing problems and collective fears unaddressed. A community in crisis may not know where they can get help, like people in a rural area who care deeply about what happened but have no access to local LGBTIQA+ services that could help them organize or seek accountability from law enforcement. Members of low-income populations might not have the availability to volunteer their time or attend awareness-raising events like those in middle-class neighborhoods; some school districts don't have the money to bring in a trained expert to address a recent tragedy. These and other issues create many complexities in community impact after gender violence occurs.

Institutions

Many of the gender-violence-related challenges faced by communities radiate out to the larger institutions to which they are connected and the regions in which they are geographically located. Entire industries may become plagued with fear, confusion, and division. Institutions may be forced to negotiate needs for safety, demands for accountability, and concerns about image management in their responses to gender violence. Leaders may or may not know how to respond supportively, help communities deal with its aftermath, or facilitate system-wide changes that could help prevent future violence. In addition to these challenges, there is an economic impact. In the following sections, I outline research on the costs of gender violence in the areas of health-care, jobs and education, housing, and the criminal system in the United States.

Health Care

Experiencing gender violence can result in out-of-pocket costs, high insurance premiums, and expensive long-term health-care treatment for large numbers of a population. Providing physical and psychological care puts demands on staff and facilities. And because this care is often made possible through state and federally funded programs, taxpayers may also feel its effects.

Case Example

Moni's Experience of Acid Violence

Masuda Akter Moni was a young, extroverted woman in Dhaka, Bangladesh, who loved art, dance, and music. In 2012 she refused a local youth's marriage proposal, and he and three accomplices attacked her with acid. She suffered severe burns on her face, eyes, chest, back, and right hand. As she received extensive treatment and four eye surgeries at hospitals, her attacker continued to live in the same community. Some people blamed Moni for being too social and for her interest in performance arts they perceived as attracting men's attention. The Acid Survivors Foundation pushed for authorities to arrest Moni's attacker, connected her with legal support, and intervened at the community level to motivate and encourage people in Dhaka to take action. Community members put pressure on Moni's attacker and his family to the point that they eventually sold their land and left the area. In 2015, the attacker and two of his accomplices received harsh criminal sentences. Moni has yet to regain her eyesight, but the support of other women with similar experiences helped her remain determined to bring her perpetrators to justice.

[a] Acid Survivors Foundation, "Masuda Akter Moni," January 12, 2020, https://acidsurvivors.org/masuda-akter-moni/.

Many forms of gender violence result in physical injury. Acid attacks usually involve extensive medical care related to disfigurement, blindness, chronic pain, and long-term complications.[7] Many patients require a specialized burn unit and multiple complex surgeries, rehabilitation, and other costly support.[8] A UK organization estimates one acid attack costs their national health system £34,500 (close to $44,000), making the cost for all known acid attacks in

---

[7] Acid Survivors Trust International, "Worldwide Problem."
[8] Sital Kalantry and Jocelyn Getgen Kestenbaum, "Combating Acid Violence in Bangladesh, India, and Cambodia," Avon Global Center for Women and Justice and Dorothea S. Clarke Program in Feminist Jurisprudence, 2011, https://scholarship.law.cornell.edu/avon_clarke/1.

just one year over £32 million ($41.6 million).[9] More research is needed to estimate expenses in other regions, though the costs of some acid attacks may be accounted for in partner violence costs.

Researchers estimate that intimate partner violence against women results in nearly two million injuries and 1,300 deaths per year in the United States, with more than 555,000 injuries requiring medical attention and more than 145,000 injuries serious enough to need hospitalization for one or more nights; 18.5 million mental health visits by women each year are a result of partner violence.[10] Many people don't seek medical care after abuse: in one survey, more than one-third of US women who experienced sexual and physical assaults by abusive partners sustained an injury, and only one-third of that group sought medical help; one-fifth of physical assaults committed against men by abusive partners resulted in injury, and only one-fifth of injured men sought treatment.[11] Millions of patients are treated annually by the US medical system after partner violence, and because each patient often requires multiple forms of care and numerous treatments for the same victimization, the number of medical personnel treating their injuries annually is also in the millions.[12] Altogether, direct medical and mental health-care services associated with intimate partner violence against women (including sexual assault, physical assault, and stalking committed by a partner) costs close to $4.1 billion in the United States every year.[13] This number does not take men and gender nonconforming victims into account.

When it comes to sexual assault, one study reports that 31.5 percent of women and 16.1 percent of men suffered physical injury after being raped.[14] Numbers of men who seek medical attention

---

[9] Frontier Economics, "Economic Impact of Acid Attacks in the UK: Methodology and Findings," July 2018, https://www.frontier-economics.com/media/egpj2bcq/20180709_economic-impact-of-acid-attacks-in-the-uk_frontier.pdf.

[10] National Center for Injury Prevention and Control, "Costs of Intimate Partner Violence against Women in the United States," 2003, https://stacks.cdc.gov/view/cdc/6543, 19.

[11] Patricia Tjaden and Nancy Thoennes, "Extent, Nature, and Consequences of Intimate Partner Violence," National Institute of Justice, 2000, https://www.ncjrs.gov/pdffiles1/nij/181867.pdf, v.

[12] Ibid.

[13] National Center for Injury Prevention and Control, "Costs of Intimate Partner Violence," 2.

[14] Patricia Tjaden and Nancy Thoennes, "Extent, Nature, and Consequences of Rape Victimization: Findings from the National Violence against Women Survey," National Institute of Justice, 2006, https://www.ncjrs.gov/pdffiles1/nij/210346.pdf, 30.

after experiencing rape are unavailable, but one study reported that 36.2 percent of women who were injured by rape sought medical care.[15] This data likely doesn't include, however, individuals who visit a health-care provider after experiencing sexual assault but never disclose what happened. Though many states enforce laws that cover medical costs associated with sexual assault, individuals may be partially or fully responsible for expenses. Collectively, sexual assault costs over nine million dollars annually for individuals and their insurance providers in the United States—and for each individual hospital visit, even women with private insurance may pay an average of 14 percent or $948 while insurance providers pay an average of 86 percent or over $5,700.[16] Even when some costs are covered or compensated through victims' rights laws, there may be long-term economic impacts for people who become pregnant, contract sexually transmitted infections, or suffer chronic injury. We don't have data on the costs of mental health care after sexual assault, but one study reported that 33 percent of women and 24.2 percent of men received counseling from a mental health professional after experiencing rape.[17]

Genital cutting causes a variety of health complications in gynecological, obstetric, sexual, and psychological health, costing $1.4 billion across twenty-seven high-prevalence countries in 2018.[18] Child marriage and early childbearing are connected to negative health impacts and associated costs: one analysis of global data suggests that based on current trends, child marriage could cost hundreds of billions of dollars worldwide between 2018 and 2030.[19] In addition, child brides are more likely to have poorer overall health, less economic security, and a higher likelihood of

---

[15] Ashley M. Tennessee, Tamala S. Bradham, Brandi M. White, and Kit N. Simpson, "The Monetary Cost of Sexual Assault to Privately Insured US Women in 2013," *American Journal of Public Health* 107, no. 6 (2017): 983–88, doi:10.2105/AJPH.2017.303742.

[16] Ibid.

[17] Tjaden and Thoennes, "Extent, Nature, and Consequences of Rape Victimization," 31.

[18] David Tordrup, Chrissy Bishop, Nathan Green, Max Petzold, Fernando Ruiz Vallejo, Joshua P. Vogel, and Christina Pallitto, "Economic Burden of Female Genital Mutilation in 27 High-Prevalence Countries," *BMJ Global Health* 7, no. 2 (2022): 1–13, doi:10.1136/ bmjgh-2020-004512, 6.

[19] International Center for Research on Women, "The Economic Impact of Child Marriage: Key Findings," 2018, https://www.icrw.org/wp-content/uploads/2018/07/EICM-GlobalS ynthesisSummary_Report_v3_WebReady.pdf.

experiencing violence by spouses or extended family members[20]—all factors that could contribute to even higher health-care expenses.

Health costs associated with other forms of gender violence are difficult to locate. We know that online harassment and cyberhate have likely cost Australians more than $330 million in health care as of 2018,[21] and there are probably studies in the works estimating costs of other forms of gender violence. We can assume there are major expenses associated with breast ironing, forced sterilization, and obstetric violence, but again the research is lacking. We don't know the costs after stalking and discrimination, but existing research gives us a glimpse of this picture: one study estimates that 30 percent of women stalking victims and 20 percent of men stalking victims seek counseling because of their victimization.[22] In a study of Belgian girls aged ten to eighteen, slut shaming was identified as a predictor of depression and other health problems,[23] and a study in one US state found that lack of legal protections and unfavorable social climate contributes to high rates of depressive disorder among LGBT youth and adults.[24] The costs of discrimination within health-care systems are also not accounted for, like those associated with mental health conditions that worsen when transgender individuals lack access to gender-affirming care like medical supplies, hormones, and surgeries.

Jobs and Education

Research shows that gender violence has a direct impact on individual employment and educational attainment. One US study reported that among people who experienced rape, 19.4 percent of women and 9.7 percent of men lost time from work after the incident, and 7.5 percent of women and 11.3 percent of men lost time from school.[25] Researchers found that US students experiencing

[20] Ibid.
[21] Australia Institute, "Trolls and Polls—the Economic Costs of Online Harassment and Cyberhate," 2019, https://australiainstitute.org.au/wp-content/uploads/2020/12/P530 -Trolls-and-polls-surveying-economic-costs-of-cyberhate-5bWEB5d_0.pdf.
[22] Tjaden and Thoennes, "Stalking in America."
[23] Goblet and Glowacz, "Slut Shaming."
[24] Christy Mallory et al., "The Economic Impact of Stigma and Discrimination against LGBT People in Georgia," Williams Institute, 2017, https://williamsinstitute.law.ucla.edu /wp-content/uploads/Impact-LGBT-Discrimination-GA-Jan-2017.pdf.
[25] Tjaden and Thoennes, "Extent, Nature, and Consequences of Rape Victimization," 31.

both physical and sexual forms of teen dating violence were more likely than other students to report carrying a weapon at school, miss classes because they felt unsafe, be threatened or injured with a weapon on school property, and have physical fights or be bullied at school.[26]

US women who experience intimate partner violence lose nearly 5.6 million days managing their households as well as 8 million days of paid work—an equivalent of more than 32,000 full-time jobs—each year; this adds up to an estimated $0.9 billion in lost productivity.[27] A study that focused on people in the United States who experienced stalking found that 13.4 percent of victims changed their route to a job or school, 16.7 percent took time off from work or school, and 9.5 percent quit their jobs altogether.[28] One in eight stalking victims who were employed lost time from work because they feared for their safety or had to spend time dealing with tasks like testifying in court or obtaining restraining orders, and more than 50 percent of victims lost five or more days of work.[29] The cost of one acid attack in the UK is estimated at £6,500 ($8,200) when lost work productivity, crisis service costs, and physical and emotional impact are taken into account; in one year this calculates to over £6.1 million ($7.8 million) for victims across the UK.[30] A study of Australians revealed that of those who experienced online harassment or cyberhate, 28 percent reported those situations having an effect on their ability to work and earn income; a low estimate of the total lost income from online harassment or cyberhate in Australia is $267 million.[31]

In one study, women who experienced unwanted touching or multiple harassing behaviors at work reported significantly greater financial stress and failure to thrive as employees—and they often felt the only way to resolve the situation was to quit their jobs.

---

[26] Alana M. Vivolo-Kantor, Emily O'Malley Olsen, and Sarah Bacon, "Associations of Teen Dating Violence Victimization with School Violence and Bullying among US High School Students," *Journal of School Health* 86, no. 8 (2016): 620–27, doi:10.1111/JOSH.12412.

[27] National Center for Injury Prevention and Control, "Costs of Intimate Partner Violence," 19.

[28] Katrina Baum, Shannan Catalano, and Michael Rand, "Stalking Victimization in the United States," U.S. Department of Justice, 2009, https://www.google.com/books/edition/Stalking_Victimization_in_the_United_Sta/vAF14C982tcC?hl=en&gbpv=1, 6.

[29] Baum, Catalano, and Rand, "Stalking Victimization," 7.

[30] Frontier Economics, "Economic Impact of Acid Attacks."

[31] Australia Institute, "Trolls and Polls," 20.

Sexual harassment contributes to the gender wage gap and can have an impact on job references, career attainment, lifetime earning potential, and stress that affects overall career trajectories.[32] From 2018 to 2021, sexual harassment charges filed with the US Equal Employment Opportunity Commission resulted in nearly $300 million in monetary benefits recovered from employers to those who suffered sexual harassment.[33] A report on lawsuits filed against colleges and universities for mishandling sexual assault cases suggests that around 10 percent of litigations between 2011 and 2015 cost institutions an average of $350,000. Some cases cost campuses between one and two million dollars, and all litigations for the approximately one thousand cases during that five-year period cost universities a total of $21.8 million.[34]

People who are married as children are less likely to complete their education, which reduces future earnings, contributes to intergenerational cycles of poverty, and leads to less knowledge about HIV and AIDS.[35] In an analysis of fifteen countries with high rates of child marriage, the estimated total of women's earnings lost from marrying early was $26 billion in 2015.[36] Experts suggest that national governments in just eighteen countries could collectively save up to $17 billion per year by 2030 if they provided universal secondary education.[37]

Productivity losses may hit certain groups especially hard. LGBTIQA+ people of color in the United States may be more likely than those who are White to live in poverty, experience employment and credit discrimination that leads to less income, and experience a lack of family recognition that contributes to unfair taxation, denial

---

[32] Heather McLaughlin, Christopher Uggen, and Amy Blackstone, "Economic and Career Effects of Sexual Harassment on Working Women," *Gender & Society* 31, no. 3 (2017): 333–58, doi:10.1177/0891243217704631.

[33] US Equal Employment Opportunity Commission, "Sexual Harassment in Our Nation's Workplaces," 2022, https://www.eeoc.gov/sites/default/files/2022-04/Sexual%20Harassment%20Awareness%20Month%202022%20Data%20Highlight.pdf.

[34] Canopy Programs, "The High Cost of Student-Victim Sexual Assault Claims," United Educators Insurance, 2017, https://static1.squarespace.com/static/53e530a1e4b021a 99e4dc012/t/590501f74402431ac4900596/1493500411575/FN-+RE-+2017.04-+High +Cost+of+Student-Victim+SA+Claims.pdf.

[35] Girls Not Brides, "Economic Impact of Child Marriage: An Information Sheet," November 2018, https://www.girlsnotbrides.org/documents/880/Economic-Impact-of-CM-Final -LR.pdf.

[36] International Center for Research on Women, "Economic Impact of Child Marriage," 3.

[37] Ibid.

of Social Security benefits, inequitable access to retirement savings, and inability to inherit income.[38] LGBTIQA+ college students may encounter more barriers obtaining financial aid than students who are not, and combined with unsupportive campus environments, they may experience lower educational attainment and accumulate more college debt. In addition, lesbian, gay, bisexual, and transgender individuals who are African American or Asian/Pacific Islander are less likely to complete college.[39]

Racial stereotypes and biases contribute to educators setting lower academic expectations for Black girls; Latina students may experience unfair perceptions from adults as well as experience anti-immigrant sentiments.[40] Restrictive dress codes often target girls of color with unfair disciplinary consequences for violations. They are more likely to attend underresourced schools, experience harsh disciplinary policies, have their achievements undervalued, and feel less safe at school than White girls.[41] Black and Latina girls also often have more familial obligations and caretaking responsibilities that make it more difficult to pursue their academic goals than boys.[42] All of these aspects of educational discrimination toward girls of color contribute to lower graduation rates and low-wage work, unemployment, and future incarceration.[43]

There are likely additional effects of other forms of gender violence on jobs and education—especially as they intersect with discrimination based on size, disability, religion, citizenship status, and other aspects of identity. Girls might experience street harassment every day on their way to school. People seeking career opportunities and promotions may become the victims of sexual exploitation, and others may be unaware they are being paid less than coworkers due to sexist, homophobic, or transphobic discrimination. People coerced into sex trafficking may forfeit their entire wage-earning and educational potential to traffickers. All of

---

[38] Center for American Progress and Movement Advancement Project, "Paying an Unfair Price."
[39] Ibid.
[40] National Women's Law Center, "Let Her Learn: Stopping School Pushout for Girls of Color," 2017, https://nwlc.org/wp-content/uploads/2017/04/final_nwlc_Gates_Girlsof Color.pdf.
[41] Crenshaw, "Black Girls Matter."
[42] Ibid.
[43] Ibid.

these challenges exacerbate how being a woman or LGBTIQA+ can already make it harder to obtain work and have safe and equitable access to education.

Housing

The impact of gender violence on health, jobs, and education is closely connected to housing security. People may face challenges in finding safe and affordable housing when leaving abusive relationships, losing a job due to discrimination, recovering from long-term injuries after a hate crime, or escaping sex trafficking. Sixty-four percent of people surveyed about their human trafficking experiences reported that lack of affordable housing was a barrier to them being able to leave their situation.[44] Financial abuse and exploitation connected with partner violence, sexual assault, and stalking can limit people's access to safe places to live and lead to housing insecurity.[45] In just one day in the United States in 2023, there were over 44,600 adults and children staying in a partner violence emergency shelter, transitional housing, or other provided accommodations after fleeing an abusive situation; in that same day, there were over 7,300 requests for housing help that could not be met due to lack of staff, funding, or other resources.[46]

Regardless of the reason for moving, lesbian, gay, bisexual, and transgender people may experience more discrimination while seeking housing. One report estimates that housing discrimination costs just one state around $477,000 in homeless shelter expenditures every year.[47] Another study found that 22 percent of transgender individuals surveyed were mistreated when trying to buy or rent housing.[48] LGBT people of color often experience even higher levels

[44] Polaris, "On-Ramps, Intersections, and Exit Routes: A Roadmap for Systems and Industries to Prevent and Disrupt Human Trafficking," 2018, https://polarisproject.org/wp-content/uploads/2018/08/A-Roadmap-for-Systems-and-Industries-to-Prevent-and-Disrupt-Human-Trafficking-Housing-and-Homelessness-Systems.pdf, 21.

[45] Institute for Women's Policy Research, "The Economic Cost of Intimate Partner Violence, Sexual Assault, and Stalking," 2017, https://iwpr.org/wp-content/uploads/2020/10/B367_Economic-Impacts-of-IPV-08.14.17.pdf.

[46] National Network to End Domestic Violence, "18th Annual Domestic Violence Counts Report," March 2024, https://nnedv.org/content/domestic-violence-counts-18th-annual-report/.

[47] Mallory et al., "Economic Impact of Stigma and Discrimination," 4.

[48] Harvard, Robert Wood Johnson, and National Public Radio, "Discrimination in America."

of housing discrimination because of racially restrictive covenants (contract language that excludes people of color from renting or owning property), predatory real estate and lending practices, and unfair treatment that leads to limited options when seeking places to rent or buy.[49] They are also more likely to experience longer and more expensive housing searches and higher loan and insurance costs than other groups.[50] Among youth, those who are LGBTQ are more likely to be housing insecure, and the number is even higher for Black LGBTQ youth.[51]

Unfortunately, housing insecurity also increases the risk of experiencing gender violence. One review of research suggests that when they experience housing insecurity, both women and men are more likely to experience partner abuse, sexual violence, or violent victimization, and youth are more likely to enter prostitution.[52]

Criminal System

The US criminal system bears a heavy burden for gender violence response. All forms of gender violence present a challenge for balancing investigation of crimes with awareness of victim needs. Criminal processes often take months or years to complete at a financial cost to taxpayers. Even though reports of gender violence to law enforcement are generally low, costs are likely high when investigation, forensic evidence collection, prosecution, and incarceration are taken into account. The cost of testing forensic evidence collected after sexual assault is high: in the state of California where testing is mandated by state law, the estimated annual cost is between $7.5 and $10.8 million.[53] Numbers of backlogged evidence collection kits—submitted to crime laboratories across the country but untested sometimes for five years or more—are so numerous the issue has been identified as a nationwide problem. Though many states do not have systems in place for counting or

---

[49] Center for American Progress and Movement Advancement Project, "Paying an Unfair Price."

[50] Ibid.

[51] National Sexual Violence Resource Center, "Housing, Homelessness, and Sexual Violence: Annotated Bibliography," June 2020, https://www.nsvrc.org/housing-homelessness-and-sexual-violence-annotated-bibliography.

[52] Ibid.

[53] California Legislative Analyst's Office, "The 2023–24 Budget: Sexual Assault Evidence Kits Testing Mandate," February 27, 2023, https://lao.ca.gov/Publications/Report/4714.

tracking untested sexual assault forensic evidence collection kits, it is estimated that the total is at least in the hundreds of thousands.[54] We don't have specific data on other gender-violence-related costs, but we do know that in 2017, state and local governments in the United States spent over $91 billion on policing,[55] and as of 2016, it cost federal and state governments $80 billion per year to operate prisons and jails.[56]

Politics and intersecting oppressions affect how criminal court processes play out and who bears the financial burden for gender violence cases. Because unsuccessful prosecution costs taxpayers money and often hurts chances for the reelection of state's attorneys, prosecutors may refuse to take on cases that are not easily winnable—or file less severe charges than what may fit the circumstances—due to stereotypical perceptions of gender violence, racial and class dynamics, or other issues. Individuals who may not fit the image of a "perfect," "innocent," or "traditional" victim due to their identity or decisions they made before the victimization occurred may also deter prosecution. Failure to prosecute may mean less state compensation provided to victims, less support offered by communities and institutions, and more negative effects on someone's health, employment, and education after experiencing gender violence. Stereotypes and biased attitudes can lead to more successful prosecutions against people of color, those with lower socioeconomic status, immigrants, or people who identify as LGBTIQA+. People with power and privilege may be able to afford legal protections and avoid accountability easier than marginalized populations, leading to higher numbers of Black, Brown, and poor people in jails and prisons. Being incarcerated for committing gender violence also leads to higher risk of experiencing gender-based discrimination and sexual violence.

---

[54] End the Backlog, "What Is the Rape Kit Backlog?," Joyful Heart Foundation, http://www .endthebacklog.org/backlog/what-rape-kit-backlog.

[55] Bureau of Justice Statistics, "State and Local Government Expenditures on Police Protection in the U.S., 2000–2017," July 2020, https://bjs.ojp.gov/content/pub/pdf/slgeppus0017 .pdf.

[56] Bureau of Justice Statistics, "Justice Expenditures and Employment in the United States, 2017," July 2021, https://bjs.ojp.gov/sites/g/files/xyckuh236/files/media/document/jeeus17 .pdf.

Additional Information

Being incarcerated increases the risk of experiencing

- Sexual assault
- Forced sterilization
- Inadequate menstrual health management
- Lack of gender-affirming medical care
- Inadequate access to HIV-related services

In addition to these issues, people who experience gender violence may themselves be criminalized. Arrests and incarceration of adults and youth who are trafficked are common: in one survey of people who had experienced human trafficking, 62 percent had been cited, arrested, or detained by police at least once, and 54 percent of that group said their arrests were related to their exploitation by traffickers;[57] 22 percent had been in the juvenile criminal system, and 56 percent of that group said they were in the system while they were being exploited by traffickers.[58] People who are abused by their partners may also be arrested, prosecuted, and incarcerated based on actions they took to defend themselves. An unintended consequence of relying on the criminal system to address partner violence is that, at least in the United States, more women—especially Black women and rural women—are being arrested and incarcerated than ever before,[59] which also drives up taxpayer costs.

States and Countries

The constant shift in gender-violence-related laws set by state and federal governments demonstrates the practical and economic

---

[57] Polaris, "In Harm's Way: How Systems Fail Human Trafficking Survivors," January 2023, https://polarisproject.org/wp-content/uploads/2023/07/In-Harms-Way-How-Systems-Fail-Human-Trafficking-Survivors-by-Polaris-modifed-June-2023.pdf, 41.

[58] Ibid., 26.

[59] Leigh Goodmark, "Gender-Based Violence, Law Reform, and the Criminalization of Survivors of Violence," *International Journal for Crime, Justice and Social Democracy* 10, no. 4 (2021): 13–25, doi:10.5204/ijcjsd.1994.

challenges associated with keeping people safe and holding people accountable when they harm others. Some legislation defines criminal behavior and outlines penalties for breaking the law, like a state statute that defines human trafficking or an institution-specific law like Title VII of the Civil Rights Act of 1964 that makes employment discrimination illegal. Other legislation may amend how requirements are met: Marsy's Law, for example, strengthens the enforcement of crime victims' rights in states across the United States.[60] Laws may clarify things like jurisdiction, or allocate resources for enforcement, like the VAWA Reauthorization of 2022 that restores tribal authority to hold non-Native perpetrators accountable for sexual violence, sex trafficking, and stalking against Natives and reimburses tribal governments for the cost of adjudicating these cases.[61] Some laws set mandates but leave the expenses up to the organization, like the Campus SaVE Act that requires most college campuses to provide sexual violence prevention education to first-year college students.[62] Enforcement is complicated: the existence of a law doesn't necessarily mean more protection if its language isn't carefully crafted, investigators and prosecutors aren't adequately trained, or juries aren't knowledgeable about the realities of gender violence.

On state and national levels, gender violence has an economic impact. In the United States, the cost of intimate partner violence for individuals in one year alone is estimated at more than $8.3 million when medical care, mental health services, lost job productivity, and premature death are taken into account.[63] Sexual violence likely costs even more; in Michigan alone, sexual assault is estimated to cost government agencies, insurance companies, hospitals, and citizens more than $6.5 billion per year.[64] This

---

[60] Marsy's Law for All, "About Marsy's Law," 2024, https://www.marsyslaw.us/about_marsys_law.

[61] Office of Public Affairs, "Justice Department's Office on Violence against Women Publishes Regulation Governing Special Tribal Criminal Jurisdiction Reimbursement Program," U.S. Department of Justice, May 3, 2023, https://www.justice.gov/opa/pr/justice-department-s-office-violence-against-women-publishes-regulation-governing-special.

[62] CampusSaveAct.org, "Campus SaVE Act," 2024, http://campussaveact.org/.

[63] Wendy Max, Dorothy P. Rice, Eric Finkelstein, Robert A. Bardwell, and Steven Leadbetter, "The Economic Toll of Intimate Partner Violence against Women in the United States," *Violence and Victims* 19, no. 3 (2004): 259–72, doi:10.1891/vivi.19.3.259.65767.

[64] Lori A. Post, Nancy J. Mezey, Christopher Maxwell, and Wilma Novalés Wibert, "The Rape Tax: Tangible and Intangible Costs of Sexual Violence," *Journal of Interpersonal Violence* 17, no. 7 (2002): 773–82, doi:10.1177/0886260502017007005.

number includes tangible losses—the cost of medical and mental health services, insurance administration, policy and prosecutorial processes, correctional system expenses, and loss of individual job productivity—as well as intangible losses associated with victims' psychological pain and suffering.

Sex and labor trafficking are intertwined with economies. One study estimates that in 2007 the underground commercial sex economy's worth in just eight US cities was somewhere between $39.9 and $290 million.[65] Internationally, human trafficking generates over $236 billion in illegal profits every year, $173 billion of which is from forced sexual exploitation.[66] Research on the cost of hate crimes against LGBTIQA+ people in the United States is lacking, but one preliminary analysis estimated the total cost of all types of hate crimes (including those motivated by racism or other biases) in 2019 as nearly $2.4 billion and crimes against property as almost $7.7 billion.[67] US grants for victim services and justice solutions related to sexual violence, partner violence, and stalking cost the Department of Justice nearly $225 million in 2022.[68] This number doesn't account for implementation: in 2023, the US Office on Violence against Women requested a one-billion-dollar budget to manage and administer grants, research, evaluation, and victim-related programs and services in 2024.[69]

To put things in perspective beyond the United States, it is estimated that physical and sexual violence against women and their children cost Australian victims, their friends, family members, and

---

[65] Meredith Dank, P. Mitchell Downey, Cybele Kotonias, Debbie Mayer, Colleen Owens, Laura Pacifici, and Lilly Yu, "Estimating the Size and Structure of the Underground Commercial Sex Economy in Eight Major US Cities," Urban Institute, March 12, 2014, https://www.urban.org/research/publication/estimating-size-and-structure-underground -commercial-sex-economy-eight-major-us-cities.

[66] International Labour Organization, "Profits and Poverty: The Economies of Forced Labour," 2nd edition, 2024, https://www.ilo.org/publications/major-publications/profits -and-poverty-economics-forced-labour.

[67] Michael E. Martell, "Economic Costs of Hate Crimes," Bard Center for the Study of Hate, March 13, 2023, https://bcsh.bard.edu/files/2023/03/BCSH-Economic-Cost-of-Hate_3-13 -23_Online-.pdf, 12.

[68] Office of Public Affairs, "Justice Department Announces Nearly $225 Million in Grants to Support Coordinated Community Responses to Domestic and Sexual Violence on the 28th Anniversary of the Violence Against Women Act," September 13, 2022, https://www.justice.gov/opa/pr/justice-department-announces-nearly-225-million-grants -support-coordinated-community.

[69] Office on Violence against Women, "FY 2024 Congressional Justification," March 13, 2023, https://www.justice.gov/d9/2023-03/ovw_fy24_pres_bud_narrative_omb_cleared _3-13-2023.pdf.

the economy at least $12 billion over a year from 2015 to 2016. Emotional abuse and stalking cost at least an additional $10 billion.[70] In the UK, the cumulative total cost of acid attacks to victims and criminal and health systems was estimated to be at least £60 million ($76.6 million) in 2017.[71] It is not difficult to imagine, then, the economic costs of gender violence in other countries around the world—and none of these estimates includes costs related to various forms of gender-based discrimination and ideologically motivated gender violence.

Additional Information

Estimated costs of gender violence per year:

- Intimate partner violence in the United States: > $8.3 million
- Partner and sexual violence in Australia: > $22 million
- Acid attacks in the UK: > $76.6 million
- Sexual assault in Michigan: > $6.5 billion

Global Community

Billions of individuals around the world experience gender violence and its numerous physical and psychological effects. Potentially millions more encounter hardship as they witness these effects on those close to them. First responders and service providers negotiate daily trauma exposure response. Communities struggle, and individuals and institutions are affected by educational, employment, and housing challenges. Health-care and criminal systems are expensive and often contribute to further discrimination or victimization. This is the collective impact of gender violence.

The total financial cost of all gender violence across the globe is unknown, but in the European Union alone, the total cost per

---

[70] KPMG, "The Cost of Violence against Women and Their Children in Australia," May 2016, https://www.dss.gov.au/sites/default/files/documents/08_2016/the_cost_of_violence _against_women_and_their_children_in_australia_-_summary_report_may_2016.pdf.
[71] Frontier Economics, "Economic Impact of Acid Attacks."

year—including expenses related to physical and emotional impact, lost economic output, criminal and civil justice services, housing aid, and child protection—is €366 billion (nearly $465.9 billion).[72] Analysis of research by the United Nations suggests that the cost of violence against women is around 2 percent of the global domestic product, which is equivalent to $1.5 trillion, or the size of the economy of Canada.[73] As staggering as these figures are, they still don't capture the enormity of the problem. If researchers were able to estimate the total global cost of all forms of gender violence against all genders of people, the number would be astronomical. Taking this further, suppose we were able to multiply the direct impact of gender violence (its statistical prevalence and individual impact) by its collective effects (see figure 5.2). We would begin to feel the density of gender violence all around us. Our senses might become more heightened to identify the aftershocks of each singular act of gender violence. The ripples of impact that once seemed subtle might now crash all around us like overlapping waves surging into one another in a tumultuous sea of repercussions. The devastation of gender violence would be unavoidable, demanding urgent and collaborative action.

Statistical Prevalence   ×   Individual Impact   =

MASSIVE DIRECT IMPACT ON LARGE NUMBERS OF THE POPULATION

×

COLLECTIVE IMPACT

=

WORLDWIDE AFFLICTION OF PANDEMIC PROPORTIONS

Figure 5.2. Imagining the Global Impact of Gender Violence

If you are feeling overwhelmed at the size of this problem, you are not alone. Even as someone who has been involved in the movement to end gender violence for decades, I continue to be amazed

---

[72] European Institute for Gender Equality, "Gender-Based Violence Costs the EU €366 Billion a Year," *EIGE Newsroom*, July 7, 2021, https://eige.europa.eu/newsroom/news/gender-based-violence-costs-eu-eu366-billion-year?language_content_entity=en.

[73] UN Women, "The Economic Costs of Violence against Women," September 21, 2016, https://www.unwomen.org/en/news/stories/2016/9/speech-by-lakshmi-puri-on-economic-costs-of-violence-against-women.

at the sheer magnitude of this issue and how it manages to be so pervasive in so many areas of our lives. As massive as the problem is, here's what I'm encouraged by: more research is being done on gender violence every day, and more people are talking about it than ever before. I'm hopeful that one major outcome of all of this is that more people are feeling less alone as they navigate their experiences. As you continue to grow in your understanding, you too can help raise awareness about the collective impact of gender violence around the world.

CHAPTER 6

The System of Gender

When I lead trainings and teach classes about the foundations of gender violence, a lot of people ask me why this problem is still so huge. Answering this question begins with a focus on the *gender* part of gender violence. The dynamics of power and control shared by every type of gender violence are rooted in shared social expectations about what it means to be a man or woman, and these are ideas that are central to most people's lives around the globe. They influence what we wear, how we think, and how we communicate with others. This is the system of gender.

Most cultures around the world reflect a system of gender based on binary understandings of biological differences, gender roles, and the socially prescribed behavior that follows. In other words, gender is usually divided into two categories, and the category to which a person is designated in infancy often dictates how they should—according to society—express themselves throughout the rest of their lives. Consider the gender you were labeled as a baby and how that influenced what toys others bought for you, the way you were dressed, the rules you were given as a child and teenager, and the hobbies and activities you were encouraged to pursue. Now that you are older, what health or beauty products are marketed to you? What jobs or career paths are most accessible? What do others usually expect for your dating or committed relationships? It is likely that your answers reflect expectations associated with being either a woman or a man—and if they don't, it's probably because you or others have rejected these expectations.

Researchers in sociology, psychology, communication, and gender and sexuality studies have been examining gender expectations for decades. Gender differences aren't inherently a problem, but assigning value to those differences is. Remember that gender violence is disproportionately committed by individuals with more systemic power and privilege against those with less power. It is most commonly committed by men toward women, other men, and people who are transgender or gender nonconforming. This suggests a gendered power dynamic that values certain bodies and expressions of gender over others.

A system of gender is characterized by rigid gender roles and expectations that influence individual expressions of identity, interpersonal communication, group and family dynamics, institutional norms, and socialized patterns in society. When people commit gender violence, they do so as a way to *do gender*[1]—to assert, maintain, or regain power and control—in this gendered system. This means that gender violence does not happen outside of a cultural context. Instead, high rates are committed as a result of, or an expression of, a system of gender. Epidemics of gender violence are symptomatic of this system: they are indicators of a massive cultural condition plaguing entire populations of people. Because doing gender is such a seemingly normal and everyday experience, the system of gender is often not called into question as the bedrock of gender violence. A medical professional would not view an illness separate from its symptoms. If we want to analyze why gender violence occurs, we need to understand the system of gender.

In this chapter, I unpack this system: how gender is learned, how gender roles are maintained and enforced, and how this relates to why people commit gender violence against others. As you read, you might find it striking how normal the system of gender seems even though it is the foundation of such a terrible global problem. You might find yourself reflecting on ways that you learned to express gender in your life and moments when you felt limited. You might experience frustration and anger at this system. It may be helpful to keep in mind that like other systems of inequality and oppression, the system of gender is socially constructed. This means we collectively maintain this reality through communication, behavior, and institutional norms. This also means we can change it.

---

[1] Merry, *Gender Violence*, 11.

Learning Gender

Researchers use various theories to explain how gender is learned in childhood and beyond. Many biological theories suggest that gender is innate, determined by sex, and resulting differences are natural and neutral, but psychological theories argue that children learn gender from their parents and other social relationships; sociological theories assert that gender is socially constructed and that differences are never neutral but influenced by power.[2] The differences among these theories suggest the complexities in analyzing gender as well as the pervasiveness of cultural attitudes that contribute to gender being an unquestioned system within larger societal contexts. Some scholars suggest that because communication is so central to the creation, maintenance, and changes that occur in identities and relationships, gender should be viewed as a communicative process rather than an unchanging identity or attribute that simply produces certain types of communication.[3]

People learn how to do gender throughout their lives, and this process begins at or shortly before birth. Every individual is born with sexual characteristics that, depending on the cultural context, are viewed in particular ways. The term *sex*—or, more accurately, *sex designated* (or assigned) *at birth*—refers to the label given to individuals based on culturally defined and visible sex characteristics like genitals, body shape, and musculature. Cultures often use binary terms to label someone's sex, usually making those categories the only two acceptable options: this is why medical establishments and parents may be pressured to support medically unnecessary surgeries on infants. It also explains why people may be intersex and never know, or not realize it, until later on in life. In contrast to binary designations, a *continuum of sex* acknowledges the biological diversity of human bodies when it comes to chromosomes, hormonal makeup, and the size of genitals and other body parts—and promotes their acceptance as normal.

Once a label is given to an individual based on their visible sex characteristics, a societal expectation of gender often follows.

---

[2] Catherine Helen Palczewski, Victoria Pruin DeFrancisco, and Danielle Dick McGeough, *Gender in Communication: A Critical Introduction*, 3rd ed. (Thousand Oaks, CA: Sage, 2019), 51.
[3] Ibid., 53.

Gender, or *gender designated* (or assigned) *at birth*, is used to describe the expectations for behavior that result from the labeled sex at birth. Based on culturally defined expectations of masculinity and femininity, a person's designated gender suggests how they should act, communicate, and express their gendered-ness as a person. A person's *gender identity*—their internal sense of gender not visible or always known to others—may be different than the ways they outwardly express their gender or the ways their expression of gender may be facilitated by others. *Cisgender* individuals feel their designated gender at birth matches their personal gender identity; *transgender* individuals feel their designated gender does not match their gender identity (see table 6.1 for examples).

TABLE 6.1. **Applying Gender and Sexuality Terms**

These lists represent aspects of gender and sexual orientation for two hypothetical individuals. For anyone, each category may or may not be directly related to one another. A person may change how they feel internally or choose to identify, sometimes multiple times throughout their life. They may also shift how they express themselves numerous times daily based on context. It is possible for someone to feel a certain way internally but not express it externally, or never use a particular label even though they feel differently than what people assume about them. The pronouns a person uses may or may not match up with these descriptions.

Category	Jack
Sex Designated at Birth	Male
Gender Designated at Birth	Boy/Man
Gender Identity	Girl/Woman (Transgender)
Gender Expression	Nonbinary; changes daily
Sexual Orientation	Queer Allosexual
Sexual Expression	Occasional sex with casual partners who are men

Category	Jamie
Sex Designated at Birth	Female (Intersex)
Gender Designated at Birth	Girl/Woman
Gender Identity	Cisgender (Girl/Woman)
Gender Expression	Very Feminine
Sexual Orientation	Pansexual and Demiromantic
Sexual Expression	Lots of sex with one committed partner

Gender expression refers to outward displays of gender and may include personal grooming practices, clothing choices, and verbal and nonverbal communication styles; it may also refer to ways that a person responds to cultural expectations for behavior and expression of emotion. Gender expression can be masculine, feminine, androgynous, or a combination of all three. It can change daily depending on context, like being at work, school, home, or social events, or with family, friends, children, or a significant other. In many cultures, masculinity is associated with physical strength, assertiveness, stoicism, dominance, toughness, rationality, independence, boldness, sexual prowess, physical activity, and being in control; femininity is associated with submissiveness, compassion, softness, quietness, emotionality, caretaking, docility, modesty, attractiveness, obedience, dependence, and fragility. These expectations usually overlap with aspects of sexual identity and behavior through presumptions of heterosexuality. Specific gendered expectations vary somewhat based on race, class, nationality, ethnicity, religion, age, and other factors.

Individuals learn how to do gender through their social interactions with others. Expected gender expression often comes into play immediately after a child is born in the way they are presented to others in how caretakers dress and interact with them; for example, caretakers may be more physically active with boys and more nurturing with girls. Children learn from communicating with parents, family, teachers, peers, and toys they are gifted or games they are taught by others. Children learn gender through the ways it is modeled for them by the people around them, formal or informal instruction through institutionalized systems like education and religion, and messages they receive about gender through news, music, television, and film.

Once gender is learned, it may be internalized as individuals repeat gendered patterns of behavior over and over again. Sometimes referred to as "a stylized repetition of acts,"[4] doing gender may feel normal, natural, or subconscious—people often do it without thinking—unless their behaviors are called into question. In a

---

[4] Judith Butler, "Performative Acts and Gender Constitution: An Essay in Phenomenology and Feminist Theory," in *Performing Feminisms: Feminist Critical Theory and Theatre*, ed. Sue Ellen Case (Baltimore, MD: Johns Hopkins University Press, 1990), 270–82.

Case Example

The Love Monster

When I was a full-time prevention educator, I used to facilitate a coloring activity with kids in early elementary school classrooms. My goal was to help them learn how to express fear and anger in healthy ways and where to get help if they needed it. I would give them coloring sheets with an outline of a monster and invite them to think about something that makes them scared, mad, upset, or sad—then I would ask them to name their monsters, share what sound their monsters would make, and speak back to them. A girl in a kindergarten class I visited named her picture "The Love Monster." Unlike many of the other children's scary or angry monsters, hers was cute and covered with red and pink hearts. When I asked her the reason for her picture's name she explained that a boy at school was "in love" with her and would not leave her alone, even though she had told adults about what was happening. This made her super frustrated and angry, and I could understand why. At a young age, many girls are taught to tolerate repeated unwelcome touch, advances, harassment, stalking, and abuse from boys and men. Instead of framing those situations as problems, many girls are taught to be polite, smile through their anger, and minimize potential or actual violence when it happens. Meanwhile, boys' boundary-crossing and fear-inducing behavior is passed off as normal—even endearing. This six-year-old girl was learning to believe that love was supposed to feel like a boy's relentless actions that made her uncomfortable and scared. This is how the acceptance of gender violence is taught and internalized very early in our lives.

system of gender, an individual's sex, gender, gender expression, and gender identity are expected to match, and deviations may be considered transgressive, unnatural, and abhorrent. The pressure to do gender in a specific way may be reinforced through prescriptive instruction, rewarding normative behavior, or subtle microaggressions. A boy's siblings may teach him that boys don't play with dolls, a girl may be praised by parents for being "ladylike," and friends may tease a young girl for dressing androgynously and playing contact sports. Many people may also be punished for violating gender norms. This could involve shaming, name-calling, exclusion, physical violence, public or online harassment, stalking, sexual violence, acid attacks, honor killings, or murder. An aspec individual may be repetitively questioned and ridiculed for not seeking intimate relationships. A man who cries at a film may be called a bitch by his friends, a nonbinary teen may be mistreated by teachers at school, and a woman may be stalked and harassed by her attackers after defiantly reporting a sexual assault to authorities.

Gender and Inequality

Gender is often made central to how an individual is expected to behave in relationships, families, peer groups, jobs, and other areas of social life. If most individuals adhere to binary gender expectations, larger patterns of gendered division will follow. In most cultures bound by a system of gender, men and women are positioned as unequal opposites. While men are often expected to be strong, women are expected to be fragile. Masculinity implies dominance and being in control, femininity suggests submissiveness and obedience. Men are rational, women are irrational; men are stoic and women are overemotional. Men are often encouraged to demonstrate sexual prowess (have lots of partners), but women are expected to be modest (one or very few sexual partners). In Western cultures, because men are assumed to be rugged and tough, there is an expectation for men to like and play sports, have a job outside the home, refrain from showing emotions considered feminine, and engage in physical fighting behavior when threatened. Women are expected to value their appearance, prioritize having husbands and children over careers, do the majority of housework and childcare, cry frequently, cause dramatic interactions with others, and need or seek protection from men.

Because of this binary system, men and women are assumed to be incredibly different from one another even though research suggests they are psychologically alike in most ways and that differences are vastly overinflated.[5] They are assumed to have difficulty communicating with one another based on differences in

---

[5] Janet Shibley Hyde, "The Gender Similarities Hypothesis," *American Psychologist* 60, no. 5 (2005): 581–92, doi:10.1037/0003-066X.60.6.581.

conversational style, conflict management, and leadership techniques—with the challenges so great that men and women are often thought of as two completely different cultural groups whose members are born on different planets,[6] have little in common with one another, and are involved in a constant "battle of the sexes." Media and popular culture perpetuate this stereotype. Men and women actually have many similarities in their communication styles, but the *assumption* that they are so different often overshadows the influence of social context and other aspects of culture on decision-making.[7] Put another way: race, class, age, geographical location, social environment, and other factors have such a great influence on how people communicate that it is impossible to single out gender. As a result, people often communicate with one another based on *perceptions* of gender differences when, in reality, communication might not be all that different when considering gender alone.

Rigid gender roles and expectations are indicative of *sexism*, a system of oppression based on gender. In this system, masculine gender roles are typically considered more positive, powerful, and autonomous, while feminine gender roles are associated with negativity, weakness, and dependence on others—especially men. Bodies, behavior, and communication associated with femininity or feminine stereotypes are devalued while masculine expressions are viewed as superior. *Heterosexism* (a system of oppression based on sexual orientation), *cissexism/cisgenderism* (a system of oppression based on gender identity and expression), and *allosexism* (a system of oppression based on sexual and romantic attraction) are closely intertwined with sexism because they are also based on gendered norms. People who cannot successfully perform masculinity, heterosexuality, cisgender, or allosexual identity are more likely to experience *gender-based prejudice*—preconceived opinions or judgments about gender—that leads to material differences in how they are treated by others in almost every aspect of their lives. Men who express their gender in stereotypically masculine ways are usually awarded more benefits and power than those who do not, or cannot, successfully perform the socially constructed

---

[6] John Gray, *Men Are from Mars, Women Are from Venus* (New York: HarperCollins, 1992).
[7] Palczewski, DeFrancisco, and McGeough, *Gender in Communication.*

masculine standard. *Gender privilege* is a recognition of the benefits an individual experiences because of their perceived gender, which includes aspects of their designated gender at birth, gender expression, sexual orientation, and sexual behavior. It is common for people with gender privilege to have better careers and salaries, more recognition and acknowledgment of contributions and perspectives, increased personal credibility, more personal safety, and a greater chance for upward social mobility than people without it. The same may be true for people with heterosexual, cisgender, or allosexual privilege.

Gender privilege on a societal level creates the conditions for a *patriarchy*—a cultural context in which men or those who most closely embody the traditional masculine norm have the most power. The men who benefit most from gender privilege and occupy the highest positions of power and influence in the United States and Western cultures are usually White, cisheterosexual (or perceived that way), and upper class. They hold the majority of government and elected offices. They are likely to be the CEOs of the most successful corporations, make the most money, have the most purchasing power, and be the most valued when it comes to public opinion. Their bodies, perspectives, and needs are prioritized most in biological research and health care. Their interests are reflected most in major news media and their bodies most visible as anchors and writers. They are the most likely to be the producers, directors, and actors in the film industry, which usually features stories and content representative of their experiences. In a patriarchy, cisheterosexual upper-class White men are the most successful, most powerful, most valued, and most visible.

Individual Choice in a Gendered System

Because sexism—and the prejudice, gender privilege, and patriarchal conditions that follow—operates on a systemic level, individual behavior is often influenced by historical and social context. Combined with capitalism, transnational economic inequalities, and other systems of oppression, patriarchy and sexism have become intertwined in the social fabric of most cultures around the world. Patriarchal societies were not always the norm; many anthropologists believe that some men-dominated cultures emerged eight to ten thousand years ago as humans were learning to master some aspects of nature and, by extension, women's fertility; this resulted in defining masculinity as exercising power over women, nature, and other men.[8] It is also possible women *chose* to engage in valued labor at home that involved less risk, heightened the chances of their offspring's survival, and resulted in men becoming the predominant hunters outside the home—and that it wasn't until centuries of social, ecological, climactic, and demographic changes that patriarchy evolved into what it is now.[9] In some precolonial societies multiple genders and same-gender sexual activity and marriage were common before war and colonialism driven by men in quests for power and control over land and groups perpetuated oppression and gender inequality.[10] Even cultural groups with long histories of women-centered or gender-equitable social structures (like some Indigenous groups in the northern hemisphere) shifted into patriarchal ones as a result of generations of colonization and racist oppression by others.[11]

For patriarchal and sexist social structures to stay intact, individuals are often overtly or subconsciously pressured to conform. For example, a statement that "women belong in the kitchen" reflects historical attitudes about the role of middle- to upper-class (and often White) women as primary caregivers of children and keepers of home spaces. Even when spoken without much thought, this sentiment contributes to rigid gender expectations that may limit women's confidence in pursuing demanding careers or dissuade men from becoming stay-at-home dads. Another example is cultural practices common in patrilineal societies that prioritize men's lineage and require social exchange upon marriage. Though

[8] Michael Kaufman, *The Time Has Come: Why Men Must Join the Gender Equality Revolution* (Berkeley, CA: Counterpoint, 2019), 53.

[9] Gerda Lerner, *The Creation of Patriarchy* (New York: Oxford, 1986).

[10] Rebecca L. Stotzer, "Family Cohesion among Hawai'i's Māhūwahine," *Journal of GLBT Family Studies* 7, no. 5 (2011): 424–35, doi:10.1080/1550428X.2011.623935; Angela Wei, Yang Bo Zhang, Emma Robertson, Jeremy Steen, Christopher Mushquash, and Christine Wekerle, "Global Indigenous Gender Concepts, Gender-Based Violence and Resilience: A Scoping Review," *Child Abuse & Neglect* 148 (2024): 1–14, doi:10.1016/j.chiabu.2023.106185; Mohammed Elnaiem, "The 'Deviant' African Genders That Colonialism Condemned," *JSTOR Daily*, April 29, 2021, https://daily.jstor.org/the-deviant-african-genders-that-colonialism-condemned/; O'Toole, Schiffman, & Kiter Edwards, preface to *Gender Violence*.

[11] Deer, *Beginning and End of Rape*, xiv; Wei, Zhang, Robertson, Steen, Mushquash, and Wekerle, "Indigenous Gender Concepts."

dowries are illegal in many parts of the world, they still remain common in some regions. In Western societies, it is often expected for women to take husbands' last names or be "given away" (a ritual that began as a transfer of women as property) by their fathers at weddings. These practices also contribute to perceptions of same-gender weddings as deviations from the norm.

All genders of people can participate in behaviors that encourage conformity within a system in gender. Depending on the specific context, people may not feel they have a choice to opt out of gendered expectations and often learn there are benefits to adhering to them. Culture-influencing structures and institutions like capitalism, media, education, law, government, religion, employment, the fashion industry, and others suggest or reinforce attitudes and values that contribute to gender-based oppression and patriarchy. Individuals may struggle to negotiate power, success, and survival if their behaviors are perceived as resistant to these systems. Many individuals without gender (or related) privilege may experience *internalized sexism* (or heterosexism, cis-sexism, or allosexism), in which they accept and act on negative stereotypes of themselves.

In a system of gender, pushback or punishment for violations of expected gender expression is so common it is not often questioned. Violence may even be expected by people aware they are transgressing the norm. Some laws and policies allow or encourage discrimination based on gendered expectations, especially for LGBTIQA+ individuals. The level of constraints placed on an individual in a cultural context—and how much *agency*, or decision-making ability, they have or perceive they have in how they do their gender—may vary based on numerous intersecting factors like race, class, ethnicity, age, ability, size, appearance, citizenship, and religion.

For these reasons, individuals are not solely responsible for causing or supporting systems that privilege themselves or others. The negotiation of gender and sexual expression is complicated, and a person's perception of agency in any given situation may vary. Subversion and deviance in response to these oppressive systems may involve relational, social, economic, or legal consequences, any of which may limit current and future agency. People under the age of eighteen, for example, may be subject to the decision-making of their parents and guardians. People who break the law—even if the law is unjust or perpetuates inequality—may be punished through incarceration or other legal penalties. People at the intersections of multiple systems of oppression may have less agency; people with racial and class privilege may feel freer to express themselves with less risk in a gendered system. Family units, social groups, and organizations may create conditions for more personal agency, and some individuals may create or participate in subcultures that resist status quo expectations. The responsibility for systemic change, however, is carried most by institutions that have the power to influence cultural norms and values. Without broad change, the social reality of gendered inequality, sexism, and patriarchy remains.

Case Example

Malala Yousafzai's Fight for Girls' Education

In 2008, the Taliban forbade girls from attending school in Pakistan. Malala Yousafzai was fifteen years old when she spoke out publicly in defiance of the ban in 2012. Soon after, a masked gunman shot her on the left side of her head while she was on her way home from school.[a]

Malala's story is a stark example of a group's violent enforcement of strict gender roles. When Malala refused to submit to the Taliban's ideologically motivated gender discrimination, the group used physical violence in an attempt to silence her and send a message to others girls about the consequences of disobedience.

This didn't stop Malala. After relocating to England and recovering from her injuries, she established a charity dedicated to supporting education for girls around the world and wrote a book about her experience. In 2014, she became the youngest recipient ever to be awarded the Nobel Peace Prize.[b] Over a decade later, she remains dedicated to changing beliefs, behaviors, and legislation that prevent girls from accessing educational opportunities.[c]

---

[a] Malala Fund, "Malala's Story," 2024, https://malala.org/malalas-story.
[b] Ibid.
[c] Malala Fund, "Our Work," 2024, https://malala.org/our-work.

Making Sense of the System of Gender

As individuals, we are born into ongoing cultural and social norms that we did not create. Depending on your *positionality*—all the ways you identify yourself and the groups to which you belong, or are perceived to belong to—you may feel more or less freedom in this system. When I discuss gendered expectations with students in my classes, we often marvel at how these dynamics have affected big things in our lives, like our educational experiences or relationships with our parents, and small, everyday things, like how we sit in our chairs or get ready for work or school. For some of you, it might be empowering to discover language that describes your gendered experiences moving through the world. For others, it can feel heavy to put together why you may have been treated so harshly by people around you. It can also be tough to grapple with realizing, perhaps for the first time, your privilege in a gendered system and how you can use it to help others. However you relate to the system of gender, self-reflection on how you behave and communicate is key. Keep in mind this system wasn't created overnight, and changing it will take time. We all carry some responsibility in shifting gender from something that gets policed to something that can be celebrated in its diverse forms. Depending on our positionality and the levels of privilege and influence we have in our jobs, schools, and communities, we might at some point even be able to take on a big role in making a difference.

The problem with a gendered system is not that differences exist but that they are used to limit, exclude, and harm others. Gender itself isn't a bad thing. Doing gender can be fun, creative, and freeing. It can be motivating, informed by positive values, and meaningful to our relationships and the various roles we take on in our lives. It can change based on the situation or stage of someone's life. Doing gender can be contradictory and complicated. Doing gender can be beautiful. I try to reflect on this when the system of gender gets me down, and I hope it helps you too. Perhaps it might even inspire you to wear that skirt, lift those weights, sing that falsetto, or enjoy that meal with more self-acceptance than ever before, whatever your gender identity. Finding joy in doing gender can be especially helpful as we continue to explore how other cultural attitudes and contributing factors—built on a foundation of a rigid system of gender—lead to epidemics of gender violence.

CHAPTER 7

Culture of Gender Violence

The system of gender is the underlying root of gender violence, but it doesn't give us the full picture for why gender violence happens so frequently. After all, gender itself doesn't necessarily lead to violence. It is more likely to occur, however, when the acceptance of gender violence is all around us. Unfortunately, it thrives in cultural conditions that promote it in everyday life. Attitudes and values related to the acceptance of gender violence are constantly communicated by media, various other institutions, and people around us. They exist in so many of the places we spend our time that they may feel acceptable until we stop to consider their profound harm.

Think of it like this: the system of gender is the bedrock for a *culture of gender violence*—an environment in which gender violence is minimized, normalized, and often encouraged. Closely related to the term *rape culture*, a culture of gender violence inclusively refers to all types of gender violence that flourish in a sexist and patriarchal culture. Consider planting a seed for a noxious weed (a plant that is harmful to habitats and ecosystems) in dirt (see figure 7.1). First it needs a place to grow, and the system of gender violence serves as this container. Next, it needs nutrient-rich soil: a culture of gender violence provides ideal conditions for making acts of gender violence acceptable. Other materials like sunshine and rain help it along. These are additional contributors to gender violence we will explore in chapter 8.

Why is there a huge lack of accountability when people commit gender violence? Why is there widespread blame toward people who are victimized? It is because in a culture of gender violence, people become desensitized to the harm, severity, and urgency of the problem. Speaking from experience, I can attest that it may be

GROWING A CULTURE OF GENDER VIOLENCE

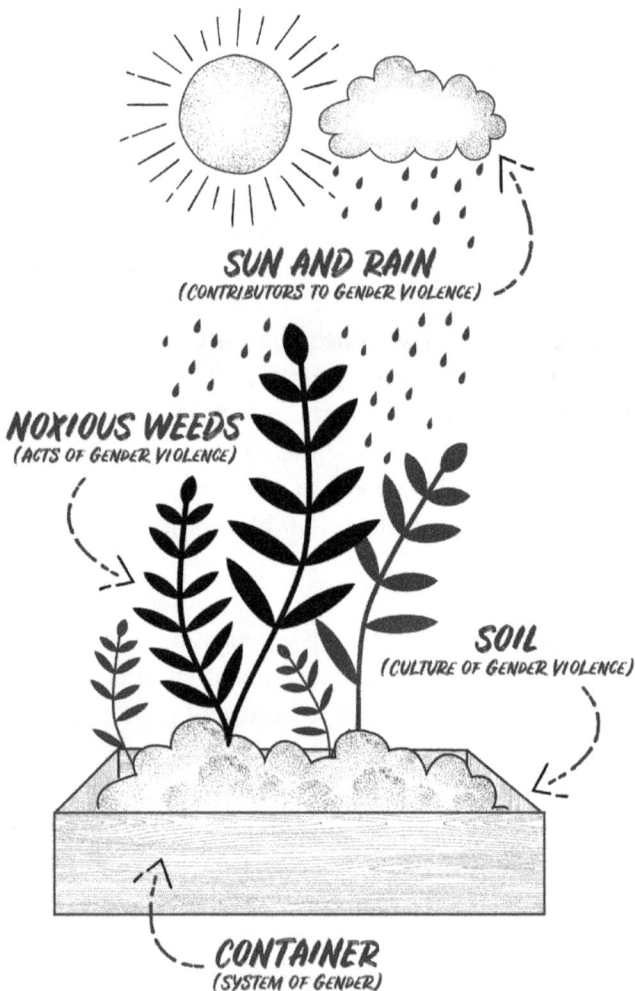

SUN AND RAIN
(CONTRIBUTORS TO GENDER VIOLENCE)

NOXIOUS WEEDS
(ACTS OF GENDER VIOLENCE)

SOIL
(CULTURE OF GENDER VIOLENCE)

CONTAINER
(SYSTEM OF GENDER)

Figure 7.1. Growing a Culture of Gender Violence

overwhelming to take on all that this means. It can feel bewildering, disappointing, and maddening. Strangely, it can also put things into perspective. The bigger picture of gender violence makes so much more sense when we understand how its acceptance is virtually everywhere. People who have experienced gender violence may even feel validated in learning that disbelief, blame, and poor treatment by others is a symptom of this cultural reality rather than a fault of their own.

In this chapter, I overview the history, characteristics, and impact of a culture of gender violence. I focus particular attention on the role institutions play in this reality and how ongoing normalization, minimization, and victim-blame contribute to cycles of gender violence. This phenomenon explains why rates of gender violence are astoundingly high and its effects so devastating, yet it is still a drastically underacknowledged problem.

A Gender-Violent History

A culture of gender violence is based in historical foundations of patriarchy, sexism, cisheterosexual prejudice, and oppressive violence. Sexual violence against women by men was—and in some places remains—common in the midst of war, colonization, global trade, and genocide. In the United States, colonization and slavery created and normalized racism and a culture of gender violence in the distant and recent past. Rape was used as a form of conquest that accompanied genocidal massacre and forced removal of Indigenous populations from their native lands. Today, members of Indigenous communities are among the most vulnerable to sexual assault and partner violence because they have often lacked clear or effective legal pathways to hold US citizens accountable for crimes against them.[1] During slavery, Black women were routinely raped by their White masters. Today, Black women who experience sexual violence still struggle to be valued and legitimized as much as White women. Black girls—especially between the ages of five and fourteen years old—often struggle against harmful perceptions that they are more adultlike and less innocent than White girls of the same age, and this has profound effects on their education and treatment by the criminal system.[2] White men's lynching of Black men during slavery and Jim Crow was often justified as

---

[1] Deer, *Beginning and End of Rape.*
[2] Rebecca Epstein, Jamilia J. Black, and Thalia González, "Girlhood Interrupted: The Erasure of Black Girls' Childhood," Georgetown Law Center on Poverty and Inequality, 2017, https://www.law.georgetown.edu/poverty-inequality-center/wp-content/uploads/sites/14/2017/08/girlhood-interrupted.pdf.

protection of White women and response to Black men's rape of (or sexual attraction to) White women—whether or not that was actually the case.[3] Today, Black men are still stereotyped in similar ways and much more likely than White men to be incarcerated for gender-violent crimes. Additionally, Black boys are more likely to be misperceived as older than they are, dehumanized, considered guilty of crimes, and subjected to violence by police.[4]

Class and property ownership issues established a legal precedent for the commonality of partner violence in the United States. Prior to White women's suffrage, women were considered men's property without rights to change the cultural conditions that allowed abuses against them. Despite them gaining the vote in 1920, Native Americans and many women of color were not able to exercise that right until the 1960s. Women's lack of financial independence made leaving violent relationships difficult, and class prejudice led to victims' accounts of abuse being perceived as less credible in a court of law. Marital rape was not outlawed in the United States until the 1990s. Since then, women have continued to struggle for the same economic opportunities as men, often earning lower wages and experiencing higher rates of discrimination. These widespread historical struggles have often been worse for people of color, LGBTIQA+ individuals, displaced populations, people without citizenship, and those with disabilities.

Current forms of ideologically motivated gender violence are often rooted in community and institutional practices with long cultural histories of gender-based inequality and oppression. People have committed acid attacks, honor killings, and partner violence in response to rigid religious and cultural attitudes about the social and sexual value of women. Economic inequality has contributed to sex trafficking, forced marriage, and dowry-related abuse. Power and control over gender expression, sexual behavior, fertility, and

---

[3] Ida B. Wells-Barnett, *The Red Record: Tabulated Statistics and Alleged Causes of Lynching in the United States* (1895; repr., Project Gutenberg, 2005), chap. 6, https://www.gutenberg.org/files/14977/14977-h/14977-h.htm.

[4] Phillip Atiba Goff, Matthew Christian Jackson, Brooke Allison Lewis Di Leone, Carmen Marie Culotta, and Natalie Ann DiTomasso, "The Essence of Innocence: Consequences of Dehumanizing Black Children" *Journal of Personality and Social Psychology* 106, no. 4 (2014): 526–45, doi:10.1037/a0035663.

childbearing have been enacted through genital cutting, forced sterilization, and state-limited access to reproductive rights.

Struggles faced by LGBTIQA+ individuals in the United States during the 1960s—like employment and housing discrimination and unfair treatment by law enforcement—are still issues today. In fact, many forms of harassment, gender-based discrimination, and gender-based hate crime stem from prejudicial beliefs about who has been and who is now allowed to be visible or welcome in certain spaces of public and private life. Together, a history of colonization, conquest, slavery, property ownership, institutional practices, and LGBTIQA+ discrimination plays a role in current cultural contexts that accept and normalize gender violence.

Characteristics of a Culture of Gender Violence

A culture of gender violence enforces cisheterosexist and patriarchal power dynamics through rigid gender roles, limits sexuality and sexual behavior in cisheterosexist ways, creates toxic social scripts for sexual and romantic behavior, and capitalizes on and reinforces gendered inequalities and intersecting oppressions. These four characteristics help us consider how a culture of gender violence grows from a system of gender.

Acceptance of gender violence is symptomatic of cisheterosexist and patriarchal power dynamics. Rigidly defined gender roles can teach and justify behaviors that perpetuate gendered inequality and violence against those without gender privilege. For example, boys may feel pressured to prove their masculinity through physical

Additional Information

Characteristics of a culture of gender violence:

- Enforces cisheterosexist and patriarchal power dynamics
- Limits sexuality and sexual behavior
- Creates toxic social scripts for sexual and romantic behavior
- Builds on and reinforces gendered inequalities and intersecting oppressions

altercations or bullying behavior, especially of boys deemed less masculine; the popular adage that "boys will be boys" is often used to minimize situations in which boys behave in ways that harm people of all genders. Individuals seeking to prove or maintain their gender privilege may feel they need to do gender in certain ways continuously, especially when they perceive their power is threatened. This means rejecting activities perceived as feminine or countering with physical violence in response to being name-called a "sissy" (or other language synonymous with "woman" and "girl," including homophobic slurs) by peers. Individuals who internalize rigid gender roles in the most extreme ways may use intimidation, manipulation, harassment, physical force, or sexual violence to assert or maintain their power.

A culture of gender violence is a direct result of the ways a gendered system defines and limits norms of sexuality and sexual behavior. When the prescribed norms are cisheterosexuality and allosexuality, individuals may commit gender violence as an attempt to demonstrate their rejection of LGBTIQA+ identities or the possibility they may be perceived as LGBTIQA+. Someone might, for example, participate in a group rape to prove their heterosexuality to others. Toxic social scripts for sexual and romantic behavior, especially between heterosexual individuals, are produced by a culture of gender violence. When men are expected to be dominant and assertive sexual initiators and women are expected to be submissive, obedient, quiet, and polite, this creates a dangerous power dynamic that enables system-supported sexual violence. Men may feel more entitled to coerce women into sex, women may be socialized to expect that their boundaries will be violated, and asexual individuals of any gender may feel pressured to participate in sexual activity. When gender roles in heterosexual dating and long-term relationships are interpreted and internalized in extreme ways, they can be used to justify abuse: a man may use verbal or physical violence to assert his dominance and keep "his woman" in line, or not allow his partner any access to their finances as a way to assert power and control. Sex itself is even conflated with violence: verbal and physical aggression may be expected as natural by-products of love and passion.

Case Example

Lock Up That Onesie

Several years ago I was in a Walgreens store when I discovered a display of infant onesies clad with handcuffs and a warning: "Lock Up Your Daughters." Though these little rompers were marketed as adorable and playful, I was struck at the multiple messages they communicated about gender and sexuality. First, they assumed that men and boys are sexually aggressive and that women and girls will need protection from them. Second, they normalized sexual aggression as long as (unwelcome) advances come from cute, innocent-looking packages (like babies or attractive grown-ups). Third, they sexualized infants before they are able to do much more than eat, cry, and poop—and if that wasn't disturbing enough, they emphasized that the solution to the wearer's inescapable sexual prowess is to physically restrain girls and women (consider the unsettling image of women and girls in handcuffs or locked in houses). Fourth, they literally put an expectation of heterosexuality on the body of a baby. Sadly, you can still find these onesies for sale across the internet alongside others that communicate sexist attitudes and objectify women's bodies: "That's What She Said." "My Daddy Is Jealous . . . I Had BOOBies for Breakfast and He Didn't." "I'm with the MILF."

Because masculine exertions of power are rewarded in a gendered system, even relationships or interactions with same-gender or gender nonconforming partners may involve gender violence that is culturally accepted. In these situations, behaviors might be motivated by or result in gendered norms, cisheterosexism, or internalized oppression, like an individual who exploits and targets aspects of their partner's intersex identity as part of abuse rooted in fears, insecurities, and desire to exercise control in their own life. Adults' abuse of children (often influenced by *adultism*, the systemic oppression of children and young people) may also involve gendered dynamics that either contribute to reasons for committing the abuse or promote the acceptance of the abuse in a gendered system. For example, a woman who sexually abuses boys may do so, in part, as an attempt to gain power and control not easily available to her in a patriarchal system of gender.

A culture of gender violence builds on and reinforces gendered and other inequalities. The extent to which gender violence is accepted in a specific cultural context is related to larger, macro-level dynamics that affect the distribution of wealth, power, opportunity, health care, and political participation. Unfair distribution of benefits and responsibilities based on gender and sexuality, unequal treatment in laws and policies, and lack of access to resources can increase the likelihood and acceptance of gender violence.[5] More constraints on sexual expression and behavior mean more social and legal punishment for deviation. When a government does not criminalize same-gender sexual activity, people are freer to engage in same-gender romantic and sexual relationships with less fear of arrest or explicit discrimination from others. Race, class, age, religion, size, citizenship, and other factors also influence negotiations of masculinity and femininity that make gender violence more or less acceptable in a specific environment. Overlap with other systems of oppression makes dominant cultural groups more likely to use gender violence to assert power. A culture of gender violence capitalizes on these power dynamics to remain in place.

Impact of a Culture of Gender Violence

Acceptance of gender violence on a cultural level plays out in four main ways: its effects are downplayed in popular culture, it is normalized in everyday communication, people who experience it are blamed or not believed, and acts of gender violence are often allowed or encouraged by individuals, groups, and institutions. In a culture of gender violence, these things occur simultaneously and continuously to influence mainstream attitudes about gender violence as a whole, perceptions about specific acts that have occurred, and ideas about what should be done to prevent future violence from happening.

---

[5] World Health Organization, "Promoting Gender Equality to Prevent Violence against Women," 2009, https://iris.who.int/bitstream/handle/10665/44098/9789241597883_eng .pdf.

Additional Information

Impact of a culture of gender violence:

- Gender violence is downplayed in popular culture
- Gender violence is normalized in everyday communication
- Victims are blamed for what happened to them
- Gender violence is allowed or encouraged to occur

First, the severity of gender violence is downplayed in popular culture. Many films, songs, television shows, music videos, books, and memes involve depictions of gender violence that are never explicitly discussed or addressed. Violent scenes or references may be included as entertainment and never commented on by characters, actors, or directors. Homophobic, transphobic, and aphobic language and behavior is often supported and used as a comedic device. Prison rape jokes ("Don't drop the soap in the shower!") are rampant. Pornographic videos often involve aggressive, degrading, and violent sex. Films and shows may use gender violence as a plot device without any discussion of its effects on the characters who experience it or accountability for those who commit it. Little consideration and empathy may be invited on behalf of the people who experience gender violence, and protagonists may be celebrated for abusing others. Acts of gender violence may be gratuitous and occur without substantive reason, or they may be depicted as inevitable or sexy. Sometimes references to gender violence are so commonplace that viewers might not realize they are watching a scene or listening to a song that is violent. And because audiences encounter normalizations of gender violence over and over, they may not consciously process the effects of what they are taking in on a regular basis.

Acceptance of gender violence in pop culture can take more subtle forms that influence attitudes about gender and gender violence. Characters may be created to reinforce rigid gender norms, commercials may threaten social punishment for behavior outside of cisheterosexuality, and song lyrics may objectify and hypersexualize certain groups of people. When an alcohol advertisement

Case Example

Gender Violence through the Lens of Entertainment Media

In the United States, most people's knowledge about gender violence is heavily influenced by entertainment media. Television crime dramas sensationalize femicide and hate crimes, and characters joke about prison rape. The *Taken* film trilogy contributes to fears of abduction when traveling abroad even though sex trafficking is an everyday occurrence in communities across the United States and most victims are recruited through people they know. Stalking is sexy if Adam Levine is doing it in a music video. Forced sterilizations are rarely mentioned in films and shows about incarcerated women. The real history of the Native Powhatan woman Pocahontas—especially how colonists kidnapped her, murdered her husband, made her give up her child, sexually assaulted her, and forced her to marry John Rolfe—is erased in the popular children's movie.[a] No wonder perceptions about gender violence are skewed.

[a] Vincent Schilling, "The True Story of Pocahontas: Historical Myths versus Sad Reality," *Indian Country Today*, February 16, 2023, https://indiancountrytoday.com/archive/true -story-pocahontas-historical-myths-versus-sad-reality.

depicts a man who asks for a "girly" drink at a barbeque being promptly pounded into the ground by a massive beer can from the sky, this communicates a message about the need to do masculinity correctly or risk the consequences. When women are constantly labeled bitches and hoes on the radio, this can have an effect on how people view women. The lack of gender and sexual diversity in mainstream film, music, and television can influence public opinion. When gay and bisexual characters are underdeveloped in scripts, included only as tokens, and portrayed without depth, viewers may be more likely to engage in stereotypical thinking about all gay and bisexual people. When transgender people of color are always the targets of attacks in the popular imagination, it can be difficult for the public to think of them otherwise. When positive depictions of people who are transgender, gender nonconforming, intersex, or aspec are missing, the general public may be less likely to regard them positively in their daily lives—if they think about them at all.

Unfortunately, even when tactful and empathetic stories of gender violence *are* told in music, film, and television, they tend to reinforce existing stereotypes. Victims are often heterosexual, cisgender, White, middle- to upper-class, able-bodied and conventionally attractive young women and girls. Without other depictions, it can be difficult for people to recognize that gender violence can happen to anyone, let alone certain populations at higher rates. In addition, acts of gender violence committed against these characters are often the primary focus of their identities, making "victim" or "survivor" a character trait rather than part of a larger and more complex reality of who they are. If these characters get any justice after what happened, it is often because the criminal system either worked in their favor or they undertook extreme measures to exact violent revenge. In real life many people neither possess the resources nor the immorality required for success down either of these paths—especially if the physical or psychological effects of the gender violence are severe or they lack the wealth, privilege, or influence to attain justice, even outside of the criminal system.

Second, gender violence is normalized and its effects minimized through everyday communication among partners, families, friends, and social groups. Men may boast of real or fictional sexual conquests of women in single-gender spaces like gym locker rooms and college fraternities. Classmates and coworkers may use homophobic slurs or tell others not to "act gay." Women and teenage girls may experience casual slut shaming or policing behaviors by friends. Families may use dehumanizing language to mock gender and sexual nonconformity at the dinner table. People may claim that rates of gender violence are exaggerated, that women should just protect themselves more, and that "boys will be boys." Sexually aggressive behavior may be deemed normal ("men just cannot control themselves when they get aroused"), and abusive behavior may be deemed a private matter ("what happens between spouses in their own home is none of our business"). When genital cutting, forced marriage, and honor killings come up in conversations, people may justify them through calls to tradition ("this is how it's always been done") and dignity ("people need to know they will bring shame upon others if they act in certain ways"). Gender violence as a whole may be dismissed as something that happens "over there" (in other parts of the world), making it seem irrelevant despite its huge impact everywhere.

Jokes about gender violence—such as a group of employees telling their coworker, "Wow, buddy, it looks like your wife beat you up," after he experiences a car accident—can make it seem like these issues are not something to be taken seriously. People may use comedy to justify comments that perpetuate acceptance of gender violence (as in someone claiming, "It was just a joke," after being called out for an inappropriate story that minimizes sex trafficking and blames a victim). Everyday language can minimize the significance of gender violence; when people use the word "wifebeater" to refer to sleeveless undershirts, describe an apartment as being "pimped" out, or tell their friends they felt "raped" by an exam, the severity of partner violence, sex trafficking, and sexual assault is minimized. Common idioms like "bend over and take it" and "git 'r done" also have gender-violent associations.

The normalization and minimization of gender violence in popular culture and everyday communication contribute to a third area of impact: the blaming of and disbelief of people who have experienced it. When gender violence is thought of as a regular, no-big-deal kind of occurrence, actual situations involving violence are more easily dismissed by those who witness them, receive disclosures, or experience them themselves. Consider a man who was sexually assaulted by an ex-girlfriend. He might not recognize what happened as a serious situation because his friends tell him "guys can't be raped" and "there is no way a dude would ever turn down sex." Perhaps he has never heard about men who have experienced something like he did, or he blames himself for not being "man enough" to deal with the situation in a different way. Or it is possible he feels distressed or threatened, but because his friends laughed when he explained the situation, he experiences more isolation and is hesitant to reach out for assistance for fear he will experience further shame or disbelief.

Minimization of gender violence leads to dismissal of people who have experienced gender violence through suggestions that victims not "make a big deal about it"—or worse, that what happened to them was their own fault. Consider someone telling a friend that they experienced homophobic street harassment on their way to school only for the friend to tell them they are overreacting, or a supervisor refusing to believe their employee's reports of harassment and doing nothing to respond. In a culture of gender violence, we are so inundated with messages that rates are overexaggerated and people lie about what happened that it can be difficult for someone without an awareness of these issues to believe victims immediately and take these situations seriously. In many instances, a focus on individual decision-making is used to blame victims for acts of gender violence they have experienced rather than focusing on the actions of those who committed the harm. People may dismiss victims if they sought a sexual interaction prior to an assault, loved and trusted the partner who abused them, didn't report harassment earlier because they thought they could handle it, or ran away from home into the economic conditions that made them more vulnerable to sex trafficking. Victim-blame helps explain why so few people are punished after committing gender violence and why people in positions of power are able to keep their jobs, leadership positions, and public adoration after accusations have been made against them. It also explains why there is often a culture of silence surrounding gender violence.

This leads us to the fourth area of impact: the allowance and encouragement of acts of gender violence by individuals, groups, and institutions. Mainstream disbelief, blame, and shame of people who have experienced gender violence have direct effects on how gender violence is perceived as a general issue, how people respond to a private or public disclosure, and how they react to situations of gender violence they witness. People are less likely to report gender violence or speak up about it, loved ones are less supportive, bystanders are less likely to intervene, and institutions are less likely to hold offenders accountable. This, in turn, empowers people to commit violence because they know that negative consequences for their abusive behavior are unlikely and avoidable. If those around them don't challenge their behavior or attempt to intervene, they can more easily continue to harm others.

In a culture of gender violence, individual acts of gender violence are often allowed through tacit approval or threats of more violence. Bystanders who witness abuse may not recognize what is happening as a problem—or at least not one urgent enough to require intervention or outside involvement. For example, a family member might laugh off an argument they witnessed between their sister and their sister's wife as a "catfight" even though it involved verbal abuse and manipulation. People who receive disclosures of gender violence might not acknowledge situations as serious or requiring any action on their part, like a work supervisor who ignores an employee's claims of transphobic abuse because they believe the employee brought it on themselves through their clothing choices. People may feel social pressure to remain quiet about situations they *do* view as problems, lack resources or skills for intervening or telling someone else about the violence, or fear the material repercussions of getting involved. A college student at a bar may not agree with his friends that slipping a drug in a woman's drink is okay, but his fear of appearing less masculine, going against the group, or not knowing what to say might lead to his complicity in the act. An individual may decide not to report a hate crime they witnessed for fear they will be the next target of violence.

Acts of gender violence can be both implicitly and explicitly encouraged. Subtle digs at virginity or in-group competitions to have the most sex may influence men's views of sex as conquest. A woman may be emboldened by friends to "take the power back" in her relationship by any means necessary and translate that to a use of abusive tactics. Friends may cheer on their popular buddy every time he sends a threatening text message to a person he is stalking. College students may make it a ritual to get first-years drunk at parties in order to target them for sexual assault. A family may conspire to facilitate an honor killing after a daughter is slut shamed. An organized group might target an outspoken activist for LGBTIQA+ rights through doxing, DoS attacks, and swatting. Gender violence may be promoted as a normal part of being in an organization, career, or social status—like employees who are expected by their peers to participate in the harassment of coworkers to show power as they move up in a company—or boards of directors who participate in corporate-affiliated sex trafficking rings. In contexts like these, it may be common knowledge that people with high levels of power and authority commit acts of gender violence regularly and are protected by people around them who enable and hide their behavior.

Altogether, the downplaying of gender violence in popular culture, normalization in everyday communication, blame of victims, and encouragement of gender violence often occur simultaneously and in relationship with one another—creating a synergistic cycle of acceptance (see figure 7.2). Pop culture trends influence tacit acceptance of gender violence, victim-blame plays a role in rationalizing gender-violent behavior, silence about gender violence leads to less reflection on communication about it, and discriminatory jokes lay the groundwork for someone to evade accountability for committing gender violence. At the *micro* or individual level, these areas of impact may shape a person's attitudes about and reactions to gender violence. At the *meso* or institutional level, an entire organization, system, or industry may use their influence and resources to reinforce the acceptance of gender violence across large groups of people.

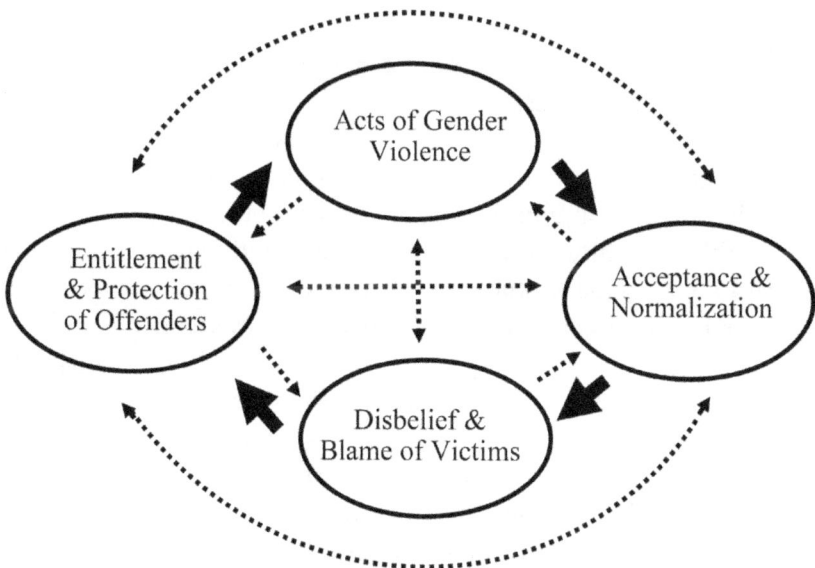

Figure 7.2. Gender Violence: The Cycle of Acceptance

The Role of Institutions

Institutions—formal social structures that influence individual behavior through implicit and explicit rules and norms—can be powerful enforcers of or resisters to the *macro* or large-scale systems of gender, cisheterosexism, and patriarchy. A culture of gender violence cannot easily be changed when rigid gender roles, narrow interpretations of sexuality, toxic social scripts, and gendered inequalities are introduced and reinforced by institutions central to our lives. Governments, educational systems, news and entertainment media, health-care systems, religious institutions, families, places of employment, organizations, and cultural groups can all play a role in maintaining a gendered system that promotes the cultural acceptance of gender violence. Institutions dictate and enforce guidelines for doing gender appropriately. Implicitly, a high school club may institute a "no pussies" rule for behavior in their group, a school may leave same-gender sexual attraction out of its health and relationships curriculum, or an organization might not support women in leadership roles even though there isn't a written rule against it. In a more explicitly harmful way, family members may demand a large dowry and abuse a bride until it is paid, a classmate may bully a child perceived as gay without consequences from school administration, hospital staff may neglect a birthing person experiencing life-threatening symptoms, or a state government might pass a law restricting transgender individuals from being able to access lifesaving medical care.

Institutional values, policies, and rules create and maintain norms that affect how people think and talk about gender violence itself. Families, community groups, or smaller organizations may use established patterns of communication and values from other institutions to guide attitudes about gender violence. For example, it might become commonplace for a couple's extended family to pretend they don't hear a partner committing abuse against the other because a church's doctrine communicates negative views about divorce. Larger institutions often dictate how much attention is paid to gender violence, how reports are handled, and what, if anything, is done to prevent it from happening in the first place. Companies may dismiss disclosures of pay inequity outright with claims that "those things don't happen here." Social media platforms might refuse to institute or follow through on policies to stop instigators of online abuse. Medical centers might not allocate resources for training staff on how to prevent mistreatment of people who identify as gender nonconforming or intersex.

Media institutions have an especially profound influence on the cultural acceptance of gender violence because of their widespread reach and accessibility. Radio, film, music, comics, magazines, and advertisements do more than entertain or sell products—they influence cultural attitudes and beliefs. Stand-up comedians that joke about dating violence minimize the seriousness of emotional abuse. A music video with scantily clad women, fully dressed men, and song lyrics suggesting that women always want sex even if they say no contributes to troubling ideas about consent (as in both versions of Robin Thicke's 2013 "Blurred Lines" featuring T.I. and Pharrell). News and social media discussion of gender violence influence ways communities respond to and process gender violence—often informing the public about current events but doing so in biased ways that leave out information and prioritize certain perspectives. News stories and social media debates about gender violence often lack complexity, nuance, and evidence-based research on the issues. When public messages about gender violence are not carefully prepared or well informed, they may sensationalize incidences of gender violence (capitalize on the unbelievable aspects of an event to create newsworthy drama for viewer consumption), normalize the incident (make an event seem isolated and unique despite research to the contrary), minimize what happened (approach the event in a matter-of-fact way or ignore it entirely), participate in victim-blame (focus on a person's choices, like their drug use, rather than the actions of their attacker), or offer simple, reductive solutions ("Women should just not go out alone at night to prevent things like this from happening"). Corporate news outlets tend to prioritize people in dominant power groups, often focusing more attention on young, White, educated, stereotypically attractive women who are the victims of gender violence rather than people of color, men (unless the case is "sensational"), or members of LGBTIQA+ populations. News outlets are also more likely to show more pictures of Black or Brown perpetrators than their White counterparts. The choices involved in framing gender violence—deciding which situations get coverage, how content is edited, and what language is used to describe them—can hurt victims of gender violence, misrepresent the problem, and contribute to stereotypes of marginalized populations.

All of these issues contribute to low rates of reporting gender violence to institutional authorities. When it comes to the US criminal system, one study found that 63.2 percent of men and 59 percent of women who experienced stalking did not report it to law enforcement; 93.2 percent of men and 86.1 percent of women who experienced harassing behaviors that fell short of meeting the legal definition for stalking didn't report it either.[6] Another study demonstrates that 80.9 percent of women who experienced rape did not report what happened to police;[7] another found that 73.3 percent of women and 86.5 percent of men who experienced physical assaults by intimate partners did not contact law enforcement.[8] As the criminal system is the institution with the most responsibility for holding individuals accountable for acts of gender violence, this is troubling. Not only is the US criminal system often viewed as unsupportive to victims, it is also largely ineffective in achieving widespread justice. Even when rape is reported in the United States, the vast majority of perpetrators will not go to jail or prison: one organization uses US crime statistics to estimate that out of 1,000 rapes, 310 are reported to police, 57 lead to arrest, 11 get referred to prosecutors, 7 lead to a felony conviction, and 6 rapists are incarcerated.[9] Individuals most likely to be prosecuted, incarcerated, and fully serve their assigned sentences are people of color, undocumented immigrants, and people without the economic means to afford strong defense attorneys.

Low reporting rates and lack of accountability play out similarly in campus judicial processes, primary and secondary educational environments, places of employment, and culturally specific contexts. Barriers to reporting on college campuses, for example, result in an estimated 80 percent of sexual assaults that women

---

[6] Baum, Catalano, and Rand, "Stalking Victimization," 9.
[7] Tjaden and Thoennes, "Extent, Nature, and Consequences of Rape Victimization," 34.
[8] Tjaden and Thoennes, "Extent, Nature, and Consequences of Intimate Partner Violence," 49.
[9] Rape, Abuse, and Incest National Network, "The Criminal Justice System: Statistics," 2024, https://www.rainn.org/statistics/criminal-justice-system.

do not report to police[10]—and universities may use low reporting rates to justify why meaningful prevention efforts are not necessary. In many institutions, hierarchical power structures function to protect those with the most power and influence, like how the culture of Hollywood often shields abusive men from accountability even when gender-violent behavior is known or witnessed by many people (like Harvey Weinstein, whose actions were referred to by many as "an open secret").[11]

Organizations can reproduce cycles of violence through policies and procedures that place emphasis on individual acts to detract from institutional responsibility for a culture of gender violence.[12] Without attention on the wider culture of an institution, even seemingly productive changes and prevention measures may fall short in decreasing rates or changing attitudes about these issues. A college may fire a coach after team members disclose sexual abuse, but in order for future violence to be prevented, the entire campus culture should be assessed, including its policies for hiring, reporting, and monitoring practices between coaches and athletes. Whether institutions are proactive, reactive, or inactive on issues of gender violence, they communicate powerful messages about it that cannot be denied.

Changing a Culture of Gender Violence

When considered outside of its cultural context, it is obvious to nearly everyone that gender violence as a whole is wrong. Violence, abuse, trauma, injury, death—no one would argue these are good things no matter how uninformed they might be about the scope or cause of the problem. I often start speeches and trainings acknowledging this common ground for that reason. But acts of gender violence don't happen in a vacuum. Like noxious perennial weeds that regrow every spring, gender violence will continue to occur at astronomically high rates unless the entire environment is addressed. Instead of snipping them at the stems, we need to pull

---

[10] Sinozich and Langton, "Rape and Sexual Assault."

[11] Sam Levin, "'We're All Complicit': Were the Harvey Weinstein Allegations an Open Secret?," *Guardian*, October 7, 2017, https://www.theguardian.com/film/2017/oct/07/harvey-weinstein-sexual-harassment-allegations-hollywood-rumors.

[12] Kate Lockwood Harris, *Beyond the Rapist: Title IX and Sexual Violence on US Campuses* (New York: Oxford, 2019).

them out from their roots and change the conditions that caused them to grow in the first place.

It can be uncomfortable and even shocking to realize how surrounded we are by cultural acceptance of gender violence and how we—as individuals, groups, or institutions—have participated in it. I think it's important to remember that the situation we are in is not the fault of one individual or group. The biggest issue is the simultaneity of so many individuals, organizations, and institutions normalizing, minimizing, and encouraging gender violence. Where the work usually begins, however, is at the individual level. The more we reflect on our own role in a culture of gender violence, the more we can begin to raise awareness in our communities and institutions. If enough shifts occur at the institutional level, groups and industries and governments can collaboratively reject the cultural acceptance of gender violence to the extent that accountability and victim support become the norm.

CHAPTER 8

Contributors to Gender Violence

In my experience as a trainer and dialogue facilitator, discussions about the *why* of gender violence often begin with questions like these: Is abuse an anger management problem? Are people who commit gender violence born monsters? Do abused people go on to abuse others? What role does alcohol play? Are men naturally more prone to commit violence? These important inquiries reveal curiosity about the nuances of individual behavior and take us into even more complex territory in examining these issues. The garden analogy from the beginning of chapter 7 helps us visualize the widespread effects of a system of gender and culture of gender violence, but individual acts are also fueled by a variety of contributing factors. They are like the raw materials of sunlight and rain used by a noxious weed to grow: the more present they are, the more acts of gender violence are likely to occur.

In this chapter, I describe a variety of biological, sociological, psychological, and communication-related factors that contribute to why an individual or a group commits gender violence (see table 8.1). Researchers and gender violence prevention and response experts have generated a lot of knowledge about these contributors I have grouped together in the following areas: biology, early life experiences, social and emotional skills, difficult life experiences, ideas about sex, and misuse of power. I offer a summary of what we know about each contributor, but depending on the individual, group, or specific act of gender violence, the influence of any of these factors may be huge or insignificant. After all, the reasons people commit gender violence are multidimensional, and even researchers disagree on what factors matter most. For this reason, it is best to think about these contributors not as isolated components but as overlapping elements that have a synergistic

TABLE 8.1. **Contributors to Gender Violence**

Area	Type of Contributor
Biology	The brain Genetics Hormones
Early life experiences	Quality of parenting Role modeling Peer modeling and bonding Patterns of behavior in early relationships Intergenerational transmission of violence
Social and emotional skills	Unhealthy coping Lack of empathy Underdeveloped interpersonal communication skills
Difficult life experiences	History of abuse Aggregation of adversities Systemic oppression Drug addiction Mental illness
Ideas about sex	Sexual objectification and dehumanization Sex negativity
Misuse of power	Entitlement Prejudice Grooming Drug-facilitated violence Illusion of safety Opportunity

relationship with one another, the system of gender, and the cultural acceptance of gender violence.

Biology

The Brain

Historically, researchers believed that higher levels of aggression in men—and more empathy in women—were linked to brain sex differentiation, or the differences thought to exist in the prenatal brain development of men and women.[1] More recent research argues that

---

[1] Lise Eliot, "Brain Development and Physical Aggression: How a Small Gender Difference Grows into a Violence Problem," *Current Anthropology* 62, no. S23 (2021): 66–78, doi:10.1086/711705.

there are no clear-cut biological differences that cause aggression; in fact, studies reveal a variety of conflicting conclusions when it comes to the impact of brain size and various neurochemicals. In other words, we don't yet understand the brain enough to be able to determine its relationship to gender-violent behavior.

Many biological explanations of gender violence simplify the complexities of neurodevelopment and do not take the role of environmental factors into account. Behaviors basic to human survival like blinking, coughing, and heart rate control are hardwired in our programming, but practically all other brain development is shaped by environmental factors.[2] Researchers use the term *neuroplasticity* to describe how the brain is malleable, especially in childhood. This means that exposure to gender roles, social demands, and cultural teachings early in life can increase or decrease gendered differences in brain development and their connection to physically aggressive or violent behavior in adolescence and adulthood.[3]

Analysis of previous studies is changing how researchers consider the brain's impact on aggression. In the past, low resting heart rate was used to predict aggressive and antisocial behavior, but most studies focused exclusively on White men and recent research found there is no significant relationship between these factors in Black men.[4] Results like these call into question many other established generalizations about the relationship between human biology and aggressive behavior; many researchers now advocate for more racial diversity and incorporation of socio-contextual factors into future studies.[5]

Genetics

Studies on the impact of genetics on violent behavior primarily focus on monoaminergic neurotransmitter systems (specific networks of nerve cells that communicate messages throughout the body related to our moods and motivations) and the endocrine

---

[2] Ibid., 71.
[3] Ibid., 75.
[4] Jill Portnoy, J. Richard Jennings, Karen A. Matthews, Dustin Pardini, and Adrian Raine, "The Relationship between Resting Heart Rate and Aggression in Males Is Racially Variant," *Aggressive Behavior* 46, no. 2 (2020): 170–80, doi:10.1002/ab.21879.
[5] Ibid.

system's response to stress.[6] Though research suggests there may be genetic differences in these systems for women and men that can result in different types of aggression, scientists are not yet able to isolate the influence of specific systems or genes.[7] Genetics are likely involved in pathological (extreme or abnormal) aggression, but studies on children reveal that gendered differences in these systems are not significant early in life—meaning that aggression is a product of both genetic predisposition and environmental factors.[8] This is why many researchers advocate for biosocial approaches to gender violence that combine a study of personality traits at the molecular level with behavior influenced by environment.[9] Though some specific genes have been identified as potential keys to better understanding violent behavior, there is still a need for more innovative methods, consideration of harmful environments on child development, and exploration of individual differences in biological sensitivity to environmental context.[10]

Biosocial approaches are also important for avoiding *racial essentialism*, or the idea that racial differences determine a person's inherent characteristics or behavior. Many scientists have inaccurately conflated Blackness with higher aggression rather than the underlying issues that lead to social inequality: one review of research reveals that social factors like poverty and living in homes contaminated by lead or other harmful substances actually affect genes and neurotransmitters.[11] Criminology researchers argue that when race is considered an innate biological difference rather than

[6] Marjolein M. J. van Donkelaar, Martine Hoogman, Elena Shumskaya, Jan K. Buitelaar, Janita Bralten, and Barbara Franke, "Monoamine and Neuroendocrine Gene-Sets Associate with Frustration-Based Aggression in a Gender-Specific Manner," *European Neuropsychopharmacology* 30 (2020): 75–86, doi:10.1016/j.euroneuro.2017.11.016.
[7] Ibid.; C. Nathan DeWall and Baldwin M. Way, "A New Piece to Understanding the Intimate Partner Violence Puzzle: What Role Do Genetics Play?," *Violence against Women* 20 no. 4 (2014): 414–19, doi:10.1177/1077801214528585.
[8] Regina Waltes, Andreas G. Chiocchetti, and Christine M. Freitag, "The Neurological Basis of Human Aggression: A Review on Genetic and Epigenetic Mechanisms," *American Journal of Medical Genetics* 171, no. 5 (2016): 650–75, doi:10.1002/ajmg.b.32388.
[9] Patricia A. Janssen, Tonia L. Nicholls, Ravinesh A. Kumar, Harry Stefanakis, Alicia L. Spidel, and Elizabeth M. Simpson, "Of Mice and Men: Will the Intersection of Social Science and Genetics Create New Approaches for Intimate Partner Violence?," *Journal of Interpersonal Violence* 20, no. 1 (2005): 61–71, doi:10.1177/0886260504268120.
[10] DeWall and Way, "New Piece to Understanding."
[11] Julien Larregue and Oliver Rollins, "Biosocial Criminology and the Mismeasure of Race," *Ethnic and Racial Studies* 42, no. 12 (2019): 1990–2007, doi:10.1080/01419870.2018.1527938.

a social process, race itself becomes criminalized—and this leads to erroneous conclusions that perpetuate stereotypes and prejudicial treatment of people of color.[12] To better understand the connection between genetics and gender violence, researchers must address these and other problems, including small sample size or a research method's failure to produce similar results when replicated in other studies.

Hormones

Hormones are molecules made up of tightly bound clusters of atoms that carry messages to different parts of the body.[13] Though the difference between the sex hormones testosterone and estrogen is only one carbon atom,[14] testosterone has been thought to play a major role in aggressive and violent behavior, particularly in men. In addition to producing sperm, testosterone has various functions that include building muscle, making red blood cells, and releasing neurotransmitters in the brain.[15] It turns out, however, that there isn't strong evidence to support the claim that testosterone promotes human aggression—though it is likely connected to that behavior.[16]

In one review of various hormone studies, researchers explain that testosterone is positively but weakly correlated with human aggression, that the correlation is much stronger for men than for women, and that the results still aren't significant enough to make a case that testosterone causes aggressive behavior.[17] It may play a role in extremely violent behavior committed by men, but only when combined with other factors like a person's perceived threats to their masculinity, physical capability to harm others, and access

---

[12] Ibid.
[13] James McBride Dabbs, *Heroes, Rogues, and Lovers: Testosterone and Behavior* (New York: McGraw-Hill, 2000), 8.
[14] Ibid., 9.
[15] Ibid., 10.
[16] S. N. Geniole, B. M. Bird, J. S. McVittie, R. B. Purcell, J. Archer, and J. M. Carré, "Is Testosterone Linked to Human Aggression? A Meta-analytic Examination of the Relationship between Baseline, Dynamic, and Manipulated Testosterone on Human Aggression," *Hormones and Behavior* 123 (2020): 1–11, doi:10.1016/j.yhbeh.2019.104644.
[17] Ibid.

to firearms.[18] Testosterone levels could help predict the re-offense of sex crimes, but effects of the hormone can be decreased through psychotherapy or channeling high levels of the hormone into pro-social (healthier and more productive) behaviors.[19] In fact, some research reveals that testosterone plays a role in altruistic, positive, and heroic behavior.[20] The hormone might even be an *effect* of aggression rather than the other way around.[21] To put it simply: testosterone has not been proven to be a cause of gender violence though it may be a contributor in combination with other factors. Inconsistent methods for measuring aggression, including the failure to account for shifting hormone levels throughout the day, add to the limitations of what we know about how this hormone works.[22]

Research on other hormones also complicates previous assumptions about their relationship to behavior. The production of prolactin, for example, is commonly associated with breast lactation because it heightens human response to the needs of a baby's cries. Increased levels of prolactin have been found in men who have close contact with pregnant individuals or newborn babies, which means that people of any gender involved in active caregiving can experience hormonal shifts that make them more sensitive to the needs of infants—and the more they act on that sensitivity, the more those hormonal changes are strengthened.[23] This suggests that social environment and behavior can influence the production of hormones related to empathy.

---

[18] Conor J. O'Dea, Elliott Jardin, and Donald A. Saucier, "The Masculinity-Based Model of Aggressive Retaliation in Society (MARS)," *Psychology of Men & Masculinities* 23, no. 2 (2022): 160–72, doi:10.1037/men0000391.

[19] Lea H. Studer, A. Scott Aylwin, and John R. Reddon, "Testosterone, Sexual Offense Recidivism, and Treatment Effect among Adult Male Sex Offenders," *Sexual Abuse: A Journal of Research and Treatment* 17, no. 2 (2005): 171–81, doi:10.1177/107906320501700207.

[20] Dabbs, *Heroes, Rogues, and Lovers*.

[21] J. Martin Ramirez, "Hormones and Aggression in Childhood and Adolescence," *Aggression and Violent Behavior* 8, no. 6 (2003): 621–44, doi:10.1016/S1359-1789(02)00102-7.

[22] Ibid.

[23] Kaufman, *Time Has Come*, 114.

Early Life Experiences

Quality of Parenting

Individuals who grow up in a home without an engaged, loving parent—or who experience a lack of interest by a parent or guardian present in their lives—are more likely to grow up with behavioral problems and other issues that can contribute to a higher likelihood to commit gender violence.[24] Absent or neglectful parents or guardians can be the most detrimental.

Role Modeling

Parents, guardians, older siblings, family members, teachers, mentors, and those with various levels of fame—like community leaders, politicians, musicians, athletes, and influencers—model behavior for others and can have a profound influence on children and adolescents. Role models who demonstrate and enforce strict gender roles, commit acts of gender violence, or participate in maintaining a culture of gender violence set examples for attitudes, values, and behaviors that young people may follow.

Peer Modeling and Bonding

Apart from the influence of parents and close family members, children and adolescents learn a lot from their peers. Knowledge about gender expression, sexual behavior, and gender violence shared peer to peer may be limited and erroneous, reproducing dangerous misperceptions that can influence attitudes and behaviors. This is especially troubling in peer bonding contexts that create comradery through language and actions that police gender expression and participate in the normalization of gender violence.

Patterns of Behavior in Early Relationships

An individual's abusive behavior in intimate relationships generally begins when dating in adolescence and early adulthood. If young people perceive unhealthy or abusive behavior as successful—they get what they want in the relationship—or their actions are encouraged or accepted by peers and others outside the relationship, that

---

[24] Ibid., 123.

behavior is likely to continue into adulthood. Abusive patterns may also begin in early childhood relationships if kids have experienced or witnessed abuse among the teenagers or adults around them.

Intergenerational Transmission of Violence

Gender violence that happens in families can have deep effects on children. Partner violence witnessed as a child or adolescent in one's family of origin has a connection to similar types of violence in adult relationships.[25] People who grow up to abuse others may have learned the behavior by observing patterns of it throughout their early lives. Individuals abused by others may be less likely to recognize harmful behavior as abuse, or accept it as commonplace or inevitable, if they witnessed or experienced it as children. All of these experiences can lead to continuing cycles of violence in one's own family generation after generation.

Social and Emotional Skills

Unhealthy Coping

People who develop unhealthy or unproductive (sometimes called maladaptive) coping skills early in life may be less likely to manage general stress (like family conflict, minor financial issues, or relational tensions), acute stressors (like the loss of a job, change in living situation, health problem, or death of someone close to them), or chronic long-term stress (like immigrating to another country, experiencing a natural disaster, living in a war zone, fleeing a country due to persecution, or managing a debilitating illness). When children, especially boys, are pressured to adhere to rigid gender expectations that discourage healthy expression of emotion, downplay vulnerability, and only allow anger and aggression, the result can be a higher likelihood to hurt others as a coping mechanism. When maladaptive coping is taught or modeled by parents, family members, and older siblings, individuals may be less likely to learn

[25] David S. Black, Steve Sussman, and Jennifer B. Unger, "A Further Look at the Intergenerational Transmission of Violence: Witnessing Interparental Violence in Emerging Adulthood," *Journal of Interpersonal Violence* 25, no. 6 (2010): 1022–42, doi:10.1177/0886260509340539.

self-control, strategies for processing anger productively, healthy perseverance, and perspective shifting.

Lack of Empathy

People without empathy may subtly or explicitly violate personal boundaries without regard for the feelings, thoughts, and harm they inflict on others. Sometimes lack of empathy is associated with developmental or personality disorders with biological causes; other times it is the result of social and environmental factors. Because empathy is often associated with femininity and it may lead to feeling or being perceived as vulnerable, it is often a behavior discouraged in masculine gender expression. Empathy and empathetic communication may also be culturally and contextually specific: people may learn to have more or less empathy for certain groups of people based on systems of oppression or in certain social environments that emphasize competition and aggression, like the military, sports, or the corporate business world.

Underdeveloped Interpersonal Communication Skills

Individuals with poor or underdeveloped communication skills may have difficulty expressing and responding to the wants and needs of themselves and others. Skills in clear verbal communication, assertiveness, active listening, self-awareness, perception, and conflict negotiation are important for creating and maintaining mutually beneficial relationships. They are especially important for communicating emotional and physical personal boundaries, building intimacy, negotiating divergent wants and needs, and handling various forms of rejection. Lack of these skills can lead to nonlistening, dismissal of nonverbal cues, verbal aggression, and manipulative communication. Combined with maladaptive coping, lack of empathy, and societal pressures on gender expression, poor interpersonal communication skills can contribute to why and how an individual may commit gender violence. They can also contribute to nonintervention in escalating situations of gender violence, passivity when faced with attitudes that promote their cultural acceptance, and unsupportive responses to people who disclose their experiences of gender violence.

Difficult Life Experiences

History of Abuse

Individuals who experience abuse, especially when they are young, may face difficulties negotiating relationships with others later in life. If a maltreated child's early relationships are structured as victimizer-versus-victim, they may defer to others using this template. This can make them more vulnerable to bullying, harassment, and coercive forms of control by others,[26] or it may mean they take on the victimizer role in later relationships as a way to regain a sense of power. Abuse and unhealthy relational dynamics in the home—or bullying and harassment from peers—during childhood and adolescence may create distorted gender expectations, potentially leading an individual to embrace rigid gender roles as a way to attempt acceptance and avoid abuse. As a result, individuals may communicate this rigidity in ways that disparage others. They may also learn to view violence as a legitimate response to threat and conflict.[27]

These relational dynamics help to explain why many people who experience abuse go on to abuse others. When it comes to sexual assault, for example, people who experience it as children may be more likely to commit general and violent crimes than people who were not abused.[28] Though most victims of abuse do not go on to commit gender violence against others, many abusers have themselves been victimized.

---

[26] David A. Wolfe, Claire C. Crooks, Debbie Chiodo, and Peter Jaffe, "Child Maltreatment, Bullying, Gender-Based Harassment, and Adolescent Dating Violence: Making the Connections," *Psychology of Women Quarterly* 33, no. 1 (2009): 21–24, doi:10.1111/j.1471-6402.2008.01469.x.

[27] Ibid.

[28] Nina Papalia, Stefan Leubbers, and James R.P. Ogloff, "Child Sexual Abuse and the Propensity to Engage in Criminal Behaviour: A Critical Review and Examination of Moderating Factors," *Aggression and Violent Behavior* 43 (2018): 71–89, doi:10.1016/j.avb.2018.10.007.

Case Example

Chris Brown and Performing Masculinity

When R&B singer Chris Brown is mentioned among people working to end gender violence, it is usually in reference to his felony assault conviction after attacking his then-girlfriend Rihanna in 2009.[a] Brown's physical attacks and threats toward ex-girlfriend Karrueche Tran—and the restraining order granted against him by a judge in 2017[b]—might also be part of the discussion. Brown has been accused of various physical and sexual assaults against women as recently as 2021.[c]

Many people might not know that Brown was likely a victim of sexual abuse as a child. In a 2013 interview, he bragged about losing his virginity when he was eight years old to a girl who was fourteen.[d] Brown's framing of the experience was probably influenced by his childhood exposure to pornography[e] and the massive pressure men are under to perform traditional heterosexual masculinity. While a victimizing experience is not a justification for violence that someone commits against others, this particular situation offers a glimpse into the challenges boys and men may face after being abused, especially by girls or women.

[a] Alan Duke and Ted Rowlands, "Chris Brown Pleads Guilty in Rhianna Assault Case," CNN, June 22, 2009, https://www.cnn.com/2009/SHOWBIZ/Music/06/22/chris.brown.hearing/.
[b] Robyn Autry, "Chris Brown Told the World Who He Was with Rihanna. We Didn't Listen," NBC News, June 27, 2021, https://www.nbcnews.com/think/opinion/chris-brown-told -world-who-he-was-rihanna-we-didn-ncna1272430.
[c] Elise Brisco, "Chris Brown Accused of Hitting a Woman in Los Angeles, Reports Say," USA Today, June 23, 2021, https://www.usatoday.com/story/entertainment/celebrities/2021 /06/23/chris-brown-faces-battery-allegations-after-hitting-woman/5318410001/.
[d] Decca Aitkenhead, "Chris Brown: 'It Was the Biggest Wake-Up Call," Guardian, October 4, 2013, https://www.theguardian.com/music/2013/oct/04/chris-brown-rihanna-interview-x.
[e] Ibid.

Aggregation of Adversities

Individuals who experience multiple forms of hardship especially as children may be at a higher *cumulative risk* to commit serious crimes. Hardships could involve family dysfunction, socioeconomic struggle, maltreatment, family members with substance abuse or mental illness, or other issues.[29] When children experience multiple co-occurring childhood adversities—especially those involving abuse or that result in damaged relationships with caregivers—and they lack social support to navigate those challenges, they may be more likely to abuse others.[30] Research on men who have committed partner violence reveals that for many perpetrators, adverse childhood experiences were associated with the development of low self-worth, self-blame, feelings of powerlessness, and beliefs that justified the use of physical violence in order to overcome powerlessness. These may be amplified by the absence of strong primary attachments, lack of social support, and expectations for traditional masculinity.[31]

Systemic Oppression

Like many other hardships that contribute to an aggregation of adversities, the racism, classism, ableism, heterosexism, allosexism, or other systemic oppression a person might experience can make their life immeasurably harder than the lives of people in dominant groups. The prejudicial attitudes, discrimination, and violence they may face based on their membership in nondominant groups can be difficult to manage, especially if they result in less opportunity, lower income, and chronic stress or trauma—*and* a person's coping skills are underdeveloped. Combined with co-occurring adverse childhood experiences, high levels of social isolation and discrimination experienced by members of marginalized communities may have more severe consequences on their psychological health and relationships with others than for those who don't belong to marginalized groups.[32] This is how systemic oppression may *at times* contribute to the reason someone may feel an especially strong

---

[29] Ibid.

[30] Natalie Hoskins and Adrianne Kunkel, "'I Didn't Really Have Anybody to Turn To': Barriers to Social Support and the Experiences of Male Perpetrators of Intimate Partner Violence," *Journal of Interpersonal Violence* 37, nos. 7–8 (2022): NP5317–NP5343, doi:10.1177/0886260520961869.

[31] Natalie Hoskins and Adrianne Kunkel, "'I Don't Even Deserve a Chance': An Ethnographic Study of Adverse Childhood Experiences among Male Perpetrators of Intimate Partner Violence," *Qualitative Report* 25, no. 9 (2020): 1009–37, doi:10.46743/2160-3715/2020.3938.

[32] Ibid., 1033–34.

need to gain power and control in their life, even at the expense of others.[33] On its own, however, systemic oppression does not cause gender-violent behavior.

Drug Addiction

People who struggle with addictions to alcohol and drugs like cocaine, amphetamines, and phencyclidine (PCP) may impulsively cause harm without in-the-moment regard for how it affects others. According to a review of research on drugs and aggressive behavior, heavy drug use can modify cognitive functions, emotional states, hormones, and other physiological systems that would typically restrain someone from being violent.[34] Alcohol can alter the brain's ability to adapt to new situations and problems, affect neurochemical systems in the body that connect to behavior, and trigger aggressive acts by people already prone to be aggressive, especially when combined with the use of other drugs.[35] Chronic alcoholism can lead to personality changes in which people develop a higher tendency to blame others. Stimulants, amphetamines, and PCP can alter the nervous system in ways that impact communication and lead to more escalating situations of violence. For all drugs, withdrawal can cause irritability, agitation, and less tolerance for stressors.[36]

Most drug use is by people who are not violent, and violent behavior is strongly influenced by personal history and gender; men, for example, are more likely to act aggressively while binge drinking.[37] Alcohol and other drugs affect everyone differently, and people may adapt their behavior in certain environments, meaning that people under the influence may have more control over their behavior than others might assume. People also often use being under the influence as an excuse for misreading communication

---

[33] Linda L. Ammons, "Mules, Madonnas, Babies, Bathwater, Racial Imagery, and Stereotypes: The African-American Woman and the Battered Woman Syndrome," in *Critical Race Feminism: A Reader*, ed. Adrien K. Wing (New York: New York University Press, 2003), 263.

[34] Sharon M. Boles and Karen Miotto, "Substance Abuse and Violence: A Review of the Literature," *Aggression and Violent Behavior* 8, no. 1 (2003): 155–74, doi:10.1016/S1359-1789(01)00057-X.

[35] Ibid.

[36] Ibid.

[37] Ibid.

signals or engaging in violent behavior.[38] All of these issues make the relationship between drugs and aggression a complex one, especially given that addiction is a disease and early decisions to use substances can be influenced by abuse, trauma, and aggregation of adversities.

Mental Illness

Though mental illness may be one contributor to gender violence, it is usually not a cause of violence on its own. According to research, mental illness does contribute to the risk of someone behaving violently, but this is often only the case for people with severe mental illness or psychotic disorders. In actuality, people with mental illness make up a small proportion of violent offenders.[39] When mental illness does play a role in someone's violent behavior, it is often in relationship with a variety of combined risk factors, including past violence, juvenile detention, parental arrest record, perceived threats, experiences of abuse, and other life struggles—with substance abuse disorders being the greatest predictor of violence when someone also has a mental illness.[40] Unfortunately, the connection between mental illness and violent behavior continues to be exaggerated even though it is far more likely that individuals with a serious mental illness will be victims of violence rather than those who commit it.[41]

Ideas about Sex
Sexual Objectification and Dehumanization

Gender violence is more likely to occur in contexts in which people are treated like objects or commodities rather than individuals who deserve dignity and respect. Sexual objectification involves treating people, and parts of their bodies, as objects of desire for the sexual gratification of others. Sexual objectification can take the form of

---

[38] Ibid.
[39] Mohit Varshney, Ananya Mahapatra, Vijay Krishnan, Rishab Gupta, and Koushik Sinha Deb, "Violence and Mental Illness: What Is the True Story?," *Journal of Epidemiology & Community Health* 70, no. 3 (2016): 223–25, doi:10.1136/jech-2015-205546.
[40] Ibid.
[41] Heather Stuart, "Violence and Mental Illness: An Overview," *World Psychiatry* 2, no. 2 (2003): 121–24, https://www.ncbi.nlm.nih.gov/pmc/articles/PMC1525086/.

language that reduces people to their sexualized parts (like referring to someone as "Legs") or gratifying function (like saying a person is a great lay), media images that use the sexualization of bodies and body parts to sell products or ideas (like advertisements that feature a shapely feminine figure or a music video that zooms in on breasts), or the commodification of sexual desire and sex itself (like in many strip clubs, pornographic films, and sex work contexts).

Sexual objectification on its own doesn't necessarily lead to violence, but people and groups who commit gender violence often use sexual objectification to degrade others or make them feel less human. Dehumanization occurs when people with privilege or perceived entitlement treat people with less perceived power as undeserving of agency, bodily autonomy, and respect. Dehumanization makes acts of gender violence more justifiable to the people who commit them, especially if they view victims as deserving of violence.

Sex Negativity

Cultural attitudes about sex can influence how people think about gender violence and empower groups and individuals to commit it. When sex is considered dirty, transgressive, shameful, and dangerous in some contexts but sacred and pure in others, this can result in discriminatory attitudes and actions against people based on their sexual desires and experiences. In a sex-negative culture, sex is rarely explicitly discussed and sexual behavior is discouraged unless it takes place in specific contexts: in its most extreme form, this is only within the confines of heterosexual marriage for procreation. Sexual desire and expression outside of heterosexuality, monogamy, marriage, reproduction, and socially prescribed couplings involving no more than two individuals are often demonized. This leads to secrecy and shame around sex that has multiple implications. First, when sex cannot be discussed openly in nonjudgmental ways, it is more difficult to facilitate accurate education on healthy sexuality, consent, and gender violence. Second, people are more likely to be discriminated against if they express sexual desire or engage in behavior in culturally unacceptable ways, even when they do not harm others. Third, people who experience discrimination based on their sexual orientation, behavior, or perceived sexual expression—or who experience gender violence—are less likely to disclose or report it to others. Fourth, victims of gender violence are more likely to be shamed for what they experienced or worse: deemed as deserving of the acts committed against them.

Misuse of Power

Entitlement

People with power due to wealth, popularity, leadership position, success, fame, or (gender, racial, or other type of) privilege may harm others because they feel entitled to do so. Their self-perception of superiority may cause them to act in ways that violate the boundaries of others without a regard for bodily autonomy. They may believe they deserve things that others do not and justify using resources, influence, manipulation, coercion, or force to get what they want. Organizations and institutions may also use entitlement backed by wealth, longevity, influence, and various forms of privilege to commit gender violence against entire groups of people. They may create or continue traditions, rituals, events, policies, or practices that knowingly ignore bodily autonomy and harm their members, then use their power to evade accountability. Entitled individuals and groups may buy or maneuver loyalty of bystanders to avoid accountability for their unethical behavior. As a result, they may be able to retain a positive public image despite allegations made against them or others' common knowledge of their harmful behavior. If they are successful in abusing others without consequences, their sense of entitlement may increase and motivate continued or more severe harm of others.

Prejudice

Biased attitudes about race, class, disability, religion, size, appearance, and other aspects of identity may increase a person or group's motivation for committing gender violence. Feelings of discomfort, intolerance, superiority, contempt, or hate that stem from these attitudes may cause someone to believe their discrimination or violence is warranted against members of certain groups. They may use privilege to harm someone without as much of it, then use their privilege as protection against any repercussions for their behavior.

A lean White man, for example, might make hateful verbal attacks against a Brown woman he views as overweight sitting next to him on an airplane, then rely on his gender and racial privilege to talk White flight attendants out of considering the woman's complaints about him legitimate. He is likely aware there are no legal protections based on body size (further empowering his behavior), and he may draw on restrictive or inequitable aspects of the environment like small plane seats or narrow cabin aisles to strengthen his attacks. People and groups who commit gender violence at least partly due to prejudicial attitudes rely on systems of oppression to support their harmful actions or increase their severity. The combination of entitlement, prejudice, and support from others through ideologically charged groups or systems of oppression may enable particularly dehumanizing forms of gender violence.

Grooming

Acts of gender violence are often premeditated. Abusers and attackers may target individuals they perceive as vulnerable and easier to take advantage of than others, then build their target's trust through complimenting, flirting, gift-giving, and over-the-top demonstrations of care or affection. Grooming can be short (over the course of one evening) or long term (over a period of years) and can occur in all kinds of relationships. It creates a false sense of safety and care that can mask or desensitize others to early signs of abusive behaviors. This enables an abusive person to exploit a target's vulnerabilities—things like having low self-esteem, being in new surroundings, lacking emotional maturity, experiencing financial or housing insecurity, having a disability, being without a support system, or having some other need—and manipulate their trust.

Individuals who have been groomed by an abusive person may feel conflicted about the harm they are experiencing because they did not expect the behavior and have grown to trust, care for, or love the person abusing them. They may fear negative repercussions from resisting the abuse or telling others about it. Groomers rely on these conflicted feelings to discourage people from seeking help or reporting their behavior to authorities. Grooming often occurs in abusive dating or committed relationships, planned sexual assaults, sex trafficking recruitment, sexual exploitation, and gender-motivated kidnappings and homicides. Abusers may also groom people close to those they harm as a way to boost their image, manipulate others, deflect blame, and make themselves more invincible so they can continue their abuse. This type of grooming is common in the midst of partner violence, sexual violence, sexual harassment, and other types of sexual exploitation.

Drug-Facilitated Violence

Premeditated forms of gender violence may involve the use of drugs to facilitate an attack. Abusive individuals may target those they perceive to be vulnerable due to their use of alcohol or other drugs, like someone who notices a person getting intoxicated at a party, taking an illicit drug for the first time, or leaving somewhere alone while under the influence. Whether to facilitate sexual violence, emotional manipulation, stalking, or gender-based hate crime, an abuser's passive use of drugs in these situations is still strategic. One study observed that when initiating aggressive behavior at bars, men were more likely to target women they perceived as intoxicated—leading the researchers to suggest that initiators' sexual aggression was intentional rather than an effect of their own alcohol use.[42]

Drugs may also be used in active ways to deliberately make targets more vulnerable to abuse, like pressuring someone to drink beyond their limit, spiking someone's drink without their knowledge, or manipulating someone into taking a drug without knowledge of its effects. These tactics are common in situations involving sexual assault, exploitation, nonconsensual distribution of sexual content, and sextortion. An abusive person may also strategically facilitate someone's addiction to drugs—or exploit an existing addiction—as a way to control and manipulate them. This strategy is commonly associated with partner violence and sex trafficking.

---

[42] Kathryn Graham et al., "'Blurred Lines?': Sexual Aggression and Barroom Culture," *Alcoholism: Clinical and Experimental Research* 38, no. 5 (2014): 1416–24, doi:10.1111/acer.12356.

Illusion of Safety

The continuous minimization of gender violence leads many people to presume that they and those closest to them are safe from it. An *illusion of safety* involves believing that gender violence rarely happens, and when it does, it only happens to others who have made decisions that led to their victimization. Though this belief may initially shield individuals from dealing with the harsh, daily realities of gender violence, avoiding its existence means less preparation for potentially troubling situations and higher risk of victim-blame toward oneself or others.

Unfortunately, people and groups who commit gender violence often rely on a presumption of safety to harm and get by with harming others. A predator may target individuals (especially young people) without education on boundaries and safe touch in the hope that their abuse goes unquestioned. Health organizations or medical providers may evade informed consent for drugs and procedures that result in infertility or sterility. Attackers might use someone's lack of knowledge about gender violence ("it never happens") or sense of immunity from it ("it could never happen to me") to catch them off guard and take advantage of them more easily. If gender violence does occur, people without knowledge of its dynamics and the resources available may not know how to talk about issues that arise, where to get help, and what options they have for moving forward. Teens might not know how to respond to something that doesn't feel right, family and friends might not share what happened with one another, and individuals may try to press on without assistance from anyone. Predators rely on this silence to avoid accountability and continue their abuse. They also rely on victim-blame to shift attention away from their behavior and protect themselves against allegations of wrongdoing. People unfamiliar with gender violence dynamics may be likelier to disbelieve a disclosure, think a victim brought the situation on themselves, or quickly come to the defense of the person accused of the abuse. Self-blame may be more automatic: those who have internalized a false sense of security may be more likely to deny the seriousness of what happened, shame themselves, and decide against seeking help.

People who recognize the pervasiveness of gender violence—but believe it is preventable if enough precautions are taken—may be more likely to blame themselves if they do experience it despite all of their efforts. Risk-reductive behaviors like wearing modest clothing, staying sober, not going out alone, taking self-defense classes, carrying a weapon, or only trusting certain people may increase safety to some degree and help individuals feel safer, but they are not a surefire way to avoid experiencing gender violence. Some actions may make someone less likely to be targeted or help them fight off an attack more successfully, but there are numerous factors that influence whether they are effective. In addition, risk-reductive behaviors are not as likely to be used in situations with people they know and trust. As a result, individuals who put their faith in risk reduction as prevention may feel a deeper sense of anger and bitterness if they experience gender violence. People who knew they were engaging in what they perceived as riskier behaviors may be especially hard on themselves for what happened; this contributes even more to silence and isolation.

If victims do speak out despite these challenges, committers of gender violence may capitalize on the illusion of safety to influence others' opinions about accusations made against them. Because it can be difficult to negotiate the reality of betrayal by people who are close to us, inspire us, or have been recipients of our trust or adoration, it is often easier to remain in disbelief rather than confront the reality of their behavior. When the accused has a great deal of privilege, fame, or influence, they may sway, charm, or manipulate an entire group, community, or nation of people. For all of these reasons, an illusion of safety from gender violence can contribute to, and even enable, an individual or group's abusive behavior toward others.

Opportunity

Regardless of someone's early life experiences, social and emotional skills, difficult life experiences, ideas about sex, or other factors, they may or may not commit gender violence depending on the situations in which they find themselves. Some offenders may plan an attack for days, weeks, or months; some groups may harm others without much forethought. Individuals may not initially intend to harm others but continue to do so if they gain power, are rewarded in some way, or become solidified in their behavioral and communication patterns. Others may test boundaries, commit verbal forms of abuse, or take what they perceive as small actions to gain practice and confidence toward larger and more severe violations. Some may only commit gender violence when they are alone, in a group, or in settings they perceive as low risk for others finding out about their behavior or holding them accountable. In other words, people may encounter or actively create the opportunity to harm someone.

This means it is difficult to predict when someone may commit gender violence. They may be more likely to do it when others are most vulnerable, but it would be reductive to conclude that vulnerabilities on their own—like being young, drinking alcohol, having a physical disability, or being financially dependent on someone—always lead to gender violence. Similarly, predators may seek out people they perceive as being easier to attack or manipulate, but gender violence is not the inevitable result of walking alone at night, engaging in risky behaviors, or trusting someone. For these reasons, it is important to both acknowledge how opportunity plays a role in someone's choice to commit gender violence and understand it is just one factor that contributes to their behavior.

After all, everyone has vulnerabilities and takes risks at various points in their life, whether these are physical, emotional, social, or financial. It can help to be vigilant, maintain clear boundaries, and do things to protect yourself or others, but risk reduction cannot guarantee protection from gender violence. It's also neither practical nor healthy to close yourself off from all other people in all contexts for all time to avoid gender violence. Opportunities for harm will always exist, but our vulnerabilities are not the problem: the responsibility for committing gender violence is with the person who identifies someone else's vulnerabilities and chooses to exploit them.

Case Example

Contributors to Online Harassment against Yasmin Benoit

British model Yasmin Benoit came out publicly as asexual in 2017 and has since been an outspoken activist for asexual rights and visibility.[a] She has been asked inappropriate questions about her identity, encountered pressure to have sex from both men and women who ignore her disinterest, and been a target of street and online harassment. She uses her social media platform to raise awareness of acephobia in online spaces—even sharing screenshots of hateful comments she has received on her own posts.[b] What are the causes and contributors to acephobic online harassment like this against her?

We can start with the system of gender and the ways people learn to police sexual expression that doesn't fit the binary gender norm. Next, a culture of gender violence makes it acceptable to communicate discriminatory and violent comments. Yasmin herself discusses how the lack of asexual representation in mainstream culture, especially media, contributes to the "symbolic annihilation" of aces and their mistreatment in everyday life.[c] Add in someone's prejudicial attitudes—a possible combination of acephobia, sexism, and racism—and their active sexual objectification and dehumanization of women's bodies, especially those more on display through a modeling career like Yasmin's. Entitlement and lack of empathy likely play a role in justifying harassment, and the internet offers opportunity for people to post anonymously and remain emotionally distant from the harm their actions might cause. Perhaps, in addition, the people harassing Yasmin never observed adult or peer examples of compassionate or understanding behavior toward people who are asexual.

[a] Gabriella Ferlita, "Asexual Activist on Facing 'Inappropriate Questions' and 'Sexual Harassment,'" *PinkNews*, March 12, 2024, https://www.thepinknews.com/2024/03/12/asexual-spectrum-identities-yasmin-benoit/.

[b] Ibid.

[c] Yasmin Benoit, "Asexuals Need Media Representation," YouTube video, posted by TEDx Talks, March 25, 2021, https://www.youtube.com/watch?v=ifwRAT3DM2E&ab_channel=TEDxTalks.

Understanding the Role of Contributing Factors

A comprehensive understanding of why people commit gender violence involves exploring the complex, synergistic relationship among a gendered system, a culture of gender violence, and multiple overlapping contributors. Though all acts of gender violence share the same root causes, contributing factors help us acknowledge that every person who harms others may do so for a unique combination of reasons. Even two individuals who share the same gender, early experiences, and hardships may behave differently based on biological, psychological, cultural, social, and contextual factors. The interplay between multiple contributors is complex: gender violence is more likely to occur the more contributors are present, but possible contributors on their own do not make gender-violent behavior inevitable.

These contributors help us understand what may have led to an occurrence of gender violence and begin to predict when a person or group may be more likely to commit it. We can use this knowledge to help people who have experienced gender violence make sense of their experiences as well as provide better psychological treatment for those who commit it, more interventions into ongoing situations, and early identification of behavior that may be escalating toward harm. As biological research continues and new theories about human behavior continue to be examined in the social sciences, I hope others add to these contributors so we can respond to and prevent gender violence in more effective ways.

CHAPTER 9

Misperceptions about Gender Violence

In addition to the system of gender, culture of gender violence, and numerous contributing factors, pervasive misperceptions of the issue play a big role in maintaining cycles of gender violence. They distort the problem, oversimplify its causes, and misrepresent the people who commit it and those who are victimized. When believed by most of the public, they operate like grease on the hub of the wheel of gender violence, helping to power its root causes and contributors. Mistaken assumptions about gender violence perpetuate suspicion and hostility for people who disclose their experiences and lack of accountability for those who commit it and allow it to occur. When not corrected, these commonly held beliefs may be used by an abuser justifying their actions, a first responder refusing to believe a victim's story, a bystander deciding not to intervene, or someone blaming themselves for the violence that another person committed against them.

The misperceptions I examine in this chapter occur in everyday communication about gender violence, all of which I have witnessed throughout my professional and personal life. They may be expressed by someone discussing a situation learned from the news, believed by a friend of a victim, indirectly suggested by a medical professional, spread through social media by anonymous posters, implied by an attorney in legal proceedings, embraced by someone who has committed gender violence, or internalized by someone who has experienced abuse. We might even unintentionally contribute to these misperceptions in our gender violence prevention and response efforts when we avoid discussing tough realities or challenging mainstream beliefs. As you read this chapter, I encourage you to question your own previously held assumptions. When I began this work, there was a lot I didn't realize because I was socialized to believe certain "truths" about gender and unaware of how my racial, cisgender, and ability-based privilege affected how I viewed these issues. Even now, I am grateful to others who help me to continuously reflect on my own understanding.

The Problem of Gender Violence

Many people without an in-depth knowledge of gender violence may believe the problem is exaggerated. This often happens through public distrust of statistical data about victimization rates, strong adherence to an illusion of safety, or disdain for loud, confrontational social justice activists attempting to raise awareness. As you may have experienced reading the early chapters of this book, encountering the full reality of gender violence can be shocking and disorienting. Now imagine being faced with these issues for the first time through an angry social media post or group of shouting protestors. Many activists have learned that these strategies are often necessary for getting people's attention even though they may provoke defensiveness. After all, individual and collective anger are legitimate responses to gender violence, and their absence from the public sphere may actually indicate that a community, institution, or nation is in denial of the problem, ignorant that it exists, or effective in silencing people from speaking out. Even when gender violence does get discussed, its realities are often obscured by political power grabs, media spin, sophisticated cover-ups, and institutional image management.

Another common misperception is that gender violence is an issue women alone are responsible for addressing. Though women represent the largest global demographic affected by gender violence, to suggest it is a *women's* issue negates its profound impact on communities of color, LGBTIQA+ individuals, people with disabilities, Indigenous people, and other marginalized populations. It contributes to victim-blame by suggesting that women should be responsible for, or can be successful in, preventing the violence committed against them. This misperception also suggests that men are neither victims of gender violence nor the demographic primarily responsible for committing it. Gender violence is a human issue. All individuals may participate in social scripts and adhere to cultural beliefs that perpetuate oppression, inequality, and harmful gender dynamics, and all people are capable of committing or experiencing gender violence.

Many people underestimate the seriousness of individual acts of gender violence. Though some forms like homicide, crimes against children, acid attacks, and physically injurious forms of sexual and partner violence are usually deemed grave and legitimate by the general public, other forms tend to be more easily dismissed or minimized. Sex trafficking is often mistaken for consensual prostitution, and in either scenario sexual violence may be minimized and viewed as "just part of the job" for people who experience it—as if sex workers cannot be raped or are undeserving of bodily autonomy. Unfortunately, these views may be influenced by racist and classist attitudes toward people who are sex workers or victims of trafficking. Even sex trafficked teenagers are often treated with disdain and insensitivity.

It is common for sexual violence to be misconstrued as hesitant, obligatory, invited, or regretted sex. Contrary to historical belief, people in established or long-term relationships are neither required to provide sexual gratification to their partners nor are acts of sexual violence committed against them any less legitimate than when experienced by other people. Hesitant or obligatory sex may be assault if consent is not continuously discussed and obtained by the people involved. This is why an individual may appear by some to regret what happened when in actuality they never wanted it or stopped wanting it at a certain point. Ignoring a sexual partner's concerns, hesitations, or boundaries leads to sexual assault. Even invited sexual attention becomes assault when consent is not granted at each level of sexual interaction.

Street and sexual harassment are often misconstrued as harmless flirtation even though they may cause severe distress or fear for one's physical safety. Online harassment and nonconsensual distribution of sexual images are downplayed. Stalking is not often discussed as a serious crime, so it is common for people to believe it is a form of flattery. Teenagers or others unaware of its seriousness may be envious of those being stalked by a partner, spouse, or stranger if they mistake it for romantic flirting, sexy obsessiveness, or loving behavior. The same may be true for a dating or committed partner's verbal abuse and psychological manipulation; considered

Case Example

Who's That Girl Stalking Her Ex? It's Jess

New Girl is one of my favorite television sitcoms, but it's far from perfect. In the fifth season of the show, its writers focused an episode on Jess's relentless pursuit of her ex, Sam.[a] The name of the episode is "300 Feet"—the distance Jess must keep away from Sam after she is served a restraining order demanding she cease all contact with him. Jess is surprised and refuses to take the situation seriously. Despite loud encouragement from her friends to leave Sam alone, Jess writes Sam a letter, goes to his place of employment, spies on him in the parking lot, and hides in the back of his truck, which he drives through an automatic car wash. After being pummeled by the water sprays and rotating scrubbers, Jess throws herself onto the hood of Sam's car, terrifying him. Outside the car wash, Sam reiterates the presence of the restraining order to Jess. She makes a fool of herself, runs into a pole, and Sam reluctantly offers to give her a ride home out of pity. When Sam orders Jess out of the vehicle a few minutes later, Jess tells Sam he was right to take out a restraining order on her because ever since she saw him again she couldn't stop thinking about him. The music shifts, and all of a sudden Sam grabs Jess and kisses her. Later Sam tells Jess that the only reason he got the restraining order in the first place was because he couldn't stop thinking about *her*—romantic, right?

Not only does this episode fail to acknowledge stalking as a serious issue (Jess's behavior would meet the legal definition in many states across the United States), it also contributes to stereotypes about what stalking looks like and who can commit it. Jess herself states, "I'm not dangerous" and "I'm not a restraining order person," before continuing to cause Sam psychological distress. Jess's stalking of Sam and his need for protection from her are meant to be laughable, which is often the mainstream response to women stalking men.

[a] Sophia Lear, *New Girl*, season 5, episode 14, "300 Feet," directed by Trent O'Donnell, featuring Zooey Deschanel, David Walton, and Lamorne Morris, aired April 12, 2016, 20th Century Fox Television, video, 22:00.

in isolation by those outside the relationship, a partner's actions may be viewed as reasonably jealous, innocently overinvolved, or harmlessly overprotective when in fact the opposite is true.

Other forms of gender violence may not be considered serious or important if they are culturally sanctioned (like genital cutting or honor killings), influenced by tradition (like dowry-related violence or forced marriage), or committed against members of marginalized populations who are unreasonably expected to accept mistreatment by others as normal (like street harassment against transgender individuals or inadequate access to menstrual health care in prisons). Seemingly minor forms of gender violence like bullying or one-time discrimination may be minimized even though they could have unimaginable effects on those that experience them. Whatever the type of gender violence, when large numbers of the public believe these issues are exaggerated, that women alone should solve the problem, or something is only worthy of our attention when it happens in certain contexts or against certain groups of people, it becomes easy to dismiss the entirety of the problem.

The Causes of Gender Violence

Though they are incredibly common and statistically likely for a large number of the global population, acts of gender violence are often misunderstood as isolated and individual behaviors that represent an aberration from the everyday lived experiences of most people in a society. This framing directs attention away from the root causes of gender violence and subtly suggests that most people are safe unless they engage in risky behaviors. It leads many to view gender violence as inevitable or reactionary—as acts that can be justified or explained away with simple explanations. For example, people may believe that men rape and abuse women because that is their biological role. Phrases like "boys will be boys" and "man's role is to spread his seed" play into the idea that men and boys are naturally aggressive toward women. This is insulting to men, contributes to an assumption that all men are violent, and suggests that gender violence is inevitable. Similarly, the misconception that men cannot stop themselves from sexual gratification is biologically inaccurate and suggests that men are governed by animal instincts and don't possess the ability to control themselves. People may also believe that individuals only commit gender violence when they are provoked—like someone who physically assaults their partner as a response to something their spouse said or did, or a person who stalks a woman who initially expressed interest but then rejected their romantic advances. This belief contributes to a misperception that gender violence only happens under abnormal circumstances, or when a committer is not acting like themselves. People might also blame poorly managed anger, drug addiction, or mental illness. Though these issues can play a role in why someone commits gender violence, they should not be used to deflect attention away from the impact of a system of gender or multiple other contributors; these assumptions also draw from harmful stereotypes about people who experience addiction and mental illness.

Framing acts of gender violence as common, culturally sanctioned, and rooted in harmful gendered and systemic power dynamics means acknowledging the horrific reality of these issues and losing an illusion of safety from experiencing gender violence. It means viewing all genders of people as capable of committing it. It requires a refusal to accept gender violence as inevitable and a rejection of oversimplified reasons that people commit gender violence. It requires engaging the breadth and complexity of these issues despite the discomfort it may cause and labor it necessitates for effective prevention.

Who Commits Gender Violence

Most people are familiar with the stereotypical images of rapists, stalkers, abusers, murderers, and sex traffickers that lead to misperceptions about who commits gender violence. Attackers are often believed to be creepy strangers who hide in the bushes or jump out in dark alleys. They are depicted in various forms of media as dirty and disheveled and are usually of low income and have strange mannerisms that "give them away" as threats to public safety. This stereotype misleads people into believing they are most vulnerable to attack by people they don't know. Though gender violence may be committed by strangers, most of the time this is not the case. Researchers suggest that 80 to 90 percent of sexual assaults on women are committed by people they know;[1] in one study, 74 percent of rapes committed against men involved acquaintances or intimate partners, and 92 percent of women stalking victims and 85 percent of men victims were stalked by someone they knew.[2] From 2003 to 2014, 55 percent of homicides against women in the United States were connected to partner violence, over 90 percent of which involved current or former intimate partners.[3] Research shows that individuals are often sex trafficked by people known to them, like boyfriends or mothers, uncles, and husbands,[4] and that victims of honor killings are murdered by siblings, parents, husbands, or extended family.[5]

The pervasive idea of "stranger danger" suggests that gender violence can be avoided by using risk reduction and flagging potential perpetrators—the *stereotypical accused*. Poor and low-income individuals, people with neurological differences or mental illnesses, individuals considered unattractive by cultural standards, or people with mannerisms considered deviant or nonnormative are often stereotyped as dangerous without good reason. Attention is deflected from the myriads of people with power, wealth, and desirable personality and appearance traits who commit gender violence every day and use these qualities to groom others to trust them. Stranger danger minimizes the threat of friends, family members,

---

[1] Fischer, Cullen, and Turner, "Sexual Victimization"; Callie M. Rennison, "Criminal Victimization, 1998: Changes 1997–98 with Trends 1993–98," U.S. Department of Justice, August 1999, https://bjs.ojp.gov/content/pub/pdf/cv98.pdf; Lawrence A. Greenfeld, "Sex Offenses and Offenders: An Analysis of Data on Rape and Sexual Assault," U.S. Department of Justice, February 1997, https://bjs.ojp.gov/library/publications/sex-offenses-and-offenders-analysis-data-rape-and-sexual-assault.

[2] Matthew J. Breiding, Sharon G. Smith, Kathleen C. Basile, Mikel L. Walters, Jieru Chen, and Melissa T. Merrick, "Prevalence and Characteristics of Sexual Violence, Stalking, and Intimate Partner Violence Victimization—National Intimate Partner and Sexual Violence Survey, United States, 2011," Centers for Disease Control and Prevention, September 5, 2014, https://www.cdc.gov/mmwr/preview/mmwrhtml/ss6308a1.htm.

[3] Emiko Petrosky, Janet M. Blair, Carter J. Betz, Katherine A. Fowler, Shane P. D. Jack, and Bridget H. Lyons, "Racial and Ethnic Differences in Homicides of Adult Women and the Role of Intimate Partner Violence—United States, 2003–2014," Centers for Disease Control and Prevention, July 21, 2017, https://www.cdc.gov/mmwr/volumes/66/wr/mm6628a1.htm?s_cid=mm6628a1_w.

[4] Dominique E. Roe-Sepowitz, Kristine E. Hickle, Jaime Dahlstedt, and James Gallagher, "Victim or Whore: The Similarities and Differences between Victim's Experiences of Domestic Violence and Sex Trafficking," *Journal of Human Behavior in the Social Environment* 24, no. 8 (2014): 883–98, doi:10.1080/10911359.2013.840552.

[5] Cynthia Helba, Matthew Bernstein, Mariel Leonard, and Erin Bauer, "Report on Exploratory Study into Honor Violence Measurement Methods," Westat, November 2014, https://www.ojp.gov/pdffiles1/bjs/grants/248879.pdf.

partners, classmates, coworkers, and acquaintances, even though these individuals are the most common perpetrators. It also reinforces other systems of oppression.

Another misperception is that people of color are most likely to commit gender violence. Racial stereotypes play into this myth: political rhetoric, media coverage, and implicit bias contribute to hatred and fear of Black and Brown men assumed to be criminals. For Black men in the United States, stereotypes about their supposed sexual aggression can be linked to the Jim Crow era, in which White men falsely accused Black men of raping White women to justify lynchings.[6] The image of a pimp is associated with Black men even though sex traffickers are usually White men. Men of color in the United States are more likely to be profiled, arrested, and incarcerated than White men even though Black and Brown men don't commit more crimes.[7]

Gay men and transgender individuals also suffer from negative stereotypes suggesting they are more dangerous than heterosexual and cisgender people. Many educational messages to US children and families in the 1960s promoted the image of child molesters as gay men; though less pervasive today, this association still has negative effects. In the 2020s, researchers documented an upsurge of social media ads and posts demonizing drag queens and people identifying across the LGBTIQA+ spectrum by calling them predators and pedophiles who groom children.[8] Contemporary debates about public bathroom use are premised on the harmful stereotype that transgender individuals are sexual predators when they are actually more at risk themselves for discrimination, physical assault, and sexual violence in restrooms and dressing rooms than many cisgender people. This belief has also capitalized on stranger danger.

---

[6] Ida B. Wells-Barnett, "Southern Horrors: Lynch Law in All Its Phases," speech given at Lyric Hall in New York City on October 5, 1892, Iowa State University Archives of Women's Political Communication, https://awpc.cattcenter.iastate.edu/2020/09/21/southern-horrors-lynch-law-in-all-its-phases-oct-5-1892/.

[7] Michelle Alexander, *The New Jim Crow: Mass Incarceration in the Age of Colorblindness* (New York: New Press, 2010).

[8] Center for Countering Digital Hate and Human Rights Campaign, "Digital Hate: Social Media's Role in Amplifying Dangerous Lies about LGBTA+ People," 2022, https://hrc-prod-requests.s3-us-west-2.amazonaws.com/CCDH-HRC-Digital-Hate-Report-2022-single-pages.pdf.

The Stereotypes That Strengthened a Case

In the early 2010s, I worked at a rape crisis services agency in the Midwest. Among my coworkers, the elected state's attorney in my county was infamous for not prosecuting any sexual assault cases for something like a decade. One morning when I got to work, people were excited to share the news: the state's attorney had finally charged someone, and this demonstrated the progress we were making in our community. I rushed to read the story on the front page of my city's newspaper. A Black man was charged with sexually assaulting a young White woman, and they were unknown to each other. These factors—the race of the perpetrator, race of the victim, and fact it was an assault by a stranger—made the case one that fit a stereotype of how these crimes happen and was, as a result, more likely to end in a conviction. I felt conflicted. The criminal system was holding a predator accountable for his actions, but how many other White men had committed similar crimes without the same consequences? The county was seeking justice for a young White woman who had experienced something terrible, but how many women of color had come forward only to be met with disbelief or blamed for what happened?

People who do not fit the stereotypical image of someone who commits gender violence—the *nonstereotypical accused*—are more likely to provoke defensive reactions from partners, family members, friends, employers, fans, and followers when someone makes an allegation against them. They receive the benefit of the doubt because they don't fit the image of the stereotypical perpetrator. They inspire scrutiny and disbelief of their accusers. They are often portrayed positively in media and defended through arguments that their actions were provoked or the accuser is overreacting or lying. People and institutions may demonstrate support for them through social media posts, rallies, job promotion, and fundraising. The nonstereotypical accused and their supporters may take offensive measures to publicly discredit, silence, threaten, and attack an accuser through smear campaigns, nondisclosure agreements, defamation lawsuits, false reporting charges, or harassment. Even when it becomes clear to the general public that the nonstereotypical accused did commit gender violence, their actions are often framed as accidents and one-time events they just happened to "get swept up into." Supporters use surface-level explanations for their actions that negate their accountability and oversimply causes and contributors. Collective refusal to acknowledge the capability of the nonstereotypical accused to commit gender violence helps maintain a collective illusion of safety and perpetuate prejudicial bias against people who fit the predator stereotype.

The People Who Experience Gender Violence

In the general public, a *victim* of gender violence is often thought of as a young, White, cisheterosexual, traditionally feminine, conventionally attractive, middle- to upper-class woman. Though individuals who fit this image are certainly affected by gender violence, atrocities committed against them tend to receive far more news coverage than other demographics. They are more likely to be treated with care by first responders and viewed as credible witnesses in the US criminal system. They tend to invite more collective empathy and outrage than members of marginalized populations. In contrast, people perceived as "bad victims"—like women who are abrasive or argumentative, aggressive toward their abusers, don't conform to traditional gender roles, or who are women of color, lesbians, transgender, or sex workers—are more likely to be arrested and labeled as criminals.[9] Ableism, sizeism, ageism, and other systems of oppression contribute to the invisibility of many people's experiences to the extent that they may not be perceived to qualify as victims deserving of empathy, support, or justice. This helps to explain why law enforcement and prosecutors sometimes accuse victims of lying about the abuse they experienced.

Men and boys are often dismissed as potential victims, but for different reasons. When men are expected to exert masculinity through assertiveness, self-determination, and physical aggression, it can be difficult to imagine them in moments of vulnerability and weakness. Boys who experience sexual abuse as teenagers may be

---

[9] Goodmark, "Gender-Based Violence."

perceived as having enviable sexual prowess at a young age, or may feel pressured to reframe their experiences as empowering rather than risk a hit to their masculine image. People may mistakenly believe men are biologically incapable of being raped or physically abused—especially by women—even though men's musculature and body size vary and abuse may be verbal, psychological, drug facilitated, or occur in a variety of physical and sexual forms. When men and boys *are* deemed to be legitimate victims of gender violence, their cases are more likely to be sensationalized in media as particularly shocking and harrowing. Though it is important that these cases receive public attention, they often gain it because they defy stereotypical expectations as members of a dominant group, especially when they are White, cisheterosexual, middle to upper class, and conventionally attractive. As such, many men who speak publicly about their experiences of gender violence are often deemed more credible and heroic than women, people of color, or gender nonconforming individuals who come forward.

Even when individuals are believed to have experienced gender violence, they may be viewed as accessories to what happened to them through secretly desiring the behavior, provoking it, or not preventing or fleeing the situation. The argument that women secretly want to be raped or abused is sometimes used to exempt men from the responsibility of gaining consent or controlling their actions. No one wants to be in a situation in which they have no control and are being harmed by another person. Anyone's desire for sexual attention, expression of sexuality, assertion of independence, or engagement in seemingly "risky" behaviors is never a justification for abuse. Individuals who flirt, dress to attract attention, frequent bars and parties, use drugs, travel alone, out themselves as LGBTIQA+, or make decisions to kiss or have sex should not be blamed for someone else's violent actions against them.

It is important to distinguish provocation of abuse with consensual erotic practices, kink, and roleplay like bondage/discipline/sadomasochism (BDSM) in which all parties explicitly negotiate permission and enforce respectful boundaries.[10] Though power differences are central in the roles people may take on in these

---

[10] Mika Galilee-Belfer, "BDSM, Kink, and Consent: What the Law Can Learn from Consent-Driven Communities," *Arizona Law Review* 62, no. 2 (2020): 507–38, https://arizonalawreview.org/pdf/62-2/62arizlrev507.pdf.

interactions, like being a submissive (agreeing to give up control in an activity, scene, or relationship), consent is a central tenet and details of interactions are often heavily negotiated and detailed.[11] Guidelines for consent in BDSM communities are actually often clearer and more useful than those found in US state laws.[12] Still, consent to kink and roleplay does not justify engagement in anything to which an individual has not explicitly given permission—those actions would be considered stalking, harassment, or assault.

The cultural impulse to hold victims of gender violence responsible for what happened is often so strong that their own natural and traumatic reactions to abuse get used against them. Victims are often expected to resist or fight their attackers, vocalize their rejection of permission, flee the situation immediately, report what happened to authorities, and react in stereotypical ways. If they don't, these behaviors may be used by others in attempts to discredit them or minimize the harm they experienced. People may offer less empathy to victims who don't cry or act weak. They may view people who didn't flee as exaggerating situations even though research shows that trying to leave can be incredibly dangerous: women abused by their partners may face a high risk of homicide when leaving,[13] and common barriers to escaping a sex trafficker are physical and sexual violence and threats of violence against them and their loved ones.[14] The dynamics of sexual violence are often so misunderstood that victims may be blamed for not fighting back "hard enough" against attackers even when they were coerced by someone they trusted, caught off guard by what happened, or intentionally passive to avoid further violence. Even misperceptions about genital arousal and pregnancy are sometimes used to suggest an individual in some way wanted the violence that happened to them. Though arousal can occur in moments of nonconsensual contact and individuals can become pregnant after rape, neither should be used to suggest permission for someone else's abuse.

---

[11] Ibid., 509–10.

[12] Ibid., 523.

[13] Jacquelyn C. Campbell et al., "Risk Factors for Femicide in Abusive Relationships: Results from a Multisite Case Control Study," *American Journal of Public Health* 93, no. 7 (2003): 1089–97, doi:10.2105/AJPH.93.7.1089.

[14] Rebecca Pfeffer, Kelle Barrick, and Terri Galvan, "Barriers and Facilitators to Leaving a Trafficker: A Qualitative Analysis of the Accounts of People Who Have Experienced Sex Trafficking," *Victims & Offenders* (2023): 1–20, doi:10.1080/15564886.2023.2214814.

Paradoxically, many people who fight back against their attackers also face intense scrutiny, especially if they cause injury or fatal harm. Individuals who lash out verbally or physically against abusive partners may be gaslit into believing they too are abusive or judged by the general public as participating in a "mutually abusive" relationship even though their partner clearly holds the power and control. Some people exercise the limited power they have in a relationship with an abuser, harasser, or trafficker by angering them at particular times in order to suffer less physical harm or shorten its duration, keep others from finding out, or protect their children; they may be misjudged by others as instigators. People who threaten violence, defend themselves with weapons like guns and knives, or use violence as a way to escape may be misperceived as overreacting or having ulterior motives even when they fear for their lives. If they seriously injure or kill their attackers—or even threaten to do so—they may be charged with crimes and incarcerated, especially if they are Black women. Cyntoia Brown-Long was tried as an adult and incarcerated for fifteen years after killing a man who bought her for sex despite the fact she was sixteen and trapped in the sex trafficking industry.[15] Marissa Alexander was incarcerated for three years after firing a gun into the air as a warning shot against her abusive partner.[16] And CeCe McDonald served nineteen months in a men's prison for defending herself against a racist and transphobic attack.[17] Without an understanding of the effects of gender violence and compounded trauma, people outside these situations may not view these individuals as victims. It is also possible for police, juries, or others involved in the criminal system not to pick up on signs of gender violence, making it difficult to identify when defendants have acted in self-defense.[18] Unfortunately, all of these misperceptions are common among people who don't fit the stereotypical image of a "good" victim.

---

[15] Simon & Schuster, "Cyntoia Brown-Long," 2024, https://www.simonandschuster.net/authors/Cyntoia-Brown-Long/166812568.

[16] Zerlina Maxwell, "How Stand Your Ground Laws Failed Marissa Alexander," *Essence*, October 27, 2020, https://www.essence.com/news/how-stand-your-ground-laws-failed-marissa-alexander/.

[17] National LGBTQ Task Force, "CeCe McDonald Released from Prison," January 13, 2014, https://www.thetaskforce.org/news/cece-mcdonald-released-from-prison/.

[18] Melissa E. Dichter, "Women's Experiences of Abuse as a Risk Factor for Incarceration: A Research Update," VAWnet, July 2015, https://vawnet.org/sites/default/files/materials/files/2016-09/AR_IncarcerationUpdate.pdf.

Whatever gender violence they have experienced, if individuals *are* able to prove victimization or demonstrate enough credibility to invite empathy from others, they often then face a set of expectations for performing the role of a brave but simultaneously broken hero: a survivor. This role equates victimization with damage that requires healing, usually with the assistance of mental health professionals. *Survivors* may feel pressure to demonstrate they have recovered, perform empowerment, and speak publicly about their experience for therapeutic benefit—and in doing all of these things successfully, risk their entire identities being subsumed by that label. Though some individuals who experience gender violence embrace and draw strength from the label, *compulsory survivorship* suggests that all people should react to and move forward from these experiences in the same way, regardless of cultural background.[19]

Being a "good" survivor often involves White and middle- to upper-class expectations of behavior, including reporting to authorities and seeking help through the mental health system. Individuals who do not do so, or who struggle to move forward even with support and avenues for justice, may be viewed as obstacles to their own healing. "Good" survivors find ways to regain an appearance of normalcy in their lives. They do not use unhealthy coping strategies like drug use, casual sex, or other behaviors perceived as irresponsible and do not end up unemployed, food or housing insecure, or struggling with addiction; they do not remain damaged. Many people don't feel comfortable claiming the *survivor* label in the first place. Because the language suggests enduring a life-threatening situation, it's not inclusive of all experiences of gender violence. Unfortunately, the result of all these expectations is that certain types of individuals receive more visibility, support, and justice than others.

Disclosing Gender Violence to Others

When navigating the aftermath of gender violence, people already face a variety of challenges that affects their willingness to disclose

---

[19] Jennifer L. Freitag, "Four Transgressive Declarations for Ending Gender Violence," in *Transgressing Feminist Theory and Discourse*, ed. Jennifer Dunn and Jimmie Manning (London: Routledge, 2018), 134–50.

what happened to others. The extent to which they defy stereotypical expectations, are perceived as responsible for what happened to them, or fail to perform successful survivorship can increase the risks they face in disclosure. These risks are exacerbated by misperceptions about the problem of gender violence, its causes, and who commits it. Together, all of these issues influence what anyone may believe about a victim's motivations for telling others what happened.

To start, disclosures of gender violence are often met with skepticism and disbelief. People who witness disclosures may believe that victims are exaggerating what happened or reframing the situation to cast blame on someone else for behavior they regret. They might mistakenly assume that victims are simply seeking attention or money—these reactions presume that people who make disclosures are guilty, manipulative, and deceitful. Many people who report their experiences to police, employers, campus administrators, or journalists or share what happened on websites and social media platforms seek some combination of visibility, justice, connection, social change, or safety for themselves or others. In doing so, however, they may find themselves the targets of social ostracization, public scrutiny, or backlash that changes their personal relationships, social lives, employment, and economic situations. They may lose friends and partners, be treated poorly by family, get harassed by acquaintances, sacrifice their anonymity, lose their privacy, risk their job security, or be shamed by media. They may be doxed, threatened, or stalked if they claim harm or abuse against someone with power, influence, or popularity—especially if their allegation involves the nonstereotypical accused. Those who support victims of public disclosures may also experience negative ramifications, making it difficult for any demands for accountability to be heard and considered by the public.

Sometimes people may doubt the credibility of a person's disclosure because of when they report what happened. People may suspect a situation is not serious if it is not reported right away, or at all. They might not realize it is common for individuals to hesitate or resist reporting to authorities for fear of not being believed, not wanting to get the person who attacked them in trouble, experiencing retaliatory violence, or being charged with false reporting.

They may not want to relive the experience while telling their story multiple times in detail to law enforcement officers, investigators, lawyers, campus hearing boards, judges, medical personnel, and journalists—doing so can be emotionally draining as well as trigger flashbacks and acute physical reactions to their trauma. They also might be in shock or denial, not recognize what happened as violent behavior, blame themselves for the situation, or in some circumstances not remember what happened at all. People who do not immediately make disclosures but do so later are often accused of lying, engaging in blackmail, trying to sabotage an attacker's career, or being pawns in someone else's ideological or political agenda. In reality, they may need time to decide how they wish to move forward after experiencing gender violence for their own well-being. It may take them years or decades to process what happened to them. They may become motivated to come forward when they realize others have accused the same person of violence, statute of limitations laws change, or the accused applies for a promotion, seeks an electable office, or grows in popularity and success at the expense of others.

People may view a victim's disclosure as suspect because of how they narrate what happened. If they don't show stereotypical signs of emotional distress and psychological harm, they may be immediately discounted. If they cannot remember what happened, only recall things in bits and pieces, or misremember events out of order, people might think they are being dishonest and intentionally misleading. If they suddenly remember details or recall an entire experience after years of complete repression, people may question the accuracy of their account. Suspicion of victims in these circumstances reflects a lack of knowledge about common reactions to gender violence as well as the impact of trauma on the brain. First responders, investigators, and loved ones may require that victims corroborate their stories with physical evidence or witnesses in order for them to be taken seriously. This may be impossible when the violence is verbal and psychological; it may also be difficult in situations in which a harasser deletes their social media account, a stalker only makes contact when there is no one around, an abuser hurts them in ways that will not be visible to others, or an attacker uses a condom. Bodily physical evidence may be gathered in some instances of gender violence that are injurious or sexually invasive, but in order for it to be useful in a court of law, it usually needs to be collected immediately by a trained forensic professional. If a person uses the bathroom, eats, drinks, showers, or changes clothes—all normal things someone might do in the hours or days following an attack—evidence may be lost.

The content of a disclosure may also be judged, especially if a victim cannot remember details or intentionally withholds certain information. They may be afraid to expose their attacker if they have been threatened or if their abuser is someone others may not believe could be capable of gender violence. If the attacker is a member of a traditionally marginalized population, they may not want to subject them to a racist, classist, heterosexist, transphobic, or otherwise oppressive judicial process. A victim might not disclose certain aspects of a situation because they themselves are members of an oppressed group and fear mistreatment; they may be attempting to maintain safety or privacy on behalf of someone else. People might believe that disclosing certain details will get them in trouble with significant others, parents, or friends: a spouse may be hesitant to disclose they were having an affair, a daughter might not want to out herself as bisexual to homophobic family members, a teen might not want parents to discover they are sexually active. They might also be trying to hide illegal or prohibited behavior like drug or alcohol use. Even if victims' accounts are missing information or contain inconsistencies, it is presumptive for others to dismiss their experiences of violence on those grounds alone. Victims often negotiate complex social, cultural, professional, and personal variables as they decide what details to disclose to others.

It is common for the general public to believe that when someone recants or changes their story, it is because it wasn't true or they were exaggerating. In actuality, victims may take back their stories due to negative reactions they receive from loved ones, first responders, or investigators. They may deny what happened as a way to decline participation in adjudication processes or because they are struggling to regain normalcy in their lives. They may recant because they have been pressured by others to do so. In many instances, victims sign official documents testifying they were mistaken about what happened after being threatened by abusive partners, employers, or law enforcement. Victims may also be persuaded or coerced to sign nondisclosure agreements that prevent them from speaking publicly about what happened.

Whatever form it takes, automatically presuming that people who make disclosures of gender violence are dishonest, manipulative, or opportunistic is harmful and unfair—especially considering the challenges they often encounter after sharing. Knee-jerk suspicion suggests more about the threat victims pose to the nonstereotypical accused and the maintenance of a culture of gender violence than the reliability of their accounts. This is not to suggest, however, that disclosures can never be fabrications. False accusations do occur, but not at the high rates or for the reasons the general public is misled to believe. Among the various types of gender violence, it is often believed that people lie about being sexually assaulted the most. In reality, FBI statistics and documented research proves that false accusations do not occur any more for rape than those for other crimes—between 2 and 10 percent of the time.[20] These numbers, however, do not often distinguish between findings of false accusation and unsubstantiated cases that lack certain types of evidence important for successful prosecution, even with credible victim testimony. Not advertising these details contributes to a skewed view of the frequency of gender violence and an unreasonable public standard of victim believability that mirrors that of a criminal court of law. For example, many universities' published crime rates omit the total number of reports of gender violence made by students and staff and only include cases that have been investigated and substantiated. This is misleading and conceals any institutional negligence in handling cases.

False accusations work against the respect and support victims deserve when they share their experiences with others. It is troubling to consider that anyone would lie about experiencing gender violence, but those who are able to do so without detection likely have a good amount of social standing, public influence, or privilege. Motivated by malice, personal revenge, prejudice, or a variety of other factors, they may communicate false accusations to social groups, communities, or institutions. When accusers are members

---

[20] National Sexual Violence Resource Center, "False Reporting Overview," 2012, https://www.nsvrc.org/publications/false-reporting-overview.

of dominant groups with more power than those they accuse, they are more likely to mobilize support from others. People of color, LGBTIQA+ individuals, immigrants, and people who belong to other marginalized groups have endured a history of harmful stereotypes, unfounded suspicion, and false accusations that have resulted in lynchings, hate crimes, deportation, harassment, loss of employment, and incarceration for crimes they didn't commit.

False accusations may also be made by people actively abusing others. Research shows that men who abuse women may preemptively report to police they have experienced assault by their partner in order to destroy their partner's credibility and maintain power and control. They may injure themselves and claim their partner harmed them, tell police their partner is the primary aggressor, exploit an abused partner's distressed and traumatized state to convince others she is aggressive or mentally unstable, or use her immigration status or cultural differences to increase her vulnerability.[21] In these situations, women experiencing abuse may be convinced to plead guilty to an abuse charge, especially if they have little experience with the criminal system or fear worse outcomes from the case going to trial.[22]

Navigating Complexities

Enduring misperceptions about gender violence contribute to stereotyping, surface-level understanding, and silence about these issues. In a culture of gender violence, these misperceptions create a fog of complexity that can make it hard to pinpoint exactly how to make sense of a given situation. Unless you have encountered the terrain before, finding your way through the fog can be difficult. When reflecting on someone's act of gender violence requires taking on the discomfort of a shattered illusion of safety or the racist history of false accusations, it can be much easier to disengage. Unfortunately, others are affected by these complexities whether we acknowledge them or not. Many cases that seem clear-cut are likely that way only because they fit assumptions we have been socialized not to question, like stranger danger or the stereotypical

---

[21] Dichter, "Women's Experiences of Abuse."
[22] Ibid.

predator profile shaped by classism and ableism. When account-ability prevails or systems seem to work in favor of someone who has experienced gender violence, we should ask why and highlight those factors as we continue to seek justice and safety for others who face way more challenges in being heard, believed, or pro-tected from violence.

We can light paths through the fog. We can be the ones who expose the realities of gender violence and demonstrate unflinching support for those bold enough to call others out for what they have done—especially when the people speaking up don't fit the histori-cal mold of being a "good" victim or survivor. We must reverse misperceptions about how people share their experiences while remaining diligent about the power accusations can have when they are not made in earnest. If we are not engaging complexities like this through our educational programs, professional trainings, and awareness-raising campaigns, who will?

After more than two decades in gender violence prevention and response, it is here that I've seen the most individuals and organizations get stuck. In a world of bite-size social media posts and clickbait headlines, it's difficult to facilitate in-depth discus-sions about anything, let alone the complexities of a massive global issue that many people have been culturally conditioned to ignore. If you are unsure about how to move forward, start by listening to activists and experts already leading this charge, many of whom are people of color, Indigenous people, LGBTIQA+ individuals, and people with disabilities who've been leading these conversations for decades. Seek guidance from experts in interpersonal communica-tion, dialogue facilitation, public speaking, and marketing. Keep listening, self-reflecting, and persevering; new complexities are inevitable as the movement to end gender violence evolves.

CHAPTER 10

Applying a Comprehensive Approach

The problem of gender violence is massive, complex, part of our everyday lives, and interwoven with other systems of oppression. When we examine it using a comprehensive framework, we acknowledge that all forms of gender violence share the same root causes and contributors, affect individuals similarly, and contribute to unimaginable collective impact. The system of gender, culture of gender violence, and widespread misperceptions about these issues keep cycles of gender violence in place. So what now?

To start, we can develop a greater vigilance for identifying when gender violence may have occurred and the conditions that make it more likely. This will increase early detection and help us intervene in its cultural acceptance more effectively. Next, we can consider what this approach means for how we support people affected by gender violence, especially those who belong to marginalized groups. We can rethink our policies and procedures for justice and accountability and imagine different ways forward that are more effective, less discriminatory, and more likely to create safety for everyone. We can collaborate more and take actions to improve the sustainability of our efforts over time.

The ideas I offer in this chapter are starting points meant to invite further discussion beyond the pages of this book. If you are new to learning about gender violence, I hope they help you feel out ways you can get involved in helping to end it. If you work in prevention and response, perhaps they will inspire changes in how you communicate about gender violence, provide services, or engage in strategic planning. To legislators, stakeholders, journalists, and leaders: this chapter merely scrapes the surface of what's next in this movement. Reach out to gender violence experts, organizations, and researchers for more insight—especially those working at the intersections of gender violence and other systems of oppression. To anyone personally affected by these issues, be encouraged. We've got a lot of work to do, but we're improving. Keep telling us how to do better.

Indicators of Gender Violence

Being attentive to indicators of gender violence can increase early detection and lead to earlier and more effective intervention and response. This could mean more immediate support and assistance is provided after someone experiences gender violence, or that individuals who experience it do so for a shorter duration or with less severity or compounded trauma. It could improve intervention in someone's patterns of abusive behavior early in life before they do further damage to others, and it could help us recognize the potential for committing gender violence early enough that abuse of others never occurs. It could also mean more interruption in group dynamics and institutional climates that contribute to the acceptance of gender violence.

Signs That Someone May Have Experienced It

Because gender violence is still often shrouded in a veil of secrecy, people who experience it may not disclose to others. Even so, there may be indicators that someone is experiencing its effects. Pay attention to sudden behavioral shifts. Remember that although everyone reacts to gender violence differently, it is the deviations from normal behavior that may offer clues that something is wrong. Those in close relationship with someone might notice subtle changes in stress level, communication, priorities, daily routines, and coping mechanisms. They might pick up on vague or indirect references to something that happened, increased secrecy around a person or situation, or out-of-the-ordinary defensiveness when questions are asked. But even if we never learn about gender violence happening to those around us, we can still facilitate conversations about it and let others know they will have our support if they ever experience gender violence.

Crisis workers, first responders, health-care providers, educators, and others should receive training to identify signs of gender violence among their clients, patients, and students. Police officers, attorneys, and campus officials can use these indicators to build better cases against attackers. Training should cover common reactions, effects of trauma, and misperceptions about gender violence. Extra attention should be paid to indicators of gender violence among members of groups at the highest risk of experiencing it. This means requiring training on aspects of cultural difference and interruption of prejudicial attitudes that contribute to barriers to accessing safety and accountability.

Additional Information

How to Help Someone Who Has Experienced Gender Violence

Supporting someone after their experience of gender violence can feel intimidating, especially if you are new to learning about these issues. Here are some general guidelines to help you assist them. Consider this list a starting point: depending on your relationship and where and when the incident occurred, you may need to take additional actions or adapt your communication.

1. **Assess Safety:** Ask about their safety, then help them seek medical care or get to a safe location if needed. Assist them in making a plan to get or stay safe over the next few hours or days.
2. **Listen:** Use active listening and supportive communication behaviors, allow them to share as much or little as they want at their own pace, and only ask questions important for assessing safety or other concerns that they identify.
3. **Support:** Validate their disclosure with phrases like "Thank you for sharing" and "I believe you," assure them their response to the situation is normal, tell them what happened is not their fault, and avoid making assumptions about their experience.
4. **Provide Options:** Share whatever you can about options for getting additional help and support. If you don't know the answer to something, do online research, call a hotline, or ask about resources from a trusted individual or organization.

5. **Respect Decisions:** Unless a situation requires immediate medical treatment, avoid pressuring them to make any quick or specific decisions. Respect their right to do or not do certain things (like share about the experience with others or report to authorities), and assist them with following through on their decisions (like offering to sit with them when they call a friend or family member).

6. **Maintain Privacy:** Do not share their disclosure with others unless you have permission to do so or they are in danger of hurting themselves or someone else.

7. **Engage in Self-Care:** Responding to a disclosure can be stressful and upsetting, so it is important for you to engage in self-supportive actions that might include talking to a counselor or trusted confidant. Just be sure not to share identifiable details with others.

8. **Follow Up:** Check in on them in the hours or days following their disclosure, and if necessary, work through this list again.

Signs That Someone May Have Committed It

We know that people who commit gender violence are likely to have rigid gender expectations for themselves and others, and that lifelong exposure to the cultural acceptance of gender violence through institutions like media and family can contribute to harmful behavior. We also know that multiple contributing factors—like a difficult childhood, underdeveloped coping skills, and entitlement—along with opportunity—may make someone more likely to commit gender violence, especially if they are a man. We must become more attentive to combinations of these contributors, especially among the nonstereotypical accused. This means confronting our own stereotypical thinking and becoming more cautious of any communication by people with power, privilege, and influence that could be used to groom others. When we reject the illusion of safety and pay more attention to these signs, we are more likely to detect potential instances of gender violence or ongoing harm more effectively. Use this awareness to intervene in rigid gender role adherence or prejudicial attitudes about women, LGBTIQA+ individuals, or others before they influence lifelong patterns of behavior. Especially among kids and adolescents, start early to better identify when multiple factors might be increasing someone's likelihood to harm someone—then provide better role models, social and emotional skill development, sex-positive education, help for struggling parents, or other supports that take some of these potential contributors out of play. Demand education on these signs for teachers, childcare workers, social service agencies, and mental health professionals to facilitate early intervention; demand training for law enforcement, Title IX officers, adjudicators, and human resources staff to improve investigations.

Signs That Groups and Institutions May Be Actively Contributing to It

Institutions and groups that encourage rigid gender roles and status quo acceptance of gender violence are more likely to engage in stereotyping, silencing, and victim-blaming when instances of gender violence occur. The same is likely true of organizations and networks that respond negatively when called out for contributing to problems. Institutions with hierarchical power structures, lack of (gender, sexual, racial, and other) diversity in leadership, and reliance on fear-based compliance are more likely to protect certain members from accountability or fail to implement procedures for effective prevention and response. Building cultural environments that appreciate gender and sexual diversity, advocate for equity across these differences, and actively reject a culture of gender violence takes intentional and consistent effort over a sustained period of time. When these actions are absent, it is much more likely that gender violence is happening than not. Institutions unwilling to engage in honest and critical discussion about gender violence contribute to its acceptance by default. Organizations unwilling to explore the realities of prejudice and discrimination for specific cultural groups contribute to the acceptance of gender violence committed against individuals who belong to those groups.

Some institutions may develop laws, policies, and procedures that seem to reject a culture of gender violence but continue to disempower those who experience it and protect those who hurt them. I can tell you from my work that this is happening everywhere—in higher education, the criminal system, K–12 school districts, corporations, nonprofit organizations, and the military—whether or not most people hear about it. Expect more from leadership than one-time actions that don't address acceptance of gender violence over time; critically analyze institutional messaging that prioritizes image management over accountability and safety. Leave groups that threaten discipline or violence against those who call out members for gender-violent behavior. Demand transparency, create task forces, hold teach-ins, fund trainings, organize boycotts, and support people spearheading efforts to make change.

Support for People Who Have Experienced Gender Violence

A comprehensive understanding of gender violence makes it imperative for us to support those affected by these issues with more commitment and compassion than ever before. Provision of crisis services must be made accessible to people of all gender identities and sexual orientations; our adherence to assistance premised on a gender binary excludes many individuals seeking support and ultimately reinforces the root causes of gender violence. Prioritize assistance for vulnerable populations who face culturally specific challenges in receiving help and navigating reporting and adjudication processes. Put in the work to better understand the challenges involved in intersections of various identities with gender violence.

On an interpersonal level, communication with people who have experienced gender violence needs to involve validation and respect. We must acknowledge a large diversity of reactions and how they relate to disclosure. Because these individuals often face overwhelming barriers to being believed, we should lead the charge in correcting misperceptions about their credibility. Continue emphasizing the importance of their agency in deciding whether or not to report to authorities or pursue various forms of justice. Reject compulsory survivorship, and be mindful of the language you use to describe people who have experienced gender violence and how they move forward in its aftermath.

On a community level, we can support people who publicly disclose their experiences. Amplify their voices, and discourage automatic skepticism of their accounts. Help other individuals and communities navigate the shock, frustration, anger, and devastation that accompany increased awareness about the reality of gender violence, and participate in dialogue that engages its complexities. We can be a collective voice for accountability. We can point out when prejudice is likely playing a role in disbelief and victim-blame. The same is true at the institutional level. Advocate for better training, laws, policies, and practices that support people who share about what happened to them. Pressure lawmakers to increase funding for crisis advocacy. Support more ways for people to access fully confidential support. Confront leaders who shame victims.

Accountability, Justice, and Safety

When it comes to accountability, justice, and safety in our communities and institutions, we need to explore avenues that address the limitations and failures of our current approaches, the relationship between individual behavior and institutional culpability, and the unequal distribution of punishment due to systemic oppression. Many of the reasons people don't report their experiences is because the psychological, physical, and economic costs often profoundly outweigh the likelihood of accountability. Even when institutions do acknowledge the wrongdoing of one of their members, they often spare them from harsh consequences and fail to prioritize the safety of victims and other members—especially if allegations involve the nonstereotypical accused.

Lack of consultation with people who have experienced gender violence firsthand may lead to group or institutional actions that increase immediate danger. Mere appearance of accountability can create more dangerous environments by contributing to a committer's perception of entitlement and everyone else's illusion of regained safety. Disproportionate accountability for marginalized populations in the criminal system makes Black and Brown men, LGBTIQA+ individuals, and people lacking the privilege and resources to successfully defend themselves bear the brunt of collective fear, anger, and justice seeking. This reiterates misperceptions about people who commit gender violence, contributes to apathy about false accusations against members of these populations, and decreases empathy for those who are punished for engaging in self-defense. All of this leads to higher numbers of people of color being exploited through prison labor—what scholar and activist

Angela Davis refers to as constitutional slavery—and put to death through capital punishment.[1] To top it all off, the consensus among researchers is that imprisonment doesn't deter crime;[2] it may actually contribute to higher levels of re-offense, especially when prison environments are threatening and violent.[3] Rehabilitation programs for sex offenders and people who have abused their partners may reduce recidivism for some incarcerated individuals, but on the whole research shows they are not super effective either.[4]

For these reasons, we need transformational strategies for responding to gender violence. Laws and policies on their own are not the answer, though repeals and updates are necessary. Advocate for these changes in consultation with gender violence experts using an intersectional approach. Demand trauma-informed investigatory procedures and mandatory training for anyone involved in disciplinary processes. Replace public relations strategies that defend institutional image with acknowledgment of problems and commitments to future safety backed up by actual change. Work with researchers to improve rehabilitation programs, and ask deeper questions about what justice—across all forms of cultural difference—really looks like. Explore ideas generated from the field of critical race feminism[5] and learn about comprehensive approaches to criminal sentencing,[6] race-informed approaches to partner violence laws,[7] and informal adjudication like Navajo

---

[1] Angela Y. Davis, *Are Prisons Obsolete?* (New York: Seven Stories Press, 2003).

[2] Damon M. Petrich, Travis C. Pratt, Cheryl Lero Jonson, and Francis T. Cullen, "Custodial Sanctions and Reoffending: A Meta-analytic Review," *Crime and Justice: A Review of Research* 50 (2021): 353–424, doi:10.1086/715100.

[3] Shelley Johnson Listwan, Christopher J. Sullivan, Robert Agnew, Francis T. Cullen, and Mark Colvin, "The Pains of Imprisonment Revisited: The Impact of Strain on Inmate Recidivism," *Justice Quarterly* 30, no. 1 (2013): 144–68, doi:10.1080/07418825.2011.597772.

[4] Ibid.; Roger Przybylski, "The Effectiveness of Treatment for Adult Sexual Offenders," Sex Offender Management Assessment and Planning Initiative, U.S. Department of Justice, July 2015, https://smart.ojp.gov/sites/g/files/xyckuh231/files/media/document/theeffectiv enessoftreatmentforadultsexualoffenders.pdf; Larry Bennett and Oliver Williams, "Controversies and Recent Studies of Batterer Intervention Program Effectiveness," VAWnet, August 2001, https://vawnet.org/material/controversies-and-recent-studies-batterer-intervention-program-effectiveness.

[5] Adrien K. Wing, ed., *Critical Race Feminism: A Reader* (New York: New York University Press, 2003).

[6] Paula C. Johnson, "At the Intersection of Injustice: Experiences of African American Women in Crime and Sentencing," in Wing, *Critical Race Feminism*, 209–16.

[7] Ammons, "Mules, Madonnas, Babies."

Case Example

Activist Successes in Athletics

Many changes in US and international sports have been catalyzed by the efforts of women and LGBTIQA+ athletes who have fought gender discrimination. Here are a few successes to celebrate: Tennis player Billie Jean King protested gender differences in pay and succeeded in establishing equal prize money for women at the US Open.[a] Gymnast Simone Biles called out USA Gymnastics and the US Olympic and Paralympic Committee for enabling sexual abuse,[b] then later inspired national conversations about athletes' mental health.[c] Runner Caster Semenya won an appeal in the European Court of Human Rights for discrimination related to testosterone testing, opening the door for other athletes who have DSD (differences of sex development) or are intersex to challenge similar restrictions.[d] Runner Allyson Felix spoke out about the lack of maternity protections from a former high-profile sponsor, prompting them to update their policy.[e] College basketball player Sedona Prince used social media to highlight gender disparity in NCAA tournament weight rooms, prompting a gender equity review and multiple changes.[f] Duathlon competitor Chris Mosier helped to create and pass improved International Olympic Committee guidelines for transgender athletes.[g] US Women's National Soccer Team players sued the US Soccer Federation for discriminatory pay and working conditions and reached a settlement that included back pay and a commitment to equal pay at the World Cup.[h]

[a] Liz Robbins, "Fifty Years Ago, Billie Jean King Won Equal Pay—but She's Not Done Yet," *New York Times*, July 15, 2023, https://www.nytimes.com/2023/07/15/sports/tennis/billie -jean-king-us-open-equal-pay.html.

[b] Michael Shapiro, "Simone Biles: USA Gymnastics 'Enabled and Perpetrated' Larry Nassar Abuse," *Sports Illustrated*, September 15, 2021, https://www.si.com/more-sports/2021 /09/15/simone-biles-larry-nassar-hearing-usa-gymnastics-enabled-abuse.

[c] Alice Park, "How the Tokyo Olympics Changed the Conversation about Athletes' Mental Health," *Time*, August 8, 2021, https://time.com/6088078/mental-health-olympics-simone -biles/.

[d] Karleigh Webb, "Caster Semenya Wins Appeal in European Court of Human Rights," *OutSports*, July 12, 2023, https://www.outsports.com/2023/7/12/23791579/track-and -field-semenya-echr-appeal-switzerland-world-athletics/.

[e] Allyson Felix, "My Own Nike Pregnancy Story," *New York Times*, May 22, 2019, https:// www.nytimes.com/2019/05/22/opinion/allyson-felix-pregnancy-nike.html.

f Amelia Nierenberg, "The Video That Changed the N.C.A.A.," *New York Times*, March 15, 2022, https://www.nytimes.com/2022/03/16/us/the-video-that-changed-the-ncaa.html.

g Scott Gleason, "Transgender Athlete Chris Mosier Worries about Competing in North Carolina," *USA Today*, April 27, 2016, https://www.usatoday.com/story/sports/olympics/2016/04/27/transgender-duathlon-chris-mosier-hb2-law-national-championships-north-carolina/83435260/.

h Analisa Novak, "Megan Rapino and Alex Morgon on $24 Million Settlement with U.S. Soccer Federation: 'It's Equal Pay from Here on Out,'" *CBS News*, February 22, 2022, https://www.cbsnews.com/news/womens-soccer-megan-rapinoe-alex-morgan-uswnt-settlement/.

peacemaking.[8] Get loud about victims who are prosecuted for defending themselves. Develop community-based alternatives to law enforcement to shift reliance away from police and prisons for solving the problem of gender violence.[9] Learn more about prison abolition, the decriminalization of sex work, restorative justice frameworks, and new approaches to dismantling cycles of injustice against marginalized populations that can radically transform how we respond to gender violence.[10]

Gender Violence Prevention

The problem of gender violence requires prevention efforts that respond to its enormity and complexity with rigor and skill. This means stopping the problem before it starts through awareness raising and education. For effective awareness raising, find ways to communicate the pervasiveness and impact of gender violence—especially across cultural differences—to others in ways that necessitate immediate response. Focus on widespread victimization caused by all forms of gender violence to make a powerful argument in marketing campaigns, social media activism, protests, art projects, and everyday conversation that is impossible for others to ignore. In educational efforts, prioritize addressing the root causes and contributors of all forms of gender violence rather than isolating discussion to singular types. Always start with gender

---

[8] Donna Coker, "Enhancing Autonomy for Battered Women: Lessons from Navajo Peacemaking," in Wing, *Critical Race Feminism*, 287–97.

[9] Critical Resistance and INCITE!, "Critical Resistance-INCITE! Statement on Gender Violence and the Prison-Industrial Complex," *Social Justice 30*, no. 3 (2003): 141–50, https://www.jstor.org/stable/29768215.

[10] Davis, *Are Prisons Obsolete?*

and cultural dynamics, and don't shy away from complexities. Use research-informed educational strategies that lead to long-term changes in attitudes and behavior, then encourage others to use their new understanding to initiate shifts on institutional levels.

If you are limited by grant requirements and corporate donations that make it difficult for you to embrace a comprehensive approach for prevention, consider fundraising and organizing outside of state-funded models.[11] If you have the resources, consider donating time, money, and other kinds of support to individuals and organizations tackling any causes or contributors to gender violence. If you have the influence, invite experts to provide education to your group, organization, or workplace and ensure they are compensated generously. Perhaps most importantly, continue educating yourself. Be open to new methods and listen to people who challenge us to keep doing better.

Ending Gender Violence Collaboratively and Sustainably

A problem with collective impact requires a collective response. To end gender violence, we need widespread collaboration between crisis service providers, prevention educators, activists, researchers, lawmakers, leaders, and people who have experienced gender violence. This is the only way for us to simultaneously identify gaps in our knowledge, hold each other accountable for addressing our participation in various systems of oppression, make the problem of gender violence more apparent in our communities and institutions, maximize our effectiveness in prevention and response, and ward off feelings of isolation in doing this work. Together, let's reflect on the history of our movement, communicate with one another about best practices, and become more organized toward our common goal than ever before. We can facilitate more dialogue between researchers and on-the-ground service providers. We can identify overlapping goals, troubleshoot obstacles, and pool resources. We can amplify historically underrepresented voices. We can track our progress and celebrate successes. We can

---

[11] INCITE!, *The Revolution Will Not Be Funded: Beyond the Non-profit Industrial Complex* (Durham, NC: Duke University Press, 2007).

recognize our commitment, strength, ingenuity, and resilience in the movement thus far and use it to spur us forward.

Whatever your role in taking on the problem of gender violence, prioritize self-care and preservation. Develop a plan for trauma stewardship as you witness the suffering of others.[12] Explore the liberatory power of rest as resistance.[13] Read and share stories of queer joy that counter the trauma often associated with LGBTIQA+ identities.[14] Use humor, make and witness art, spend time in nature. Make self-preservation and sustainability part of strategic planning. Scholar-activist bell hooks wrote that "one of the most vital ways we sustain ourselves is by building communities of resistance, places where we know we are not alone."[15] I remain hopeful for a future in which gender violence no longer exists. It won't be an easy road, but we'll be on it together.

---

[12] Lipsky, *Trauma Stewardship*.

[13] Tricia Hersey, *Rest Is Resistance: A Manifesto* (New York: Little, Brown Spark, 2022).

[14] Michael Tristano Jr., "Performing Queer of Color Joy through Collective Crisis: Resistance, Social Science, and How I Learned to Dance Again," *Cultural Studies/Critical Methodologies* 22, no. 3 (2022): 276–81. doi:10.1177/15327086221087671.

[15] bell hooks, *Yearning: Race, Gender, and Cultural Politics* (New York: Routledge, 2015), 231.

Index

Page numbers in italics refer to figures and tables.

J enn Freitag, Ph.D., is a writer, speaker, educator, and trainer in the areas of communication, culture, and dialogue. For over twenty years, she has been involved in anti-oppression and gender violence prevention and response work as a crisis advocate, program coordinator, prevention educator, performer, public speaker, professor, and activist. She has extensive experience working with nonprofit organizations, pre-K–12 school districts, college campuses, and law enforcement agencies. Jenn grew up in southeast Iowa and enjoys singing and playing the guitar and ukulele. She currently lives in Dayton, Ohio.

www.ingramcontent.com/pod-product-compliance
Lightning Source LLC
Chambersburg PA
CBHW030647270326
41929CB00007B/250